THE ECONOMICS OF
JOHN MAYNARD KEYNES

The Theory of a Monetary Economy

by

DUDLEY DILLARD

PROFESSOR OF ECONOMICS
UNIVERSITY OF MARYLAND

PRENTICE-HALL, INC.
Englewood Cliffs, N. J.

PRENTICE-HALL ECONOMICS SERIES

E. A. J. JOHNSON, Editor

Current printing (last digit):

21 20 19 18 17 16 15 14 13 12

PRINTED IN THE UNITED STATES OF AMERICA

23110–C

John Maynard Keynes

(1883-1946)

To

LOUISA

My wife and colleague

Preface

THIS BOOK is an exposition of the economics of John Maynard Keynes. By any test, Keynes ranks as one of the great economists of all time and as the most influential economic thinker the twentieth century has so far produced. His book, *The General Theory of Employment, Interest and Money*, published in 1936, has already become one of the classics of economic thought. Unfortunately for the undergraduate and for the general reader, the *General Theory* is addressed to professional economists and is not very intelligible to others. However, the fundamental ideas underlying Keynes' work are relatively simple and can be understood by anyone who is acquainted with broad problems of economic policy such as unemployment and inflation.

The present discussion of the economics of Keynes focuses on the forces which determine the volume of effective demand, an insufficiency of which leads to unemployment, and an excess of which causes inflation. The plan has been to follow the outline of the *General Theory* and to bring in at appropriate points the other aspects of Keynes' work which contribute to his fundamental position. Restatements and modifications made by Keynes in articles after 1936 have been incorporated into his general theory, with the last statement being taken as definitive. The chapter on war and postwar inflation is based mainly on Keynes' *How to Pay for the War* (1940). In the concluding chapter, an interpretation is given of the meaning and significance of Keynes' entire contribution to economic theory and policy.

The subject matter of this book is the economics of Keynes rather than Keynesian economics. The distinction is important. In recent years the scientific, as well as the not-so-scientific, literature in economics has been filled with books and articles refining, enlarging, criticizing, and "refuting" what is now commonly referred to as "The New Economics." The positive contributions of others in this vast literature are important, but in a book of this size and type it is not possible to encompass the field of discussion and controversy. The basic idea behind this book is the need for a simple and thorough exposition of the ideas of the one man who stands out above all others as the chief architect of "The New Economics." The extent to which Keynes dominates recent developments in economics is indicated by the fact that "The Keynesian Revolution" is a synonym for "The New Economics." Occasionally in the text and in footnotes, some of the more important extensions and refinements of Keynes' work have been introduced, but there is no systematic attempt to survey the supplementary literature or to interpret the numerous debates which have centered around Keynes. For the benefit of readers who wish to pursue these issues further, a list of suggested readings is included for each chapter, as well as a bibliography of Keynes' own writings at the end of the book.

Perhaps the chief task which confronts a writer who attempts to simplify and clarify economic theory is to discover a method which will give concrete meaning to the abstract concepts which constitute the theory. Arithmetical examples, diagrams, and summaries are all useful, but they are not enough. From a pedagogical as well as from other points of view, I am thoroughly convinced that Keynes' theories are most easily understood when they are related to the policies with which they were associated in his thinking, especially since Keynes' ideas were always oriented toward positive policy. Keynes did not forge new tools of analysis just for the love of tool-making. His ideas are operationally significant and have been translated into action by statesmen. The meaning of his abstract theory is to be discovered on the solid ground of economic policy, that is, in terms of its consequences when put into practice. Hence, if there is anything distinctive about this presentation, it is the self-conscious manner in which I have attempted to explain the somewhat complicated and, in many respects, intrinsically difficult body of theory by linking it to the policies which Keynes advocated.

Although the Keynesian tools of analysis are now being incorporated into the new principles of economics, this does not involve an acceptance of Keynes' practical policy or social philosophy. The concepts developed by Keynes are not limited to the uses to which he put them. They have proven useful tools for others with different ideas about policy. Nevertheless, it should be recognized that in the larger sense, the tools of analysis which economists use are never divorced entirely from their preferences with respect to policy. People with widely differing social philosophies make use of quite different tools. Those who believe firmly in the laissez-faire premise that the economic system of private property is self-adjusting at full employment without inflation have no positive use for most of the tools of analysis forged by Keynes. Therefore, it seems safe to conclude that the widespread acceptance of Keynes' theory is an indication of a declining faith among economists and others in the automatic, self-adjusting nature of our economic system.

Despite the widespread acceptance of his ideas, Keynes was and remains a controversial figure. In so far as matters of controversy touch the present volume, it is what would probably be called "sympathetic" to Keynes. In my judgment, a good exposition of any economist's work should be sympathetic in order to be understanding and illuminating. However, I am not unaware of Keynes' shortcomings as an expounder of the ideas of people of whom he was critical and of his impatience for detail. Keynes was an original thinker in the sense that he arrived at his ideas in his own way. The ideas he advanced were his own even though someone else may have expounded the same or similar ideas at an earlier date. For this as well as for other reasons, no attempt is made to trace the antecedents of Keynes' ideas either as they relate

to heterodox predecessors on the principle of effective demand
or to the more contemporary Anglo-Saxon and Swedish writers on monetary theory. Much more important than the influence of other people was the influence of historical circumstances in leading Keynes to his new theory. To explain this
is one of the main purposes of the final chapter. In connection
with Keynes' criticisms of what he called "classical" economics, especially the work of Professor Pigou, it should be
observed that Keynes was prone to state his case strongly in
order to lend clarity and persuasiveness to his position.

My concentrated attention was first directed to Keynes by
the late Professor Leo Rogin of the University of California,
who from the beginning recognized the revolutionary significance of the *General Theory*. Professor Rogin's untimely
death is an irreparable loss to the economics profession, which
has been deprived of one of its great minds.

The present volume was written at the suggestion of Dr.
E. A. J. Johnson of New York University and editor of the
Prentice-Hall Economics Series.

I wish to express my sincere gratitude to all who have assisted in the preparation of this book. Dr. Allan G. Gruchy
of the University of Maryland, Dr. H. Gordon Hayes of Ohio
State University, Dr. Everett E. Hagen formerly of the Bureau
of the Budget and now of the University of Illinois, and Dr.
Paul A. Samuelson of the Massachusetts Institute of Technology have read the manuscript and made valuable suggestions for its improvement. Special acknowledgment is made
to Dr. Gruchy for his keen criticisms and stimulating counsel
throughout the entire period of preparation of this book. His
generous assistance and valuable suggestions are deeply
appreciated. I am grateful to Willard O. Ash of the University
of Maryland for helpful suggestions regarding Chapter 5.
Most of all, I am indebted to my wife, Louisa Gardner Dillard, for invaluable assistance at every stage in every detail in
organizing, writing, typing, checking footnotes, preparing
bibliography, and reading proof. As a small token of my

appreciation for all she has done, this book is dedicated to her.

Harcourt, Brace and Company, the American publishers of Keynes' works, have kindly granted permission for use of quotations, especially from *The General Theory of Employment, Interest and Money*. The page numbers inserted parenthetically in the text refer to the *General Theory* unless otherwise indicated by the context. Appreciation is expressed to *The Journal of Economic History* for the use of part of my article, "The Pragmatic Bases of Keynes' Political Economy."

Dudley Dillard

Table of Contents

List of Figures

List of Tables

THE ECONOMICS OF
JOHN MAYNARD KEYNES

The Theory of a Monetary Economy

CHAPTER 1

Introduction and Fundamental Ideas

I am more attached to the comparatively simple fundamental ideas which underlie my theory than to the particular forms in which I have embodied them . . . .

J. M. Keynes, *The Quarterly Journal of Economics*, February, 1937, page 211.

WITHIN the first dozen years following its publication, John Maynard Keynes' *The General Theory of Employment, Interest and Money* (1936) has had more influence upon the thinking of professional economists and public policy makers than any other book in the whole history of economic thought in a comparable number of years. Like Adam Smith's *Wealth of Nations* in the eighteenth century and Karl Marx's *Capital* in the nineteenth century, Keynes' *General Theory* has been the center of controversy among both professional and non-professional writers. Smith's book is a ringing challenge to mercantilism, Marx's book is a searching criticism of capitalism, and Keynes' book is a repudiation of the foundations of laissez-faire. Many economists who were at first highly critical of Keynes have deserted their old position for the Keynesian camp. In book after book, leading economists acknowledge a heavy debt to the stimulating thought of Lord Keynes.

If the influence of Lord Keynes were limited to the field

of technical economic doctrine, it would be of little interest
to the world at large. However, practical economic policy
bears even more deeply than economic theory the imprint of
Keynes' thought. A few examples of the wide and growing
acceptance of Keynes' philosophy of governmental intervention, public investment, and other forms of economic policy
designed to fill the gaps in the private enterprise economy
are: the economic policies of the New Deal, the special economic message of President Truman to Congress at the close
of the second world war, the English, Canadian, and Aus-
tralian "White Papers" on unemployment policy, the Mur-
ray Full Employment Bill of 1945 and the Employment Act
of 1946 in the United States, the provision in the new French
Constitution which requires an annual employment budget,
the newer thinking in the field of fiscal policy, the International Monetary Fund, and the International Bank for Reconstruction and Development. It appears that the trend in economic policy in those countries where private enterprise is
still vigorous will be in the direction which Lord Keynes
charted. Many of his ideas and most of his theoretical apparatus can be useful in socialist economies even though his
fundamental social philosophy is anti-Marxian.

During his lifetime Keynes wrote numerous books, many
of which are outstanding contributions to special fields of
economics. Clearly, however, *The General Theory of Employment, Interest and Money* contains the essence of his
contribution to general economic theory. This work, published
when he was fifty-two years of age (he lived to be sixty-two),
is a product of his mature thought. It seems appropriate that
a book on the economics of Keynes should begin with a discussion of the fundamentals of his thinking as outlined in
the *General Theory*. The fundamental ideas are to be distinguished from the form in which these ideas are expressed.
In the first restatement of his position after publication of the
General Theory, Keynes wrote: "I am more attached to the
comparatively simple fundamental ideas which underlie my
theory than to the particular forms in which I have embodied

them . . ."[1] The theory stands or falls on these basic ideas. The forms in which the ideas are presented, on the other hand, allow for compromise. It is mainly these forms which have been the subject of debate subsequent to the publication of the *General Theory*. Once the fundamental ideas are clear, the rest falls easily into place. A full statement of the under-lying ideas involves, of course, an explanation of the frame-work upon which they are built, but for the purpose of a general introduction the framework can be temporarily neglected. These fundamental ideas center around the fol-lowing: (1) the *general* nature of Keynes' theory, (2) the role of money, (3) the relation of interest to money, (4) in-vestment, and (5) uncertainty about the future.

(1) *A General Theory:* In the title of his book *The General Theory of Employment, Interest and Money*,[2] Keynes' emphasis is on the word *general*. His theory deals with *all* levels of employment in contrast with what he calls "classi-cal" economics, which is concerned with the special case of full employment. The purpose of Keynes' general theory is to explain what determines the volume of employment at any given time, whether it happens to be full employment, wide-spread unemployment, or some intermediate level. For reasons to be explained in the following chapter, the classical school assumes there is a tendency for the economic system based on private property in the means of production to be self-adjusting at full employment. Keynes challenges this assumption and calls the classical theory which is based on it a *special* theory, applicable only to one of the limiting cases of his *general* theory. Keynes attempts to show that the nor-mal situation under laissez-faire capitalism in its present stage of development is a fluctuating state of economic activ-ity which may range all the way from full employment to widespread unemployment, with the characteristic level far

---

1. "The General Theory of Employment," *The Quarterly Journal of Economics*, February, 1937, Vol. LI, No. 2, page 211.

2. Keynes, J. M., *The General Theory of Employment, Interest and Money*. New York: Harcourt, Brace and Co., Inc., 1936.

short of full employment. Although unemployment is characteristic, it is by no means inevitable. Another "general" aspect of the general theory is that it explains inflation as readily as it does unemployment since both are primarily a matter of the volume of effective demand. When demand is deficient, unemployment results, and when demand is excessive, inflation results. If Keynes' more general theory is correct, then the special theory is at fault not only in being the theory of a limiting case, but also in being largely irrelevant to the actual world in which unemployment is obviously one of the gravest problems. Most of the significant differences between the classical theory and Keynes' theory stem from the difference between the assumption that full employment is normal and the assumption that less than full employment is normal. The one is a theory of a stationary equilibrium and the other a theory of a shifting equilibrium.

There is another equally important meaning associated with the term "general" as it appears in the title of Keynes' book. His theory relates to changes in employment and output in the *economic system as a whole* in contrast with traditional theory which relates primarily, but not entirely, to the economics of the individual business firm and the individual industry. The basic concepts of Keynes' over-all theory are the aggregates of employment, national income, national output, aggregate supply, aggregate demand, total social consumption, total social investment, and total social savings. The relationships between individual commodities expressed in terms of individual prices and values, which constitute the chief subject matter of traditional economics, are important in Keynes' general theory, but they are subsidiary to the aggregate or over-all concepts of employment, income, et cetera. A little reflection will reveal that conclusions which are valid for the individual unit may not be valid when applied to the economic system as a whole. For example, some people may get rich by stealing from others, but obviously a whole community cannot enrich itself merely by its members plundering each other.

(2) *The Theory of a Monetary Economy:* During his early career, Keynes was primarily a specialist in monetary theory and monetary policy. His greatest work prior to his *General Theory* was a two volume *Treatise on Money*. When he moved from the narrower field of monetary theory to the broader field of general economic theory, Keynes took money along with him and gave it a place of tremendous importance in the determination of employment and production in the economic system as a whole. He refers to his analysis as "the theory of a monetary economy." (pp. vii, 239, 293) Money serves three functions: as a medium of exchange, as a unit of account, and as a store of value. Of these three, the store-of-value function is most important in defining Keynes' "monetary economy." People with more income and wealth than they currently consume may store the surplus in several forms, including hoarding money, lending money, and investing in some type of capital asset. If they choose to store their wealth in the form of money, they receive no income; if they lend their money, they receive interest; and if they purchase an investment asset, they expect to receive profits. Since money as a store of wealth is barren and other forms of wealth yield returns in the form of interest or profit, there must be a special explanation why people sometimes prefer to store wealth in the barren money form. Keynes gives as an answer the fact that money may be the safest form in which to store wealth. In lending money and in buying income property, there are uncertainties which do not exist as long as one's wealth is kept in the money form. Owners of money have a type of security which owners of other kinds of wealth do not enjoy.

When wealth-holders generally express a preference for hoarding money rather than lending or investing it, the production of real social wealth is handicapped. This preference for owning money rather than owning income-yielding wealth exists to a significant degree only in a world in which the economic future is uncertain. If the world were one in which the economic future could be predicted with mathematical

certainty, there would be no sense in storing wealth in the
barren money form. Only the highly uncertain nature of the
economic future explains why there is a preference for storing wealth in the form of non-income-yielding money. As
Keynes says, the desire to store wealth in the form of money
is "a barometer of the degree of our distrust of our own calculations and conventions concerning the future. . . . The possession of actual money lulls our disquietude; and the premium which we require to make us part with money is the
measure of the degree of our disquietude."[3]

(3) *Interest a Premium for Not-hoarding Money:* The
desire of wealth-holders to store wealth in the form of money
against the risks of lending is not an absolute desire. It may
be overcome by paying a premium in the form of interest.
Interest is the reward for parting with control over wealth
in its liquid form. The *rate* of interest depends on the inten-
sity of the desire to hoard, or on what Keynes calls "liquidity
preference," for speculative purposes. The stronger the
liquidity preference, the higher the rate of interest which
must be paid. An increase in the desire of the public to hold
money increases the rate of interest, although it is possible
for the banking and monetary authorities to meet this increased desire by increasing the quantity of money. Keynes'
emphasis is not on the actual hoarding of money but on the
desire to hoard. "Hoarding" is one of those phenomena
which appear quite different when looked at from the individual, as compared with the economy-wide, point of view.
An individual wealth-holder can increase the amount of
money he holds only at the expense of someone else as long
as the total supply of money does not increase. Therefore
when the public as a whole wants more money, it cannot get
it, and the increased desire for money results in the necessity
of paying a higher premium to those who do part with their
money. But when the price that must be paid for money increases, many types of new business activity that might be

---

3. "The General Theory of Employment," *op. cit.*, page 216.

carried out at lower rates of interest will not be carried out at all. Therefore, an increase in interest rates tends to reduce effective demand and, in normal times, to cause unemployment.

Although the notion that interest is a reward for not-hoarding money may seem very ordinary from the layman's point of view, it is most unusual from the point of view of traditional economic theory. Interest has been looked upon by economists as a reward for saving, that is, a reward for postponing consumption rather than as a premium for surrendering liquidity. The importance of interest and money in Keynes' theory is indicated by their inclusion in the title *The General Theory of Employment, Interest and Money*. As further discussion will indicate, the ultimate theoretical explanation of unemployment in Keynes' theory is found in the peculiar properties of money and interest. In the absence of money or of any form of wealth with the properties of conventional money, Keynes contends the economic system would tend to be self-adjusting at the point of full employment (p. 235). Although the title indicates a theoretical emphasis on money and interest as the basis of the ultimate explanation of unemployment, from the point of view of practical policy Keynes places even greater stress on the instability of demand for capital assets arising from the irrationality of the private investment market.

(4) *Investment the Important Determinant of Employment:* In a society characterized by great inequality of wealth and income, the economic ability of the community to consume is limited. The rich have more income than they wish to consume currently and the poor have so little income that their ability to consume is narrowly restricted. As a consequence, there is a sizable potential surplus of resources in excess of what is needed to produce consumers goods. This surplus, if it is to be used at all, must be devoted to producing things that are not to be currently consumed. This production in excess of what is currently consumed is called investment. Investment includes such activity as building new

factories, new houses, new railroads, and all other types of goods which are not to be consumed as fast as they are produced. The distinction between consumption and investment is fundamental to Keynes' entire analysis. His theory reduced to its simplest terms states that employment depends upon the amount of investment, or that unemployment is caused by an insufficiency of investment. This, of course, is a great simplification. Nevertheless, it indicates the emphasis on investment. Not only do some workers receive employment directly in building new factories, houses, railroads, et cetera, but the workers so employed spend their money for the products of factories already built, pay rent on houses already built, ride railroads already built, et cetera. In brief, employment in investment activity helps to maintain demand for the consumption output of existing facilities. In order to make full use of the factories already in existence, we must always be building new factories. Otherwise, in our society with its characteristic widespread inequality of income, there will not be enough money spent to keep the old factories going. If investment falls off, unemployment results. Clearly, it is very important to understand what determines the amount of investment that actually takes place. The most important section of Keynes' *General Theory* is Book IV entitled, "The Inducement to Invest." If we mean by a "cause" that factor in a complex combination of factors which fluctuates most widely and suddenly, we may say that investment is the determinant of employment. Employment fluctuates primarily because investment fluctuates. Unemployment results primarily from an inadequacy of investment. If investment can be controlled, total employment can be controlled. A high level of employment depends upon a high level of investment. The clue to understanding the general theory of employment is found in the answer to the question: What causes investment to fluctuate and characteristically to be less than the amount required for full employment?

(5) *Psychological Irrationality a Cause of Instability:* Investment fluctuates because present knowledge about the

future rests on a precarious basis and therefore decisions which relate to the uncertain future also are precarious and subject to sudden and sweeping revision. Since investment is production other than for present consumption, it is connected with the future in a direct manner. Although investment may take the form of producing more consumers goods than are currently consumed, the more important form is investment in durable producers goods, like factories, houses, railroads, apartment houses, et cetera.[4] A decision to build a factory depends on what is expected to happen in the future. However, the outstanding fact about the future, so far as economic life is concerned at least, is that we know very little about it. The potential investor must be guided by his *expectations* in reaching his decision to build or not to build a new factory. The vague and uncertain state of our knowledge rules out the possibility that these expectations can be reduced to a rational, scientific basis. Yet as practical people living in a society whose productivity depends upon large-scale investment in durable assets, we must make and do make decisions concerning the long-term future, even though they rest on a foundation of shifting sand. Since those who make these dollars-and-cents decisions have very little confidence in the correctness of the judgment which leads to any particular investment, the prevailing attitudes which affect investment and employment so seriously are easily provoked to sudden change. If wealth-accumulation were a matter of secondary importance, the vague and uncertain state of our knowledge of the future would not matter so greatly. But under modern industrial capitalism, wealth-accumulation (investment) is the basis of the successful functioning of the entire economic system.

In the market place, entrepreneurs and other prospective investors shelter themselves from the turbulent stream of

---

4. Houses might be included in durable consumers goods, but income statistics classify them under investment. They are of such obvious importance that they have been used for illustrative purposes here, even though they are not strictly a producers good.

coming events that flows out of a dimly lit future by adopting protective attitudes that give the appearance of rational conduct. These attitudes include the assumption that the present is a much better guide to the future than a candid examination of the past would warrant. There is, in other words, a tendency to abstract from the fact that we know very little about the long-term future. The further assumption is made that existing opinions as reflected in the stock market, bond market, and other organized markets are based on a correct summing up of future prospects. Finally, because investors have so little confidence in their own opinions, they tend to rely upon the judgment of the majority or average. What Keynes calls "conventional judgments" become the basis of market-place behavior. They are conventional because they involve a general concurrence of opinion or the acceptance of a convention as a substitute for genuine knowledge which does not exist. Although investors have grave doubts concerning the soundness of action based on mass psychology, they accept it as correct behavior in the absence of any positive evidence that it is incorrect. When something new does turn up to indicate that past behavior has been incorrect, a violent shift takes place. Conventional judgments lend some stability as long as the convention is accepted, but when the convention breaks down, instability becomes the order of the day. Thus the state of expectations rests on a razor's edge and investment markets are charged with potential panic. When one conventional judgment gives way to another, all new judgments tend to move in the same direction. The sweeping nature of changes in conventional judgments stands in contrast with the classical theory of the market which assumes that the pessimistic decisions of some strong-minded individuals will offset the optimistic decisions of other strong-minded individuals.

By assuming that investors possess present knowledge about the future quite different from that which they actually possess, the classical theory underestimates "the concealed factors of utter doubt, precariousness, hope and fear."[5] The over-rationalistic psychology of the classical economists leads to a misinterpretation of behavior in the investment market, and to a neglect of the strategic role of money as a protective link between the present and the uncertain future. For as we have seen, the uncertain future which makes real investment hazardous also lends enchantment to money as a store of value.

Despite these important differences between the psychological assumptions of Keynes and those of the classical school, there is one respect in which their psychological theory is similar. The classicists assume rational behavior on the part of individuals. The individual behavior posited by Keynes is also rational, within the limitations of the given situation. It is quite rational for a bewildered investor to want to hold money during a depression-created crisis, even though this behavior brings results that are highly irrational from the point of view of the economic system as a whole. Whereas the classical economists are concerned with rational behavior in a rational world, Keynes is concerned with rational behavior in an irrational world.

Under five separate headings we have outlined the fundamental ideas of Keynes' *General Theory*. It is a general theory that pertains to all levels of employment for the economic system as a whole. It is a theory of a monetary economy in the sense that money is an important form in which to store wealth, and interest is the premium paid for not-hoarding wealth in this form. It is a theory in which fluctuations in the volume of investment account for fluctuations in employment. Fluctuations in the volume of investment are largely accounted for by the fluctuating and uncertain nature of expectations regarding the future returns from capital assets and the future terms on which money may be lent at interest. From the presentation of these basic ideas, it is apparent that they are closely related to each other. One idea cannot be discussed without

5. "The General Theory of Employment," *op. cit.*, page 222.

bringing in the others. The theory of interest and money is really one theory. Investment involves consideration of money as an alternative form of storing wealth. Investment in real capital assets occurs only if the expectations of profits are in excess of the premium that must be paid for borrowing money. The uncertain nature of knowledge about the future accounts both for the existence of money as a store of value and the precariousness of investment in real capital assets. These related ideas are all brought together into one theory of employment, which is the essence of the *General Theory*, and may be stated as follows: In a world in which the economic future is highly uncertain and in which money is an important form for storing wealth, the general level of employment depends upon the relation between the expected profits from investment in capital assets and the interest premium which must be paid to induce wealth-holders to surrender control of their money. If there is confidence in the future, real investment will occur and employment will be at a high level. Although interest will continue to be paid for not-hoarding, this premium can be paid and still enable entrepreneurs to carry out real investment on terms which they expect to be profitable. When confidence in the future is lacking and the expectations for profits are dim, the premium required to get wealth-holders to part with their money will exceed the expected rate of return. Investment and employment will fall to a low level. A depression is a period in which the premium that must be paid for not-hoarding money exceeds the rate of return expected from building new capital assets of almost every type. Therefore, men are not employed to build new factories, and lacking income, they have little money with which to buy the output of existing factories. While the economic storm is raging, no one is able to pay the premium necessary to lure away from wealth-holders their highly preferred cash. Wealth-accumulation dwindles, workers lose their jobs, and the storm grows worse.

References for Further Reading
See references at end of Chapter 3.

CHAPTER 2

The Classical Background

I shall argue that the postulates of the classical theory are applicable to a special case only and not to the general case . . . Moreover, the characteristics of the special case assumed by the classical theory happen not to be those of the economic society in which we actually live, with the result that its teaching is misleading and disastrous if we attempt to apply it to the facts of experience.

J. M. Keynes, *The General Theory of Employment, Interest and Money*.[*]

To UNDERSTAND the nature and novelty of Keynes' ideas, it is useful to know their setting. The fundamental ideas sketched in the preceding chapter represent a reaction to what seemed to him the unsatisfactory character of the prevailing principles of economics. On the first page of the text of the *General Theory*, Keynes says, ". . . the classical theory . . . is misleading and disastrous if we attempt to apply it to the facts of experience." Classical economics bears to Keynes' *General Theory* much the same relation that mercantilism bears to Adam Smith's *Wealth of Nations*. Just as it would be difficult, if not impossible, to understand Smith without knowing something about mercantilist theory and practice, so it is difficult to understand Keynes without knowing something about classical theory and practice. An insistence upon practice as well as principles is important because the ultimate meaning

[*] Harcourt, Brace and Co., Inc., 1936, page 3.

13

of the principles is to be discovered only when they are put into practice.

The term "classical economics" as used by Keynes refers to the traditional or orthodox principles of economics which have been handed down and generally accepted by academic economists since the time of David Ricardo, the famous English economist of the early nineteenth century.[1] Although these principles have been refined and elaborated by many writers of varying shades of opinion, they comprise a well-established body of doctrine which forms the core of analytical material presented in principles of economics textbooks which appeared before 1947. This set of principles has become so widely accepted over a period of more than a century that it merits the label "classical." Keynes has been criticized for viewing the classical theory as a single body of unified thought. Undoubtedly he was guilty of oversimplifying a vast body of doctrine contributed to by many able scholars. Whether his oversimplification is in general unfair to the classical position is an issue on which there is likely to be disagreement. However, the present chapter is concerned with the classical theory as background and not with what Keynes said it was. So far as possible, polemics have been dispensed with in the following discussion of the classical background.[2]

1. As Keynes points out, he uses the term "classical economics" and "classical economists" in a rather unusual sense. He means by "classical economists" the *followers* of Ricardo, including John Stuart Mill, Alfred Marshall, and A. C. Pigou. The term "classical economists" was invented by Karl Marx to refer to Ricardo and his *predecessors*, including Adam Smith. Throughout this book the term "classical" is used in the sense in which Keynes employs it, to refer to the orthodox economics of the past century and a quarter. The writings of Professor Pigou are the special target of many of Keynes' criticisms of "classical" economics because Professor Pigou is the latest of the great representatives of this body of doctrine. However, Professor Pigou, along with many other economists, has modified his position as a result of Keynes' influence. Nevertheless, he has accepted the mantle of classicism and continues to write in its defense.

2. A full understanding of Keynes' attack on classical economics presupposes a knowledge of Keynes' own theory. His more detailed criticism of the classical position will be found in the *General Theory*, Chapter 2, "The Postulates of Classical Economics." In this chapter his criticisms are specifically directed at Professor Pigou's *The Theory of Unemployment*. Keynes recognized

Whatever may be said about the fairness of Keynes' criticisms, he was not an uninitiated outsider when he launched his attack on the citadel of classicism. He was brought up on and for many years adhered to the Cambridge version of the classical theory. His father, John Neville Keynes, was a distinguished lecturer at Cambridge University and a close friend of Alfred Marshall, the greatest of all the Cambridge classical economists, whose *Principles of Economics,* first published in 1890, still stands as the landmark of classical achievement. John Maynard Keynes was a student and disciple of Marshall. During most of his career, he accepted and taught the classical principles in the form in which they emanated from Marshall. There is much in the classical principles which Keynes continued to accept as valid and useful. In his last article, which appeared posthumously in 1946, he wrote: "I find myself moved, not for the first time, to remind contemporary economists that the classical teaching embodied some permanent truths of great significance, which we are liable to-day to overlook because we associate them with other doctrines which we cannot now accept without much qualification . . . It shows how much modernist stuff, gone wrong and turned sour and silly, is circulating in our system . . ."[3] By 1946 Keynes probably felt his triumph over the classical theory was secure enough to justify this warning to the younger "revolutionaries," some of whom he felt had gone too far in throwing overboard the classical tradition. In his *General Theory,* Keynes emphasized the differences rather than the similarities between his and the classical theory in order better to drive home his main points.

It would, however, be a mistake to underestimate the fundamental significance of Keynes' attack on classical eco-

---

the shortcomings of this chapter and stated it was the part of his *General Theory* most in need of revision. Some of the changes are to be found in Keynes' article, "Relative Movements of Real Wages and Output," *The Economic Journal,* March, 1939, Vol. XLIX, No. 193, pages 34-51. His fundamental argument remains unaffected by these amendments.

3. "The Balance of Payments of the United States," *The Economic Journal,* June, 1946, Vol. LVI, No. 222, pages 185-186.

nomics. In an age in which laissez-faire is dead, it is important to divorce economic theory from laissez-faire, even though that marriage, which was performed so well by Adam Smith, has been losing ground at least since the time of John Stuart Mill. Viewing classical theory as a whole, its practical meaning is still to be found in the presumption in favor of laissez-faire. Viewing Keynes' theory as a whole, its revolutionary nature lies in the repudiation of any presumption in favor of laissez-faire. In this sense, Keynes' challenge strikes at the heart of classical theory and ramifies especially into the fields of unemployment theory, monetary theory, interest theory, price theory, inflation, business cycles, fiscal policy, international trade, foreign exchange, and other major fields of economics.

The Content of Classical Economics

Classical economic theory rests on the assumption of full employment of labor and other resources. There may be lapses from full employment, but these are regarded as abnormal and their explanation does not constitute a basic part of the subject matter of classical economics. If at any time there is not actually full employment, the classical theory asserts there is always a *tendency* toward full employment.[4] The normal situation is stable equilibrium at full employment. If disturbance does persist, it is attributed by the classical school to interference by government or private monopoly with the free play of market forces. As a general rule to which there are minor exceptions, the social policy which guarantees normal full employment is laissez-faire, the absence of government control of private enterprise. In contrast with this, Keynes takes the normal condition of laissez-faire capitalism to be a fluctuating level of employment. The primary purpose of Keynes' theory is to explain what determines the volume of employment at any time.

---

4. Pigou, A. C., *Equilibrium and Employment*, page 78. London: Macmillan and Co., Ltd., 1941. See also, *Lapses from Full Employment*, Chapter V London: Macmillan and Co., Ltd., 1945.

Instead of attempting to explain what determines the volume of employment, the classical theory assumes full employment and goes on to explain how a *given* total volume of resources is allocated in production and how the income derived from production is distributed to the different types of resources participating in production. The market forces which allocate resources in production and determine the rewards in distribution are supply and demand. The general relations of supply and demand determine the relative values of individual resources and commodities. Expressed in terms of money, these values are prices, and the pricing system is the unconscious "planning" mechanism which guides private individuals, in pursuit of maximum individual rewards, to allocate economically and fully the total resources of the economic system. This, in brief outline, is the well-known theory of value, distribution, and production, which forms the core of classical economic theory.

Classical theory focuses on the use of a given quantity of resources by individual firms and individual industries within the economic system as a whole. If more resources are employed in one industry, they are assumed to be drawn away from other industries. If more resources are employed by one firm, they are assumed to be drawn away from other firms. Thus the choice is between employment here and employment there, and not between employment and unemployment. Additions to total output in one direction are at the expense of deductions from total output somewhere else in the economic system and are not additions to total output resulting from putting to work previously unemployed resources. Thus classical economics is a study of the alternative uses of a given quantity of employed resources. When resources are ideally allocated, there is no way by which total output can be increased by reallocation. In the long run, of course, increases in population and productivity and the discovery of new resources result in increases in total employment and output. In contrast with the emphasis upon the use of a given total quantity of resources by individual firms and industries,

Keynes' general theory of employment deals with changes in output and employment in the economic system as a whole as a result of fluctuations in the quantity of employed resources.

Acceptance of full employment as the normal condition of an exchange economy is justified in classical economics by the assumption that supply creates its own demand. This assumption or "principle" is called Say's law of markets, after J. B. Say, an early nineteenth-century French economist who was one of the first to state the "law" in a dogmatic form. By supply creating its own demand is meant that every producer who brings goods to market does so only in order to exchange them for other goods. Say assumed that the only reason people work and produce is in order to enjoy the satisfaction of consuming. In an exchange economy, therefore, whatever is produced represents the demand for another product. Additional supply is additional demand. The analysis is carried on in terms of barter, but the fact that sales and purchases are made with money is assumed not to affect the process, except that exchange based on money is more efficient than exchange based on barter. When a resource is put to work a product (output) is produced and income is paid to those who contribute to its production. The sales receipts or proceeds which an employer can expect to receive from the output produced is assumed to cover the cost of the output for all levels of employment in the economic system, provided the contributors of resources are willing to accept rewards commensurate with their productivity. This does not mean that each additional worker need purchase exactly the same product which he himself produces. It signifies merely that the new income from his employment will create a sufficient demand to take off the market an amount of output equivalent to that produced by virtue of his employment. As long as production is directed into proper channels, whatever is produced can be sold. Misdirected production may result in temporary oversupply of some particular items but there can be no general overproduction as long as supply creates its own demand. If errors result in excess production of some particular items of output, this will be corrected when entrepreneurs shift from the production of things they cannot sell (at a profit) to the production of things they can sell (at a profit). In brief, Say's law of markets is a denial of the possibility of general over-production, that is, a denial of the possibility of a deficiency of aggregate demand. Therefore, the employment of more re-sources will always be profitable and will take place up to the point of full employment, subject to the limitation that the contributors of resources are willing to accept rewards no greater than their physical productivity justifies. There can be no general unemployment, according to this view, if workers will accept what they are "worth."

In an exchange economy, Say's law means there will always be a sufficient rate of spending to maintain full employment. The classical justification of full employment as "normal" rests on the assumption that income is spent automatically at a rate which will keep all resources employed. Although most people spend most of their income fairly "automatically" for things they need or want to consume, there is also in any community a certain proportion of income that is saved. This, however, is no obstacle to spending or employment in the classical analysis because what each individual saves is as-sumed nevertheless to be spent. Saving is spending for pro-ducers goods (investment). Since saving is just another form of spending, according to the classical theory, all income is spent, partly for consumption and partly for investment (pro-ducers goods). There is no reason to expect a break in the flow of the income stream and therefore supply creates its own demand.

Flexibility in the rate of interest is the mechanism which is supposed to maintain equality of community saving and com-munity investment in the classical scheme. If the amount of saving *tends* to become excessive, forces operating through the rate of interest are set in motion to reduce saving and to increase investment until they are brought to equality with each other. In the first place, the higher rate of saving will tend to lower the rate of interest, and a lower rate of interest will lessen the incentive to save. Since interest is viewed as the reward for saving, an increase in interest rates will increase saving and a decrease in interest rates will decrease saving. In the second place, the lower rate of interest will increase the incentive to invest to an extent which will absorb the additional savings which remain after the rate of interest has declined. Other influences also enter the picture to maintain the equality of saving and investment at full employment. An increase in saving represents a decrease in the demand for consumption goods and causes their prices to fall. Lower prices mean lower profits, which cause resources to shift out of the consumers goods industries into investment goods industries, where the demand has increased. It should be observed that saving is linked to investment by a delicate mechanism, yet one which bears a heavy burden in making the adjustments that preserve full employment. If it seems strange that investment should increase at the very time consumption is decreasing, this is explained in the classical theory in terms of the presupposition that a decision to consume less today is linked directly with a decision to consume more at a later date. The classical theory does not acknowledge that a fall in consumption, instead of leading to an increase in investment, may lead to a fall in total demand and thereby to unemployment. Nor does the classical theory recognize as a significant motive for saving the desire for wealth as such.

The Meaning of Full Employment and Unemployment: The assertion that classical economic theory rests on the assumption of full employment calls for definitions of "full employment" and "unemployment." It is more accurate to say that the classical position assumes there is no involuntary unemployment, as distinguished from voluntary and frictional unemployment. Voluntary unemployment exists when potential workers are unwilling to accept the going wage or wages slightly less than the going wage. Workers on strike for higher wages are an example of voluntary unemployment. They are voluntarily unemployed in the sense that by taking a lower wage than they are asking they could be employed.

There are other forms of voluntary idleness on the part of potential workers which hardly justify being classed as unemployment at all. Some wealthy persons, the "idle rich," and some habitually lazy people, the "idle poor," are of this type. When people refuse of their own volition to work, they should not be classified as unemployed, and therefore full employment can exist even though some people are voluntarily idle.

Frictional unemployment exists when men are temporarily out of work because of imperfections in the labor market. Many factors may account for frictional unemployment: the immobility of labor, the seasonal nature of some work, shortages of materials, breakdowns in machinery and equipment, ignorance of job opportunities, et cetera. In a dynamic society in which some industries are declining and others are rising and in which people are free to work wherever they wish (providing they can find a job), the volume of frictional unemployment may be fairly large at any time. In the United States, where the total labor force is approximately sixty millions, it is estimated that frictional unemployment averages at least two millions, or about three per cent, at all times. Frictional unemployment is undesirable and every possible step should be taken to minimize it within the limits of freedom of occupational choice, but it is not a major problem because employable persons seeking work will not, as a rule, remain unemployed for frictional reasons more than a few weeks or months.

"Full employment" as thus defined is consistent with voluntary unemployment and allows for a certain amount of frictional unemployment. Full employment exists in the absence of involuntary unemployment. In the classical theory, this type of unemployment does not exist.[5] While there is

5. Keynes cites the following passage from Professor Pigou's major work, the *Economics of Welfare*, to illustrate how the classical economists ignored the problem of involuntary unemployment: "Throughout this discussion, except when the contrary is expressly stated, the fact that some resources are generally unemployed against the will of the owners is ignored. *This does not affect the substance of the argument*, while it simplifies its exposition." Pigou, *Economics of Welfare*, 4th edition, page 127. Cited in Keynes' *General Theory*, page 5. The italics are supplied by Keynes.

more involved in the issue between Keynes and the classicists than mere facts, the latter cannot be ignored since, after all, issues like this must ultimately be resolved by an appeal to common sense and the hard facts of experience. In the United States at the bottom of the depression in 1932, there were approximately 15,000,000 unemployed workers, and at the top of the business cycle in 1937 there remained more than 7,500,000 unemployed. Allowing for as many as 3,000,000 frictionally unemployed, it hardly seems plausible that the remaining millions were in any significant sense voluntarily unemployed. Millions tramped the streets looking for work at almost any price and found only "No Help Wanted" signs. The same conclusion seems justified for the United Kingdom, where between the first and second world wars the percentage of workers out of employment seldom fell below 10 per cent, and ranged upward to 22 per cent of the registered workers. Since 2 or 3 per cent is considered normal frictional unemployment, is it any wonder that Keynes and others found unsatisfactory a theory which appeared to do such violence to the facts of experience?

How do the representatives of the classical school reconcile their denial of involuntary unemployment with the undeniable fact that there do exist large numbers of idle men and women who want work but cannot find it? The crux of the answer to this important question seems to be that collective action as taken by labor unions and in the form of governmental intervention creates an imperfect labor market in which wage rates are not free to fall to their competitive levels. Monopolistic behavior on the part of labor and labor's friends is responsible for unemployment. Under perfectly free competition, or what Professor Pigou calls "thoroughgoing competition," among wage earners, wage rates fall under the pressure of unemployment until all who are willing to work can find employment. As long as there is anybody unemployed, he will, under thorough-going competition, offer himself for employment and beat down wage rates until it is profitable for employers to hire everyone who wants to work.

Professor Pigou contends that these conditions substantially obtained prior to the first world war when unemployment, apart from cyclical manifestations, remained at a low level. Since that time and to some extent even in the earlier period, certain new phenomena have arisen to weaken greatly the competitive forces in the labor market. Chief among these are collective bargaining by trade unions, minimum-wage laws, unemployment insurance, increased work relief payments, and tacit agreement among workers generally not to accept lower wages than what they and the community consider a reasonable living wage. The group pressures exerted by labor unions and government intervention in the labor market have tended to maintain wage rates above the level at which the demand for work is satisfied before everyone willing to work at prevailing wage rates can find employment. Much of this unemployment is not strictly voluntary on the part of the individual unemployed worker since there is relatively little he can do about the closed shop, minimum-wage laws, or the more-than-competitive wages being received by the employed. In fact, relatively high unemployment insurance payments and poor relief remove the incentive for wage earners to work for the low wage rates which many of them must accept if they want employment. Some individuals can, of course, find employment by accepting wage reductions which other workers refuse to accept. However, many prefer to remain idle rather than be subjected to the humiliating taunts that they are despicable "scabs" who lower the standards of fellow workers. Where the union contract or the law does not restrain, the forces of class pressure may work with great effectiveness to maintain wage rates above the competitive ideal which would permit full employment. The conclusion drawn by the classical school from these considerations is that in spite of strong group pressure this type of unemployment is nevertheless voluntary in the sense that acceptance of lower wage rates would create a demand for more employment. If wage rates were lowered sufficiently, all non-frictional unemployment would disappear. Thus, according to the classical theory, labor is guilty of a type of group behavior in the form of collective bargaining and otherwise which causes many fellow-workers to suffer unemployment. The responsibility for unemployment is placed at the door of labor itself. The practical lesson is clear: Since unemployment, apart from the frictional type, is caused by wages being too high, the cure is lower wages.[6]

Keynes' Objections to Classical Theory

What Keynes objected to most strongly in the classical reasoning is the notion that unemployment will disappear if workers will just accept sufficiently low wage rates. He repudiates the assumption that the labor market is always a seller's market in which labor can be sold if workers will just be willing to accept wage cuts. There are two aspects of Keynes' objection to Pigou's view that flexible wage rates will cure unemployment. The first may be called the practical and the second the theoretical aspect.

In a practical sense labor unions are an integral part of modern democratic economics, and welfare legislation such

6. While it would be unfair to attribute the position stated in the above paragraph to many of the so-called classical economists, it is, I believe, a correct paraphrase of the meaning of Professor Pigou's *Theory of Unemployment*, upon which Keynes bases his statement of the classical theory of unemployment. In his *Lapses from Full Employment*, published in 1945, Professor Pigou says he is in favor of attacking the problem of unemployment by manipulating demand rather than by manipulating wages. This involves a major departure from the classical position and a major triumph for Keynes. Despite his position on policy, which clearly differs from that taken in his *Theory of Unemployment* (1933), Professor Pigou continues to defend the classical position, although he acknowledges some oversights in formulation. In *Lapses from Full Employment* Pigou concludes a chapter, "The Classical View," with this statement: "The final result of this discussion is to suggest that, though there are subtleties of theory which the classicists did not envisage, for broad *practical* purposes their conclusion was correct. In stable conditions, apart from frictions, immobility and so on, thorough-going competition among wage-earners would ensure the establishment and maintenance of full employment except in circumstances which we are very unlikely to meet with in fact." (page 25). It is left for the reader to try to reconcile this statement with that in the Preface, where he states: "Professor Dennis Robertson . . . has warned me that the form of the book may suggest that I am in favour of attacking the problem of unemployment by manipulating wages rather than by manipulating demand. I wish, therefore, to say clearly that this is not so." (page v).

as minimum-wage laws and unemployment insurance are probably here to stay. Therefore, it is bad politics even if it should be considered good economics to object to labor unions and to liberal labor legislation. Pigou's solution of lower wage rates could only be realized in a freely competitive labor market or in a completely authoritarian economy. In democratic societies, which both Keynes and Pigou presuppose, labor unions are not likely to be eliminated, minimum-wage laws are not likely to be repealed, unemployment compensation is not likely to be lowered, and public opinion as to what constitutes a reasonable living wage is not likely to be revised downwards in the light of the tremendous productivity of modern technology. A minimum charge against Pigou's theory of unemployment is its irrelevance as a guide to policy under conditions as they have come to exist in the actual world of the past several decades and as they will probably continue to exist in the foreseeable future.

However, even if all the conditions necessary to restore perfectly free or thorough-going competition among wage earners might, by some miracle, be realized, this would not meet Keynes' fundamental challenge to the classical school. His theory of employment and unemployment does not rest on the premise of rigid wage rates. He contends that the volume of employment is determined by effective demand and not by the wage bargains between workers and employers. Keynes' ultimate theoretical explanation of unemployment rests, as was hinted in the preceding chapter and as will be developed more fully subsequently, on the stickiness of interest rates taken in conjunction with the irrationality of business men's expectations about investment in durable capital assets. In Keynes' view, the peculiar characteristics of a developed monetary economy account for unemployment. Even if wage rates were perfectly flexible and commodity prices perfectly competitive, unemployment could still exist. His explanation of unemployment does not depend on the decline of competition of recent decades.

While the above discussion does not do justice to the rela-

tions between Keynes and the classical theory,[7] perhaps
enough has been said to indicate the circumstances which provoked him to advance *The General Theory of Employment,
Interest and Money* in 1936. The great depression of the
1930's, like all depressions, involved tremendous loss of
human and material values. Mass unemployment is second,
perhaps, only to war in the magnitude of its human degrada-
tion and physical wastefulness. The world was poor not because it lacked material resources, technical skill, or the will
to work, or even because it misallocated its employed resources; it was poor because something was radically wrong
with the way men thought and conducted their economic
affairs. The practical advice which came implicitly if not
always explicitly from the classical theory seemed misleading
and disastrous. Cutting wages and salaries seemed to Keynes
both demoralizing and unsound. He sought a means to prosperity through monetary expansion, public investment, and
other forms of governmental action. This represented a departure from traditional laissez-faire, but Keynes had no
illusions about the invisible hand that is supposed to guide
men in the right paths if they will just pursue their own self-
interest. He had long since written off laissez-faire. Keynes
disagreed with those who seemed to say we cannot do what we
must do because if we do we shall lose our freedom. Such a
view seemed to indicate a lack of faith in freedom and representative government rather than their defense. Keynes wanted
governmental action because he saw the need for rules of the
road from which all will benefit but without which people get
in each other's way and no one gets anywhere. As one writer
has aptly stated, Keynes was the first academic economist of
high professional repute since Malthus to attack the doctrine
that the economic forces of a private-property economy tend
to bring about the employment of all who wish to work at the
prevailing wage rates.[8]

---

7. This is discussed more fully in the final chapter.

8. Hayes, H. Gordon, *Spending, Saving, and Employment*, page 133. New
York: Alfred A. Knopf, Inc., 1945.

The great fault of the classical theory is its irrelevance to conditions in the contemporary capitalist world. In many significant respects, the classical theory, as summed up by Alfred Marshall, is more useful in a socialist economy, which may be assumed to conform closely to the ideal of full employment. In capitalist economies where widespread unemployment, business cycles, inflation, and other forms of instability constitute the chief problems of public policy, the basic need is for a theory which will diagnose these ills in a manner which will furnish a guide to action for their solution or alleviation. Such a new and more relevant theory has emerged in Keynes' general theory of employment, interest and money.

References for Further Reading

See references at end of Chapter 3.

CHAPTER 3

A Preliminary Summary of the General Theory of Employment

This analysis supplies us with an explanation of the paradox of poverty in the midst of plenty. For the mere existence of an insufficiency of effective demand may, and often will, bring the increase of employment to a standstill *before* a level of full employment has been reached ... Moreover the richer the community, the wider will tend to be the gap between its actual and its potential production; and therefore the more obvious and outrageous the defects of the economic system.

J. M. Keynes, *The General Theory of Employment, Interest and Money.**

A SUMMARY of Keynes' general theory of employment naturally focuses on the principle of effective demand, which embodies in a systematic manner the fundamental ideas discussed in Chapter 1 above. The purpose of this summary is to give the reader a bird's eye view of the whole theory before presenting a detailed account of its individual parts. Subsequent discussion of the individual parts will have more meaning if their relations to the rest of the theory are already understood. This appears to be the best way to resolve the dilemma which inevitably arises in explaining a systematic

---

* Harcourt, Brace and Co., Inc., 1936, pages 30-31.

body of thought: The parts have meaning only in relation to the whole, yet the whole is made up of individual parts which must be appreciated before the whole can be explained. In our preliminary survey it will be necessary to use some special terms whose full meaning must await more detailed explanation in subsequent chapters.

The Principle of Effective Demand

The logical starting point of Keynes' theory of employment is the principle of effective demand.[1] Total employment depends on total demand, and unemployment results from a deficiency of total demand. Effective demand manifests itself in the spending of income. As employment increases, income increases. A fundamental principle is that as the real income of a community increases, consumption will also increase but by less than income. Therefore, in order to have sufficient demand to sustain an increase in employment there must be an increase in real investment equal to the gap between income and the consumption demand out of that income. In other words, employment cannot increase unless investment increases. This is the core of the principle of effective demand. Since it is fundamental to the general theory of employment, it will be restated on an expanded basis in the following paragraphs.

Aggregate demand and aggregate supply

The term "demand" as used by Keynes refers to aggregate demand of the whole economic system. Aggregate demand must be clearly distinguished from the demand for the products of individual firms and individual industries which is the usual type represented in supply and demand diagrams. The demand for a firm or industry means a schedule of vari-

1. As explained below, the adjective "effective" is used to designate the point on the aggregate demand curve where it is intersected by the aggregate supply curve. There are other points on the aggregate demand curve but these are not effective in determining the actual volume of employment. "Effective" is also helpful in emphasizing the distinction between mere desire to buy and desire plus ability to buy. Only the latter has economic significance.

ous amounts of a commodity which will be purchased at a series of prices. Price means the amount of money received from the sale of a given physical quantity of output, such as a bushel of wheat or a ton of steel. Since the output of the entire economic system cannot be measured in any simple physical unit like a bushel or ton, Keynes uses the amount of labor employed as the measure of output as a whole. The aggregate demand "price" for the output of any given amount of employment is the total sum of money, or proceeds, which is expected from the sale of the output produced when that amount of labor is employed. The aggregate demand curve,

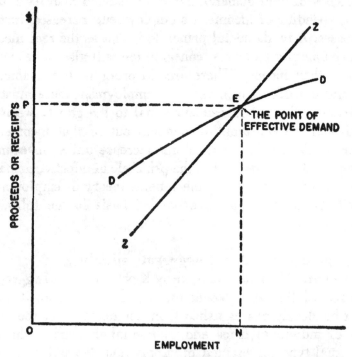

DD—The Aggregate Demand Schedule: The proceeds or receipts (P) *expected* to be forthcoming for output produced by varying amounts of employment (N).

ZZ —The Aggregate Supply Schedule: The proceeds or receipts (P) which will *just induce* given amounts of employment (N).

Figure 1. Aggregate Demand and Aggregate Supply.

or "aggregate demand function" as Keynes calls it (represented by DD in Figure 1), is a schedule of the proceeds expected from the sale of the output resulting from varying amounts of employment. As more labor is employed, more output is produced, and the total proceeds are greater. In other words, aggregate demand price increases as the amount of employment increases, and decreases as the amount of employment decreases.

In Figure 1 the aggregate demand price or proceeds is represented along the vertical axis, and the quantity of employment (N) along the horizontal axis. The aggregate demand schedule slants up toward the right, indicating that demand increases with employment. This contrasts with an industry demand curve which slants down toward the right, indicating that the quantity sold will increase as the price falls.

In a business-enterprise economy in which production is motivated by profit, each business man will employ that number of workers which will yield him the greatest profit. The total number of men employed in the whole economy is the total or aggregate of those employed by all entrepreneurs. A certain minimum amount of proceeds will be necessary to induce employers as a whole to offer any given aggregate amount of employment. This minimum price or proceeds which will just induce employment on a given scale is called the aggregate supply price of that amount of employment. The aggregate supply function is a schedule of the minimum amounts of proceeds required to induce varying quantities of employment. As the amount of proceeds increases, a greater amount of employment will be offered to workers by employers. Therefore, the aggregate supply schedule (ZZ in Figure 1), like the aggregate demand schedule, slants up toward the right as the amount of employment (N) increases. It will not, however, follow the same course. There will be some amounts of employment for which the proceeds expected will exceed the proceeds necessary to induce a given volume of employment and there will be some amounts of employment for which the proceeds expected will not be sufficient to induce that amount of employment. In between there will be some amount of employment for which the expected proceeds will just equal the necessary proceeds to make the employment profitable to entrepreneurs. At this point the aggregate demand function intersects the aggregate supply function, and the point of intersection determines the actual amount of employment at any time. This is the crux of Keynes' theory of employment. The aggregate demand schedule (DD) and the aggregate supply schedule (ZZ), as represented in Figure 1, intersect at the point E, corresponding to the amount of employment N. E at the point of intersection represents *the effective demand*. At this point, entrepreneurs maximize their expected profits. If either more or less employment were offered, profits would be less. Thus at any one time, there is, according to Keynes' theory, a uniquely determined amount of employment which will be most profitable for entrepreneurs to offer to workers. There is no reason to assume this point will correspond to full employment. The labor market is not, as a rule, a seller's market. Aggregate demand and aggregate supply might be equal at full employment, but this will occur only if investment demand happens to equal the gap between the aggregate supply price corresponding to full employment and the amount which consumers in the aggregate choose to spend for consumption out of income at full employment. According to Keynes, the typical investment demand will be inadequate to fill the gap between the amount of income corresponding to full employment and the consumption demand out of that income. Therefore, the aggregate demand schedule and the aggregate supply schedule will intersect at a point of less than full employment. This establishes an equilibrium from which there will be no tendency to depart in the absence of some external change. In the absence of a large volume of expected proceeds from the sale of investment goods, the total proceeds expected by employers will be less than is necessary to induce them to offer employment to all who are willing to work. Full employment is important only as a limiting case. It may be defined as an amount of employment beyond which further increases in effective demand do not increase output and employment (p. 26).

The maxim that "supply creates its own demand" means that *any* increase in employment will lead to an additional amount of proceeds sufficient to induce entrepreneurs to offer the increased employment. If this maxim were valid, aggregate demand and aggregate supply would be equal for all amounts of employment (N). On a diagram similar to Figure 1, the classical theory would represent DD and ZZ as equal for all amounts of employment (N). Since the expected proceeds would always be adequate to induce more employment, competition among entrepreneurs for workers and among workers for jobs would lead to an expansion of employment as long as anyone is involuntarily unemployed. The classical theory breaks down in attempting to apply Say's law to the demand for investment. For while it is true that more employment will create more income of which some will be spent for consumers goods, all of it will not be spent in this way and there is no reason to assume that the difference will be devoted to investment expenditure. If investment does not increase when employment increases, the sum of consumption demand and investment demand will be less than the aggregate supply price for the higher level of employment. Entrepreneurs will reduce employment to a level at which the aggregate supply price exceeds the consumption demand by the actual amount of investment.

Further statement of the principle of effective demand

Since there is little that is novel about the aggregate supply function, the essence of Keynes' theory is found in his analysis of the aggregate demand function. Since employment depends on demand and total demand is equal to total income, the general theory of employment is also a theory of aggregate demand or of aggregate income. Since the value of total output is equal to total income, Keynes' theory may also be called a theory of aggregate output. Employment results in the production of output on the one hand and in the creation of income on the other. Total output will have a value equal to total income. Total output consists of the production of consumers goods and the production of investment goods.[2] Total

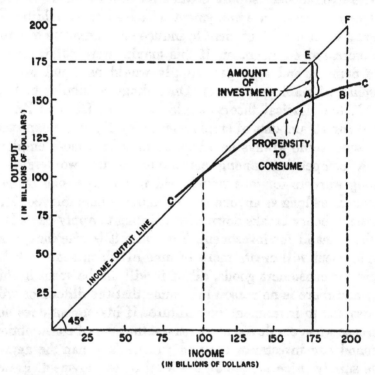

Figure 2. Income Determined by the Propensity to Consume and the Amount of Investment.

---

2. Any number of divisions of total output could be made. For some purposes it is convenient to make a three-fold division of total national product by setting the contribution of government apart in a separate category. For other problems a four-fold division into consumption, private investment, government investment, and foreign investment (net exports) is used. In the *General Theory* Keynes uses only the two-fold division into consumption and investment. At this point in our discussion it would complicate the analysis and add little to the essential meaning of Keynes' theory to depart from his simple classification of output as consumption and investment. This two-fold division is not arbitrary. It is based on the empirical premise that the behavior that determines consumption and that which determines investment are different in a way which has great practical significance. One is stable in relation to income and the other is highly unstable and largely autonomous.

income is earned from the production of consumers goods and the production of investment. If we start from less than full employment, any *increase* in employment must be divided between consumption output and investment output in a manner which corresponds to the way in which income receivers choose to divide their *increase* in income between consumption expenditure and saving.

Assuming as Keynes does the aggregate supply function to be given, the thesis of his *General Theory* is that employment is determined by aggregate demand, which in turn depends on the propensity to consume and the amount of investment at a given time.

Since employment is assumed to be uniquely correlated with income, we may show income along the horizontal axis in place of employment, which was represented there in Figure 1. The value of total output is shown along the vertical axis. Since total income is equal to the value of total output, the equilibrium adjustment must lie along the 45° line indicated in Figure 2.[3] The point of effective demand (E) will be on the 45° line at the point at which the volume of investment is equal to the distance between this line and the consumption schedule, CC.

The consumption schedule (propensity to consume) will be discussed in detail later. This schedule represents the stable relationship which Keynes assumes to exist between the size of the national income and the amount which will be spent by

---

3. The 45° line in Figure 2 is not the same as the aggregate supply schedule in Figure 1. The 45° line is merely a line along which income equals output for any value of output. Keynes did not use a diagram to explain his theory of effective demand, but geometrical drawings have been widely used for this purpose. Figure 2 differs from most of the diagrams of this type in that it shows "output" along the vertical axis. It would perhaps be more appropriate to call this the "demand for output." If Figure 2 were to be broken down into more detail, it would show income, which is along the horizontal axis, divided into two parts, consumption expenditure and saving; and output, which is along the vertical axis, divided into consumption output (or consumption demand) and investment demand. This presentation has pedagogical advantages over diagrams which show consumption, investment and saving along the vertical axis. The proportionality of the two parts of these two lines is an essential condition of an equilibrium position. It also can be used to show the meaning of the equality of saving to investment.

the public for consumption. In Figure 2 the consumption schedule is drawn to represent the following assumed relations between income and consumption, in billions of dollars:

Income	100	125	150	175	200
Consumption	100	120	137.5	150	160

This schedule follows the fundamental maxim that when income rises, consumption also rises, but less than income. The difference between income and consumption increases from zero at $100 billion of income, to $5 billion at $125 billion, to $12.5 billion at $150 billion, to $25 billion at $175 billion, and finally to $40 billion at the assumed full employment income of $200 billion.

If AE ($25 billion) is the amount of investment at a given time, the total output most profitable for entrepreneurs to pro' duce will be $175 billion. This total output will consist of two parts, $150 billion worth of consumption output in addition to $25 billion worth of investment output. Total income, which is equal to total output will also be $175 billion. If the amount of investment becomes less than AE, income must fall below $175 billion. When investment is zero, income will be $100 billion, and all output will be consumption output. The distance FB ($40 billion) represents the amount of investment that would be necessary to raise income to the full employment level of $200 billion.

Since consumption expenditure increases by less than income when income increases, there can be no increase in employment unless there is an increase in investment. This means that investment must increase to fill the gap between income and consumption. Less than 100 per cent of any increase in aggregate income will be spent for consumption goods and consequently less than 100 per cent of output must be in the form of consumption goods. Otherwise what is produced will not correspond to what is demanded out of the higher income. In the absence of an increase in the demand for investment, business men who employ additional workers to produce more output will be unable in the aggregate to sell what they produce except at losses. If newly employed workers are set to producing all consumers goods, there will be an insufficient demand to buy these goods at prices profitable to entrepreneurs because only a part of the newly created income will be spent to buy consumers goods. In the circumstances illustrated in Figure 2, let us suppose entrepreneurs were to hire the unemployed workers to produce an additional $25 billion worth of consumers goods. This would make a total output of $175 billion of consumption output and $25 billion of investment output, and a total income of $200 billion. Since out of this income only $160 billion will be spent for consumption, there will be $15 billion worth of unsold consumption output. Losses will result because all the additional workers have been employed to produce consumers goods and only part of the additional demand will be for consumers goods. But if newly employed workers are set to producing less than 100 per cent of consumers goods, there will be no market for the non-consumer (investment) goods in the absence of an increase in the demand for investment. Losses will result in either case because the proceeds received by entrepreneurs will be less than sufficient to cover the total costs (aggregate supply price) of the higher level of employment. Consequently output and employment will reach an equilibrium only at the point where income exceeds consumption by the actual amount of investment. This illustrates again the principle that employment cannot increase unless investment increases. This principle rests on the assumption that the propensity to consume (consumption function) remains unchanged.

The Propensity to Consume

Consumption demand depends on the size of income and the share that is spent for consumers goods. We have already observed that for any level of national income there is a fairly stable proportion which will be spent for consumption by the public. If the American public chooses to spend $160 billion for consumption when the national income is $200 billion, the average propensity to consume at this point is 80 per cent.

Some income recipients will spend more than 80 per cent and others will spend less than 80 per cent of their incomes for consumption, but the average (arithmetic mean) will be 80 per cent. At different levels of national income the amount of consumption will change, and the proportion which total consumption is of total income will also change. The absolute amount of consumption will increase as income increases, and will decrease as income decreases. A schedule showing the various amounts of consumption which correspond to different levels of income is the "schedule of the propensity to consume," which for the sake of brevity is referred to simply as the propensity to consume." It is a functional relationship indicating how consumption varies when income varies. Such a relationship may be shown for an individual or family consumption unit, but in Keynes' theory it is the relationship between aggregate community consumption and aggregate community income that is important.

Keynes' assumption that the propensity to consume is relatively stable in the short run is a generalization about actual experience and is an essential part of the structure of his theory. If this assumption is valid, the amount of community consumption varies in a regular manner with aggregate income. What the actual schedule of the propensity to consume will be at any time depends on the established customs of the community, the distribution of income, the tax system, and other factors, which will be discussed in Chapter 5. A high propensity to consume is favorable to employment because it leaves relatively small gaps between income and the consumption out of income corresponding to different levels of employment. If the schedule of the propensity to consume is relatively low, the gaps between income and consumption will be greater and, in order to maintain high levels of employment, the amount of investment must be relatively great. If the average propensity to consume were 100 per cent for all levels of income, full employment would be assured because no investment would be required. As income was received, it would all be spent for consumers goods. Supply would create its own demand. However, it is a characteristic of the actual world that the average propensity to consume is less than 100 per cent for all high levels of employment. Only if employment falls low enough, will a point be reached where consumption is equal to income. This is a lower limit below which employment will not fall, except perhaps temporarily. In wealthy industrial societies this level of employment is so low that it would provoke revolutionary action if long maintained. Investment is required to maintain employment above a relatively low and socially intolerable level.

The Inducement to Invest

Effective demand for investment is more complex and more unstable than effective demand for consumption. As previously indicated, investment means producing more than is currently consumed, and takes the form of adding to the accumulated wealth of society. Although investment sometimes takes the form of additions to the stocks of finished goods in the hands of retailers and wholesalers, its most important form is in expenditures by business men for factories, machinery, and other forms of producers goods. The inducement to business men to build factories and to invest in other ways arises from the expectation that such investment will prove profitable. Since these expectations are often based on precarious estimates of the future, the volume of investment is subject to wide fluctuations. Business men will borrow to invest up to the point at which the expected return from new investment is equal to the cost of borrowing funds with which to carry out the investment. The inducement to invest is determined in Keynes' analysis by the business men's estimates of the profitability of investment in relation to the rate of interest on money for investment. The expected profitability of new investment is called the marginal efficiency of capital.

The marginal efficiency of capital

The marginal efficiency of a capital asset is the highest *rate* of return over cost expected from producing one more

unit (a marginal unit) of a particular type of capital asset.
In the language of the man in the street, it may be thought of
as the expected rate of percentage profit per year on real
investments of the most efficient type. Assume that in a growing community a store building that can be built for $20,000
will yield $1200 per year in rental and has depreciation and
maintenance of $200 per year, giving a net return of $1000
per year. If the rate of interest is 4 per cent, this building is
worth $25,000 ($1000 divided by .04). A building of this
type already constructed should be worth $25,000. However,
it will be preferable to borrow $20,000 at 4 per cent to build
a new building, and receive a net return of $1000 or 5 per
cent. The efficiency of this type of capital asset is 5 per cent,
which is higher than the rate of interest of 4 per cent. If 5
per cent is the highest rate of return which can be secured
from any type of real investment, the marginal efficiency of
capital *in general* is 5 per cent. **Investment continues as long
as the expected rate of return exceeds the rate of interest.** If
the cost of construction of a new asset is less than the purchase price of the old asset of the same type, it will be profitable to build a new one rather than to buy the old one. This
explains what is meant by the expected rate of profit being in
excess of the rate of interest.

Keynes uses the term marginal efficiency of capital rather
than expected rate of profit or some other conventional term
like the marginal productivity of capital because he wishes
to emphasize the dynamic setting in which the present and
future are linked by the expectations of investors. In the
example of the store building referred to above, the fact
that the current yield from such assets is $1000 per year
does not justify the assumption that the yield will continue
at this level in the future. It may rise above $1000 in some
years, fall below $1000 in other years, or behave in almost
any other way depending on the future course of events, some
of which may be foreseen clearly but not with certainty,
others which may be only dimly anticipated, and still others
which are completely unforeseen at the time the investment

is made. In this dynamic setting, the investor is extremely cautious about investments that will realize their value, if at all, only over many years to come. The longer the period involved, the greater the chance that unforeseen events will intervene to disappoint today's investors. The role of capital assets as a link by which wealth-holders bridge the gap between the present and the future is one of the fundamental ideas underlying Keynes' entire analysis.

The marginal efficiency of capital is characterized by short-term instability and a tendency toward long-term decline. Fluctuations in the marginal efficiency of capital are the fundamental cause of the business cycle. Feverish building activity in the capital goods industries that marks the later phase of the expansion stage of the cycle results from the optimistic expectations of investors. For some time the increased activity brings larger profits and adds fuel to prevailing optimism. Meanwhile, however, great additions to the existing supply of capital goods force down the expected rate of return below the rate of interest. The cessation in capital accumulation (investment) which follows leads inevitably to collapse and depression. This transition from expansion to contraction is frequently highlighted by the gyration of the stock exchange, whose violent fluctuations are an objectification of the instability of the marginal efficiency of capital. The speculation and financial manipulation that characterize stock market activities are among the chief manifestations of the instability of capitalist economies.

Since every new investment competes with every old investment, there is a tendency in the secular long run for the growing abundance of capital assets to cause a decline in the rate of return. This tendency may be offset by unusual circumstances like those which characterized the western world during the nineteenth century when rapid growth in population, the existence of great undeveloped geographical frontiers, and great technological innovations like the railroad provided unprecedented demands for new capital, and forestalled the fall in the rate of return to capital. Geographical expansion has come to a close with the end of the frontiers in America and elsewhere, population growth has slowed down, and inventions are more of the labor-saving than of the capital-absorbing type. These underlying structural changes of recent decades provide a plausible explanation for the mass unemployment which struck capitalist economies in the 1930's. However, the unemployment trends set up by a falling marginal efficiency of capital can be offset, at least temporarily, by a corresponding fall in the rate of interest.

The rate of interest

The rate of interest, the other factor which determines the volume of investment, depends upon two things: (a) the state of liquidity preference and (b) the quantity of money. The former is the demand aspect and the latter the supply aspect of the price of money, that is, the rate of interest. Liquidity preference refers to the desire of people to hold some of their assets in the form of money. The quantity of money refers to the amount of funds in the form of coins, paper currency, and bank deposits outstanding in the hands of the public.

There are several reasons why people may wish to hold wealth in the form of money. Classified according to motive, these include the transactions motive, the precautionary motive, and the speculative motive (p. 170). The demand for money for the transactions motive refers to the use of money as a medium of exchange for ordinary transactions such as buying raw materials, paying rent, paying wages, paying dividends, et cetera. For any given level of employment, output, and prices, there is a relatively definite and stable quantity of money needed for this purpose. As the level of employment and output rises, the number of transactions will, of course, increase and thus increase the demand for money for transactions. Likewise, a general rise in prices or wages will increase the amount of money needed for transactions. The precautionary motive for holding money arises from the need for meeting unforeseen emergencies which will involve outlays greater than those involved in the usual anticipated transactions. Here again the amount of money needed to satisfy this demand is relatively stable and predictable.

The type of liquidity preference which is important in relation to the rate of interest is that arising in connection with the speculative motive. Keynes defines the speculative motive as "the object of securing profit from knowing better than the market what the future will bring forth" (p. 170). Quite apart from needs for money as a medium of exchange, people hold money as a store of wealth. They hold their assets in this form because they prefer it to any other means of storing wealth. This is a type of speculation because in holding their wealth in the barren money form, people are speculating on the chances that conditions will change so they will be able to convert their money into earning assets on better terms at a later date, and on terms which will be enough better to offset any earnings that might be made by parting with liquidity now. Chiefly responsible for this type of preference for money is uncertainty concerning the future rate of interest. If it is thought that the interest rate may rise in the future, there will be an incentive to hold money and avoid buying income-yielding securities such as bonds. A future rise in the rate of interest may wipe out an amount of the capitalized value of purchased assets to an extent that will more than offset any temporary returns in the form of interest or dividends. The lower the interest rate goes, the stronger becomes the incentive to hold wealth in the form of money. There is an increasing danger of capital loss arising from a slight rise in the interest rate. The long-term rate of interest will be especially sensitive to liquidity preference because over a long period the uncertainty of events increases in a sort of geometric proportion.

In the light of these circumstances, the demand for money to satisfy the speculative motive is subject to erratic fluctuations, in contrast with the relatively stable demand for the transactions and precautionary motives. When liquidity preference for the speculative motive weakens, the interest

rate will fall, and when liquidity preference for the speculative motive strengthens, the rate of interest will rise. Liquidity preference rises and falls according to the changing attitudes of the public toward the economic and political future.
Thus the level of the interest rate depends upon factors which
are highly psychological in nature. The so-called psychological factors are themselves conditioned by more objective
events in the economic and political arena.

A rise in the interest rate resulting from increased liquidity preference indicates that the desire to store wealth in the
form of money is not an absolute desire, but one which is
relative to the desire for rewards offered by other alternatives.
If the reward for surrendering liquidity is high enough—
that is, if the interest rate is high enough—illiquidity will
be risked. The interest rate is a price which fluctuates according to the supply and demand for money. The supply is fixed
by the banking system and the demand is determined by
the preference for holding cash. As long as the supply remains fixed, the price, or rate, varies with the demand. The
rate of interest is the price which "equilibrates the desire to
hold wealth in the form of cash with the available quantity
of cash" (p. 167). If the rate of interest were lower at any
particular time the public would want to hold more cash
than is available, and if the rate of interest were higher at
any time, the public would not wish to hold all the cash that
is available.[4] Interest is the reward paid for the use of money,
and the reward, like any price, must be neither too high nor
too low in relation to the supply.

Although the public does not control the quantity of
money, the banking system does. All the public can do when
it wants to hold more money and there is no more money is
to bid up the price, the rate of interest. But the banking
authorities are in a position to answer the demand for more
money by increasing the supply, and thus preventing the rate
of interest from rising. Consequently, the position of the

---

4. The word "cash" as used here is equivalent to "money" including demand
deposits.

banking and monetary authorities is strategic in relation to the rate of interest. By pursuing a policy of a flexible money supply, the banking system can, within limits, control the rate of interest. If the banking authorities cannot control the psychological ups and downs of the public in its attitude toward liquidity preference, they can at least offset the effects of these changes on the interest rate by letting a public which desires to hold more cash actually hold more cash. It is crucial to Keynes' position that the monetary authorities should be strong and during depressions should pursue an easy money policy which will lower interest rates and permit them to remain low.

In the transition from depression to recovery, the demand for money for transactions will be increasing. If this increased demand must be met by drawing upon money used to satisfy the speculative motive, the rate of interest will rise, and recovery will be impeded. Therefore, unless the banks are ready to lend more cash, or unless the liquidity preference of the public for the speculative motive decreases considerably, the volume of investment will fall off and recovery may be nipped before it has really begun. This shortage of money would retard investment and recovery no matter how much the desire of the public to save might increase.

The Relation of Investment to Consumption

There exists a definite relation between the amount of consumption output and the amount of investment output which it will be profitable for entrepreneurs to produce. Given the propensity to consume, the amount of consumption demand depends on the size of national income. National income is created partly from the output of consumption and partly from the output of investment. The volume of investment depends on the inducement to invest as determined by the principles discussed in the preceding section. Hence, the amount of consumption goods that it will be profitable for entrepreneurs to produce depends partly on the amount of investment output that is being produced. If the inducement to invest is such that entrepreneurs in the United States are producing $40 billion worth of investment goods, and if the propensity to consume is four-fifths, it will pay to produce $160 billion worth of consumption output in addition to the $40 billion worth of investment output. The output is divided four-fifths to consumption and one-fifth to investment because demand is in the ratio of four to one. If output is to be sold without losses, it must be proportioned between consumption goods and investment goods in the ratio which corresponds to the ratio in which income receivers choose to divide their incomes between consumption expenditure and saving. The *amount* of total output it will pay to produce in this ratio depends on the amount of investment demand.

In the arithmetical example cited in the preceding paragraph, the $160 billion of effective demand for consumption comes from the income, some of which is earned in investment activity. For example, men working on the construction of a factory (investment goods) spend part of their incomes for groceries and clothes (consumption goods) just as do men who work in factories turning out consumers goods. Thus if the number employed in building factories decreases, so will the demand for consumption goods decrease. Using the above figures, suppose investment falls from $40 to $39 billion. If the ratio of consumption to investment remains 4 to 1, there will have to be a fall in consumption to a level of 4 times $39 billion or $156 billion. From a fall of $1 billion in investment there results a fall of $4 billion in consumption, making a total fall of $5 billion. National income decreases from $200 to $195 billion ($156 plus $39 equals $195). While the ratio may not remain exactly 4 to 1, it will not change very much as long as total income remains in the neighborhood of $200 billion.

What would happen if entrepreneurs did not reduce their output of consumption goods by $4 billion when investment falls from $40 billion to $39 billion? Suppose they continued to produce the same amount of consumers goods as before, $160 billion worth. They would be unable to sell all the consumers goods produced, because the workers who lost their jobs in investment activity and other income recipients whose incomes had been lowered as a result of the falling off of investment would not spend as much for consumers goods as before. When incomes are less, consumption expenditure will be less, given the propensity to consume. The original impact of the $1 billion fall in investment is to lower income from $200 billion to $199 billion. But this is not the end of the process. Retailers and others whose sales are reduced will suffer reduced income, wholesalers who sell to retailers will also suffer reduced income, and the manufacturers who sell to wholesalers will suffer likewise. This process of cumulative income reduction will go on until the total fall in income resulting from a decline in consumption demand is 4 times the fall in investment demand. The over-all ratio of 4 to 1 between consumption and investment will be reestablished at 156 to 39, or at a total income of $195 billion. These relations between investment and consumption will be explored more fully in the discussion of the multiplier in Chapter 5.

What would be the result of applying the classical theory to the above situation? Under conditions of full employment assumed by the classical theory, income and total effective demand remain constant in the short period. Effective demand will always be sufficient to lead to full employment. Starting with an income of $200 billion, divided $160 billion to consumption and $40 billion to investment, a fall in investment of $1 billion would have to result in an *increase* in consumption from $160 billion to $161 billion. This would change the ratio of consumption to investment in a way inconsistent with Keynes' principle of effective demand. It would also seem to violate common sense because it assumes consumption will increase at the very time when men are losing jobs and spending less for consumers goods than before. Although the classical analysis may seem to violate common sense, it is not without an answer as to why decreases in investment lead to increases in consumption. The answer relates to the classical theory of the rate of interest, which brings the volume of investment to equality with the volume of saving, a subject which will be explored further in Chapter 8.

Summary of the General Theory of Employment

From the foregoing discussion and from Figure 3 it may be seen that there are several alternative ways of expressing the essence of the general theory of employment. An over-all summary may be stated in the form of the following propositions:

1. Total income depends on the volume of total employment.
2. According to the propensity to consume, the amount of expenditure for consumption depends on the level of income, and therefore on total employment (from No. 1 above).
3. Total employment depends on total effective demand (D), which is made up of two parts: (a) consumption expenditure (D_1) and (b) investment expenditure (D_2).
   $(D = D_1 + D_2)$
4. In equilibrium, the aggregate demand (D) is equal to the aggregate supply (Z). Therefore, aggregate supply exceeds the effective demand for consumption by the amount of the effective demand for investment.
   ($D = D_1 + D_2$, or $D_2 = D - D_1$. Since $D = Z$, therefore $D_2 = Z - D_1$.)
5. In equilibrium, aggregate supply is equal to aggregate demand, and aggregate demand is determined by the propensity to consume and the volume of investment. Therefore, the volume of employment depends on (a) the aggregate supply function, (b) the propensity to consume, and (c) the volume of investment.
6. Both the aggregate supply function, which depends mainly on physical conditions of supply, and the propensity to consume are relatively stable, and therefore fluctuations in employment depend mainly on the volume of investment.
7. The volume of investment depends on (a) the marginal

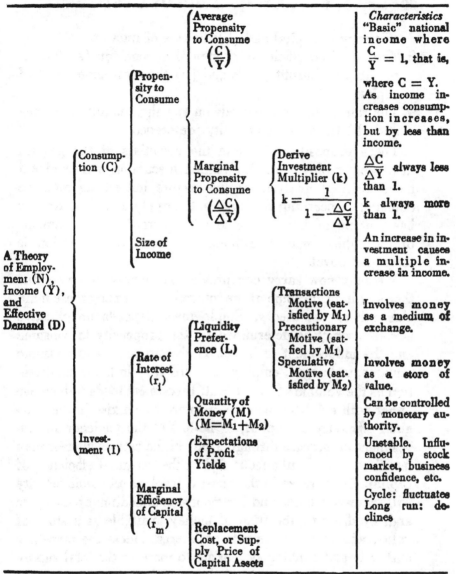

1. Employment (and income) depend on effective demand.
2. Effective demand is determined by the propensity to consume and the volume of investment.
3. The propensity to consume is relatively stable.
4. Employment depends on the volume of investment if the propensity to consume is unchanged.
5. Investment depends on the rate of interest and the marginal efficiency of capital.
6. The rate of interest depends on the quantity of money and liquidity preference.
7. The marginal efficiency of capital depends on the expectations of profit yields and the replacement cost of capital assets.

Figure 3. An Outline of the General Theory of Employment

efficiency of capital and (b) the rate of interest.

8. The marginal efficiency of capital depend on (a) the expectations of profit yields and (b) the replacement cost of capital assets.

9. The rate of interest depends on (a) the quantity of money and (b) the state of liquidity preference.

These propositions contain the essentials of the general theory of employment. Our further discussion will involve a more detailed analysis of the factors influencing effective demand. Concerning the aggregate supply function, Keynes has nothing of importance to add to traditional treatments of the subject matter, although his form of expression is somewhat novel.

We may now carry our provisional survey one step further and indicate some of the interrelations among these main elements of the theory. Employment depends on effective demand, which is determined by the propensity to consume and the inducement to invest. If the propensity to consume remains unchanged, employment will vary in the same direction as the volume af investment. Investment tends to increase either with a fall in the rate of interest or a rise in the marginal efficiency of capital, or both. But the tendency for investment to increase through a fall in the rate of interest may be offset by a simultaneous fall in the marginal efficiency of capital. An increase in the general level of economic activity will increase the demand for money as a medium of exchange and, by draining the fund of money available as a store of value, will increase the rate of interest unless the monetary authority and banking system act to increase the total supply of money. And even though the quantity of money may be increasing, the rate of interest may nevertheless rise as a result of an unfavorable shift in the attitude of wealth-holders toward liquidity. Expectations of rising future yields from capital assets will tend to raise the marginal efficiency of capital and thus raise investment and employment. This favorable effect may be offset by a simultaneous rise in the current supply price (cost of production) of capital assets.

Although rising investment will usually be accompanied by rising employment, this need not happen if the propensity to consume is falling. On the other hand, employment can rise without a rise in investment if the propensity to consume is rising. As a rule, however, the propensity to consume, or consumption function, is stable in the short run.

Finally, increases in investment bring about increases in income, and out of larger income there arises a greater demand for consumption which leads to still further increases in income. Taken in reverse, this process means that a fall in investment will decrease income and out of the decreased income there will be less demand for consumption, which leads to still further decreases in income. Once set in motion, movements of income and employment tend to be cumulative. These cumulative movements account for the fluctuating nature of employment. Limits to amplitude of fluctuation are set in the downward direction at the level at which income falls to equality with consumption, and in the upward direction at full employment. Actual fluctuations will not, as a rule, range all the way from one extreme to the other. An upward movement will characteristically stop short of full employment and a downward movement will usually stop short of the point at which income has fallen to equality with consumption. What the actual range will be depends upon the strength or weakness of the propensity to consume and the inducement to invest under the prevailing circumstances.

Practical Meaning of the Main Concepts

Among all the terms and concepts used by Keynes in *The General Theory of Employment, Interest and Money*, the three which stand out above all the rest as the strategic, independent variables are the propensity to consume (consumption schedule), the marginal efficiency of capital (investment-demand schedule), and the rate of interest (liquidity-preference schedule). The choice of these three independent variables or strategic factors arises from the nature of Keynes' interest in practical policy. The ultimate purpose of his theory is to explain what determines the volume of employment, or in terms of the practical problems involved, **what causes unemployment.** To explain the cause means, in a significant sense, to point to those factors or to a course of action which, if changed or followed, will remedy the malady. Thus when we say a common cold is caused by sitting in a draft, we usually mean that by not sitting in a draft a cold will not occur or is less likely to occur. To explain unemployment means to indicate those aspects of the economic system which need to be changed or subjected to social control in order to assure a high level of employment. Keynes says: "Our final task might be to select those variables which can be deliberately controlled or managed by central authority in the kind of system in which we actually live."[5]

Realistic theory is necessarily conditioned by the theorist's sense of values and by his ideas as to what is practicable policy. The realistic nature of Keynes' theory may be attributed largely to his vital concern with a specific type of economic program. This does not mean that Keynes' theoretical concepts are worthless in relation to policies other than those advocated by him, nor does it mean that his policies or any other policies necessarily follow from his abstract, theoretical concepts. However, a recognition of the social values and practical aims of a pioneering theorist like Keynes gives a richer insight into the meaning of his abstract theoretical concepts and propositions. A concept like the propensity to consume, or consumption function, is a formal, mathematical relationship between amounts of consumption corresponding to amounts of income for the community as a whole. But this is only the bare bones. The full meaning of this formal concept as used by Keynes emerges in terms of the use to which he puts it. He uses it to show the necessity of a high rate of consumer expenditure, which, perhaps, can be obtained by a more equal distribution of income and wealth. He uses it to indicate the desirability of steeply progressive taxation

5. Keynes, *The General Theory of Employment, Interest and Money.* New York: Harcourt, Brace and Co., Inc., 1936, page 247.

and large government outlays for social services. The propensity to consume is further refined in the form of the marginal propensity to consume, which is used to derive the concept of the investment multiplier. The common-sense meaning
of the investment multiplier is that in times of depression
when private investment lags, government investment in public works will increase the national income not only by the
amount of the public outlay but by some multiple of it.

In these terms Keynes makes a case for public works and
becomes an advocate of public spending. His theory is referred to as a "spending" theory. To call a theory a spending
theory has no meaning except in relation to some fairly specific steps or policies that may be followed to increase aggregate demand above what it would be in the absence of such
policies. When we trace the concepts to their practical consequences, the lifeless forms of abstraction begin to take on
definite shape and meaning. We see them emerging as plans
of action, altered behavior, policies. The theory is put into
practice. Only when theory is put into practice—that is, only
when we trace the theory to its practical consequences—can
we hope to test its validity by an appeal to facts and thus
arrive at an evaluation of its probable workability in the
actual world.

The operational or practical meaning of Keynes' theory
will be referred to often in this book in the belief that this
method will facilitate the understanding of what is likely to
appear to be an intrinsically difficult body of doctrine. At
this juncture we allude briefly to the operational significance
of Keynes' theories of the rate of interest and the marginal
efficiency of capital, the two independent variables which,
along with the propensity to consume referred to in the preceding paragraph, determine the level of employment. The
uniqueness of Keynes' theory of the rate of interest runs in
terms of the importance of controlling the quantity of money.
The novel concept is liquidity preference for the speculative
motive. Wealth-holders have a preference for keeping their
assets in a liquid form, the form of money, and it is this

desire to hoard which determines the level of interest rates.
An easy money policy under a strong monetary authority can
keep down the interest rates and thus stimulate investment
and employment. However, Keynes' practical sense is too
strong to lead him to attach sole importance to interest rates
and so we find a parallel stress on the marginal efficiency of
capital. The chief characteristic of the marginal efficiency of
capital is its great instability. It may fall so low in depression
that no reduction in interest rates will induce private investment. To alleviate the consequences of instability in the marginal efficiency of private capital, Keynes advocates government direction of total investment, including public investment, to compensate for the inevitable fluctuations in private
investment. A low rate of interest and a high marginal efficiency of capital are the conditions favorable to investment
and employment. Since the natural tendency is for the rate of
interest to stay up and the marginal efficiency of capital to
come down, laissez-faire policies will leave the volume of
investment short of what is necessary for full employment.
Both of these determinates of investment involve psychological attitudes toward the future which cause investment to be
much less stable than the volume of consumption. The instability of these factors determining investment leads Keynes
to say that employment is determined by investment.

The Paradox of Poverty and Potential Plenty

Keynes' principle of effective demand furnishes an explanation of the paradox of poverty in the midst of potential plenty,
one of the grave contradictions of modern capitalism. A poor
community will have little difficulty employing all its resources because it will tend to spend on consumption a large
proportion of its total income. Only a small gap needs to be
filled by investment, and since the stock of accumulated
capital assets will be slight in the poor community, the demand for investment will be brisk. A wealthy community, on

the contrary, will have great difficulty maintaining full employment because the gap between income and consumption will be large. Its investment outlets must be great if there are to be enough jobs for all. Failing to find these outlets, the potentially wealthy community will be forced to reduce its actual output until it becomes so poor that the excess of output over consumption will be reduced to the actual amount of investment. To make matters worse, the very fact that a community is rich in accumulated capital assets weakens the inducement to invest because every new investment must compete with an already large supply of old investments. The inadequacy of demand for investment reacts in a cumulative fashion on the demand for consumption. The factories that are already built cannot be used because more factories are not being built. Unemployment on a mass scale exists in the midst of potential plenty. Thus as Keynes says, "the richer the community . . . the more obvious and outrageous the defects of the economic system." Keynes finds no reason to assume that the growing gap between income and consumption at high levels of employment will be filled automatically, that is, without conscious social action, except under special historical circumstances like those existing in the nineteenth century or in time of war. War has a distinct if ironical advantage over peaceful industry in that it calls for the production of things which are to be exploded and shot away and do not remain to compete with more production of the same type at a later date. If war and threat of war are banished from the world, the capitalist countries will once more be confronted with the tasks of finding sufficient outlets for new investment to provide employment for all of its millions of workers who cannot be employed in consumption industries.

References for Further Reading

Keynes, J. M., *The General Theory of Employment, Interest and Money*. Chapters 1, 2, 3, and 18. New York: Harcourt, Brace and Company, 1936.
————, "The General Theory of Employment," *The Quarterly Jour-*

nal of Economics, February, 1937, Vol. LI, pages 209-223. Reprinted in *The New Economics*, edited by S. E. Harris. New York: Alfred A. Knopf, 1947. (This is the best statement of the essence of *The General Theory of Employment, Interest and Money* made by the author himself.)

Cassel, Gustav, "Mr. Keynes' 'General Theory,'" *International Labour Review*, October, 1937, Vol. XXVI, pages 437-445. (A critical review)

Darrell, John (Pseudonym), "Economic Consequences of Mr. Keynes," *Science and Society*, Winter, 1937, Vol. I, pages 194-211. (A Marxist review)

Haberler, Gottfried, "The Place of the General Theory of Employment, Interest and Money in the History of Economic Thought," *The Review of Economic Statistics*, November, 1946, Vol. XXVIII, pages 187-194. Reprinted in *The New Economics*, edited by S. E. Harris. New York: Alfred A. Knopf, 1947.

Hansen, A. H., "Mr. Keynes on Underemployment Equilibrium," *The Journal of Political Economy*, October, 1936, Vol. XLIV, pages 667-686. (A sympathetic review)

——, "Keynes and the General Theory," *The Review of Economic Statistics*, November, 1946, Vol. XXVIII, pages 182-187. Reprinted in *The New Economics*, edited by S. E. Harris. New York: Alfred A. Knopf, 1947. (This 1946 review is more favorable to Keynes than the one which Professor Hansen wrote in 1936.)

Harris, S. E., *The New Economics*, edited by S. E. Harris, Part I. New York: Alfred A. Knopf, 1947.

Harrod, R. F., "Mr. Keynes and Traditional Theory," *Econometrica*, January, 1937, Vol. V, pages 74-86. (A sympathetic review by one of Keynes' leading disciples)

Hawtrey, R. G., *Capital and Employment*, Chapter VII. New York: Longmans, Green, 1937. (A critical but helpful review)

Hicks, J. R., "Mr. Keynes' Theory of Employment," *The Economic Journal*, June, 1936, Vol. XLVI, pages 238-253. (A sympathetic review)

——, "Mr. Keynes and the Classics: A Suggested Interpretation," *Econometrica*, April, 1937, Vol. V, pages 147-159. (A statement of the *General Theory* in mathematical terms)

Klein, L. R., *The Keynesian Revolution*, esp. Chapter III. New York: The Macmillan Company, 1947.

Knight, F. H., "Unemployment: And Mr. Keynes's Revolution in Economic Thought," *The Canadian Journal of Economics and Po-*

litical Science, February, 1937, Vol. III, pages 100-123. (A very critical review)

Lange, Oscar, "The Rate of Interest and the Optimum Propensity to Consume," *Economica,* February, 1938, Vol. V (new series), pages 12-32.

Lederer, Emil, "Commentary on Keynes," *Social Research,* November, 1936, Vol. III, pages 478-487.

Leontief, Wassily, "The Fundamental Assumption of Mr. Keynes' Monetary Theory of Unemployment," *The Quarterly Journal of Economics,* November, 1936, Vol. LI, pages 192-197.

————, "Postulates: Keynes' *General Theory* and the Classicists," in *The New Economics,* edited by S. E. Harris, Chapter XIX. New York: Alfred A. Knopf, 1947.

Lerner, A. P., "Mr. Keynes' 'General Theory of Employment, Interest and Money,'" *International Labour Review,* October, 1936, Vol. XXXIV, pages 435-454. (An important review which was approved by Keynes)

Mount, Edward, "The Equilibrists and Mr. Keynes," *The New Masses,* September 1 and 8, 1936, Vol. XX, pages 18-19 and 17-18. (A Marxist review)

Neisser, Hans, "Commentary on Keynes," *Social Research,* November, 1936, Vol. III, pages 459-478.

Pigou, A. C., "Mr. J. M. Keynes' General Theory of Employment, Interest and Money," *Economica,* May, 1936, Vol. III (new series), pages 115-132.

Reddaway, W. B., "The General Theory of Employment, Interest and Money," *Economic Record,* June, 1936, Vol. XII, pages 28-36. (An excellent and sympathetic review)

Robertson, D. H., "Some Notes on Mr. Keynes' General Theory of Employment," *The Quarterly Journal of Economics,* November, 1936, Vol. LI, pages 168-191. (An excellent review which is critical of Keynes' theory of interest and his terminology, especially saving and investment)

Rueff, Jacques, "The Fallacies of Lord Keynes' General Theory," *The Quarterly Journal of Economics,* May, 1947, Vol. LXI, pages 343-367.

Schumpeter, J. A., "Keynes' General Theory of Employment, Interest and Money," *Journal of the American Statistical Association,* December, 1936, Vol. XXXI (new series), pages 791-795. (A brief, critical and significant review)

Shibata, Kei, "Some Questions on Mr. Keynes' General Theory of Employment, Interest and Money," *Kyoto Economic Review,* July, 1937, Vol. XII, pages 83-96.

Shibata, Kei, "Further Comments on Mr. Keynes' General Theory," *Kyoto Economic Review*, July 1939, Vol. XIV, pages 45-72. (Both of Shibata's articles are excellent.)

Takata, Yasuma, "Unemployment and Wages: A Critical Review of Mr. Keynes' Theory of Employment," *Kyoto Economic Review*, December, 1937, Vol. XII, pages 1-18.

Tarshis, Lorie, "An Exposition of Keynesian Economics," *The American Economic Review, Papers and Proceedings*, May, 1948, Vol. XXXVIII, pages 261-272.

Viner, Jacob, "Mr. Keynes on the Causes of Unemployment," *The Quarterly Journal of Economics*, November, 1936, Vol. LI, pages 147-167.

Williams, J. H., "An Appraisal of Keynesian Economics," *The American Economic Review, Papers and Proceedings*, May, 1948, Vol. XXXVIII, pages 273-290.

CHAPTER 4

Investment, Saving, Income, and the Wage–Unit

It is true, that, when an individual saves he increases his
own wealth. But the conclusion that he also increases
aggregate wealth fails to allow for the possibility that an
act of individual saving may react on someone else's
savings and hence on someone else's wealth.

J. M. Keynes, *The General Theory of Employment, Interest
and Money.**

In KEYNES' *General Theory* aggregate investment always
equals aggregate saving. This equality is a condition of equilibrium regardless of what the level of employment happens
to be. Equality between investment and saving is a consequence of changes in the level of income. If investment increases, then income will increase until the saving out of the
higher income is equal to the increased investment; and if
investment falls, income will fall until the saving out of the
lower income is equal to the reduced investment. Hence,
these concepts are geared to the fundamental idea of a shifting equilibrium as distinguished from a special, full-employment equilibrium in which investment equals saving only at
full employment. Investment, saving, and income are key
terms which must be defined more fully. Like any set of con-

* Harcourt, Brace and Co., Inc., 1936, pages 83-84.

cepts, they take on their full meaning only in relation to the whole theory of which they are a part. It is not the individual definitions in isolation that are important but the concepts in relation to each other and to the rest of the theory. If we bear in mind that Keynes' method is one which investigates the problem of unemployment in terms of an equilibrium system in which the equality of aggregate demand and aggregate supply is the fundamental condition, we may avoid the confusion that has characterized many discussions of saving and investment.

Since Keynes' theory deals with the economic system as a whole, the terms investment, saving, and income mean aggregate or total national or social investment, saving, and income. **Investment is the addition to the existing stock of** *real* **capital assets, such as the construction of new factories, new office buildings, transportation facilities, and additions to inventories.** This use of the term is to be carefully distinguished from purely financial investment such as the purchase of a stock or bond in the securities market. In the latter case, one party exchanges money for securities and another party exchanges securities for money. The additional financial investment of the party who purchases securities is just offset by the financial disinvestment of the party who sells securities. Hence, if we look at both sides of a financial investment it is consistent with Keynes' definition of (aggregate) investment because in the economic system as a whole financial investments cancel each other. No addition is made to real capital as a result of such a transaction and therefore no real investment occurs. When new securities are issued to finance plant expansion, et cetera, and labor and materials are purchased to build real capital assets, it is the latter and not the purchase of the securities as such that constitute the real investment.

The exact line of demarkation between investment and consumption is not a matter of great importance so long as it is consistently maintained. Some expenditures such as those for food and clothing are clearly consumption. Others such as the building of factories and railroads clearly represent investment. Some items such as consumers durable goods are not so easily classified. It is customary, for example, to regard outlays on housing construction as investment and outlays for automobiles as consumption, but this distinction is clearly one which might be, and has been, a subject of debate. The fact that there are no hard and fast rules for classifying some items as investment and others as consumption does not raise any important theoretical question. In statistical tabulations of the division of total output, it is, of course, important to indicate what items are placed in each category.

Investment includes additions to inventories as well as to fixed capital. These additions may be either intentional or unintentional. Intended increases are motivated by larger volume of sales or by anticipation of price changes or by other related factors which are part of the ordinary planning activities of business enterprise. Unintended investment is the accumulation of unsold finished goods (liquid capital in Keynes' terminology) arising from unforeseen changes in the market. Some writers view the distinction between intended and unintended accumulations of inventories as of prime significance but for Keynes' general theory the difference is not important (p. 76).

Saving is defined as the excess of income over consumption expenditure. This definition applies to individual saving and to aggregate saving of the economic system. An individual who has a yearly income of $2000, taxes being disregarded, and spends $1800 for consumption, saves $200. An economy which has a national income of $200 billion per year and spends $180 billion for consumption, saves $20 billion. In both cases, saving is equal to income minus consumption. However, in dealing with the over-all behavior of the economic system, account must frequently be taken of factors which may be ignored when we are concerned only with the behavior of the individual units in isolation. Saving is behavior of this type. Although individual saving and community saving are both defined in the same terms, and although community saving is the net resultant of the saving of all individual units within the community, individual saving does not always result in community saving. Individual saving is not-spending for consumption, and a failure to spend by one individual may reduce the income of others and hence impair their ability to save. Unless it is clearly understood that the kind of saving Keynes is talking about in the *General Theory* is aggregate or collective saving, the equality between investment and saving will be difficult to grasp.

The fundamental fact about saving is that its volume depends upon income. At varying levels of national income, the community will want to save amounts which are more or less stable and predictable at any given time. In other words, the propensity to save is stable. Investment, on the other hand, does not depend to any significant degree upon the size of the national income. Investment depends mainly on dynamic factors like growth of population, geographical expansion, and technological progress as these growth factors affect the profit expectations of entrepreneurs. Individuals save without any thought of building factories or otherwise making real investment. Entrepreneurs invest without ascertaining whether or not there has been an equivalent amount of saving. Despite the fact that investors and savers are, as a rule, two separate sets of persons who make their decisions freely and independently of one another, the net result of their collective behavior is to invest and to save in the aggregate identical amounts during any given period. The clue to this equality is found in fluctuations in income. Whereas experience indicates that saving is stable, more or less predictable, and induced, investment is unstable, unpredictable, and autonomous. Hence, in terms of the facts of experience, the behavior of investors is a more dynamic factor than is the behavior of savers. Investment rules the roost.

Varying levels of income cannot be sustained unless the amounts of saving at these levels of income are offset by an equivalent volume of investment. If potential savings are not offset, the potential income corresponding to these savings cannot be realized. The equilibrium level of income is realized where saving out of income is just equal to the actual amount of investment.

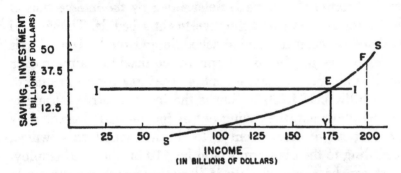

Figure 4. Saving Schedule and Investment Schedule Determine Income.

The relations between income, investment, and saving are indicated in Figure 4.[1] Income is shown along the horizontal axis and saving and investment along the vertical axis. SS is the saving schedule showing how the amount of saving increases with income. At very low levels of income, saving will be negative, meaning that consumption will exceed income. If investment is completely autonomous, in the sense that it does not vary with income, the investment schedule may be represented by the horizontal straight line II. This means that changes in investment take the form of spontaneous shifts in the entire schedule. The facts seem to be that while investment is not completely autonomous, it will not increase

---

1. Diagrams similar to Figure 4 have appeared frequently in the economics literature to explain Keynes' theory, although Keynes himself did not use such a diagram. See, for example, P. A. Samuelson, *Economics, An Introductory Analysis*, page 259. New York: McGraw-Hill Book Company, Inc., 1948; L. R. Klein, *The Keynesian Revolution*, page 76. New York: The Macmillan Company, 1947. Numerous attempts have been made to derive statistically the schedules for saving and investment. On the American data see, for example, M. Ezekiel, in *The American Economic Review*, March and June, 1942, Vol. XXXII, Nos. 1 and 2, pages 22-49 and 272-307.

as rapidly as saving when income rises. This is, of course, fundamental to Keynes' entire theory. Figure 4 concerns the simplest case in which investment remains constant for all levels of income. When investment is $25 billion, the equilibrium level of income will be $175 billion because only at this income will the amount of saving also be $25 billion. The level of national income is determined by the intersection of the saving schedule and the investment schedule. The vertical distance between the saving schedule and the horizontal axis indicates the amount of investment required to maintain each level of income. No investment is necessary for an income of $100 billion. If $200 billion is the income corresponding to full employment, the saving out of income is represented by the vertical distance from F to the horizontal axis, which, according to the diagram, would be $40 billion. Full employment can be achieved only if there is enough investment to offset this amount of saving.

There is a close relationship between Figure 4 and Figure 2. The data used in Figure 2 were, in billions of dollars:

Income	100	125	150	175	200
Consumption	100	120	137.5	150	160

The data used in Figure 4 to show the relation between income and saving are, in terms of billions of dollars:

Income	100	125	150	175	200
Saving	0	5	12.5	25	40

Thus the saving schedule, or the schedule of the propensity to save, may be found by subtracting the amounts of consumption from the corresponding amounts of income. Saving is the excess of income over consumption. The propensity to consume and the propensity to save are the same thing looked at in different ways. Figure 2 illustrates the important principle that income is determined by the propensity to consume and the amount of investment. Figure 4 illustrates the same principle in slightly different terms, namely, that income is determined by the propensity to save and the amount of investment.

Having shown that the equality of the volume of investment and the volume of saving is a condition of equilibrium, we may now restate the relations which lead to this equality. Employment results in the production of output on the one hand and the creation of income on the other. The value of total output is equal to total income. Total income (Y) is equal to the sum of the income created by the production of consumers output plus the income created by the production of investment output, (Y = C + I). Investment is that part of current output which is in excess of the value of consumption goods. Saving is the excess of income over expenditure for consumption. Therefore investment must be equal to saving since they are both equal to the excess of equal values (output and income) over consumption.

Why

I = S

Thus:

$$Y = C + I \qquad \text{Income} = \text{Consumption} + \text{Investment}$$
$$S = Y - C \qquad \text{Saving} = \text{Income} - \text{Consumption}$$

Transposing:

$$Y = C + S \qquad \text{Income} = \text{Consumption} + \text{Saving}$$

Therefore,

$$I = S \qquad \text{Investment} = \text{Saving}$$

The novelty of Keynes' treatment of saving and investment lies not in the fact that they are equal but that they can be and normally are equal at less than full employment. Whereas the classical school associates the equality between investment and saving with automatic changes in the rate of interest, Keynes associates it with changes in the level of income. The fault which Keynes finds with the classical theory is the inference that every act of not-spending (saving) by an individual will increase aggregate investment by the same amount. If this were true, any failure to spend for consumption would be offset by a corresponding increase in investment, and unemployment would not exist.

There appears to be a tendency to think of depression as a

situation in which saving is in excess of investment. Most people are so accustomed to viewing saving from their own individual point of view that it is difficult for them to think of saving from the social or community point of view. Saving is to most people putting money in the bank, or into securities, or into the mattress or an old sock. It is only by an act of conscious intellectual effort that we think far enough into the economic process of society to realize that saving is a two-sided affair. Attempts to save, which are successful so far as the individual is concerned since he adds to his individual wealth, may be self-defeating and even positively harmful so far as society at large is concerned. We plan to save for society as well as for ourselves, but in the absence of co-operation from entrepreneurs we do not assist society even when we attain our personal objectives. Putting part of a monthly salary into a savings account means only that an individual has not spent all his income. The effect of not-spending as such is to reduce the demand for consumption below what it would have been if the money which is saved had been spent. In the absence of some entrepreneur's action to invest, an act of individual saving will prove abortive for the community. It will merely reduce effective demand for consumption without any. compensating increase in the demand for investment. The decrease in effective demand for consumption reduces employment and income. One of the important lessons of the *General Theory* is that spending rather than individual saving is the essential condition of production and prosperity in an exchange economy where one man's spending is another man's income.

A further difficulty in reconciling the equality of saving to investment when there is unemployment arises from ancient mores which condition us to see in personal frugality a virtue applicable equally to society and to ourselves. That a private virtue like saving may be a public vice (unemployment) is almost as foreign to our thinking today as it was in the eighteenth century when Bernard Mandeville's *Fable of the Bees,* an allegorical poem which portrays the sad plight of a once prosperous community in which spending had been cut down in the interest of frugality and virtue, was convicted as a nuisance by a grand jury in England. Individual saving is a mere residual and is no part of effective demand. Individual saving *per se* is a withdrawal of potential effective demand. In the absence of adequate offsets to saving, thrift produces poverty and not wealth. A reluctance to spend takes on a different social significance when it is regarded not as a factor which tends to increase investment but as a factor which tends to cause unemployment (p. 185).

Income

The aggregate income of an entire economic system can be defined in any one of several different ways. Two of the figures most commonly used to refer to the over-all performance of any economy are the **gross national product** and the **net national product.** The **gross national product is the money value of all the** *final* **goods and services produced during a given period, and the net national product is equal to the gross national product minus depreciation and obsolescence** of capital assets. Final goods are finished articles which are the end products of production. They include final consumer goods like bread and automobiles and final investment goods like factories and locomotives and increases in inventory. They do not include raw materials and intermediate products like iron ore and steel which are sold, say, to automobile manufacturers. The reason for counting only final goods and not raw materials or intermediate goods in the national product is obvious. To do otherwise would involve counting the same products more than once. For example, if the value of steel sold to automobile manufacturers were added to the total market value of the automobile, which includes the cost of the steel purchased from the manufacturer, there would be double counting. This does not mean the whole contribution to national output is made at the final stage of production.

The total value of the product is the sum of the values added at each stage and is embodied in the final product.

As Keynes defines it, aggregate or national income is an amount which lies between the value of the gross national and the net national product as these terms are usually defined. He subtracts some but not all depreciation and obsolescence from the gross national product (which equals the gross national income) to arrive at his concept of "income." He chooses this definition of income because it is the concept which he believes is causally significant in the decisions that determine the amount of employment. Entrepreneurs will offer the amount of employment which maximizes their expected profits. Some depreciation on equipment inherited from the previous period will occur whether or not it is used for production during the current period. For the current period this is an involuntary expense over which the entrepreneur has no control. The entrepreneur does have voluntary control over the extra depreciation and extra maintenance which will occur as a result of the equipment being used rather than not being used. What he controls from now on governs his behavior in determining what scale of output will maximize his profits and what amount of employment will be needed to produce that output. The loss of value resulting from using equipment rather than not using it is called the user cost (p. 70). User cost is one of the expenses of production voluntarily undertaken when entrepreneurs decide how many workers to employ. For example, if a machine which is worth $1000 at the beginning of the year is used in production during the year and has a value of $750 at the end of the year, the user cost is not the full $250 decline in value. If the machine had not been used at all during the year it would have declined in value as a result of obsolescence and some forms of depreciation. Suppose its value could have been maintained at $900 at the end of the year by a small maintenance expenditure of $10 when it is not used in production. The user cost for the year is $140 ($900 — $10 — $750), or the difference between the decline in value of

$250 when used and the decline in value of $110 when not used, with allowance for the optimum amount of maintenance involved even when not used.[2]

The income of an individual business firm is therefore defined as that sum which it attempts to maximize and in terms of which it decides how much employment to offer. To arrive at this sum, the firm must subtract from its total proceeds the user cost plus the amounts paid out to other factors of production in the form of wages, interest, and rent (factor cost). Since these latter costs (wages, interest, and rent) represent the income of the rest of the community, the total national income is equal to the aggregate proceeds of all business firms less the aggregate user cost. If gross national income is represented by A and the aggregate user cost by U, the income of the economic system is A — U.

Although income as just defined is the important concept in determining how much employment entrepreneurs will offer, *net income* is the important concept in relation to the amount which will be spent for consumption. Since expenditure for consumption is an important element of effective demand, net income as well as income has a significant place in Keynes' general theory of employment. Net income, either for the firm or the whole economy, is equal to income minus the rest of the expected depreciation and obsolescence which is not included in user cost. This extra depreciation and obsolescence is called the *supplementary cost*. Since supplementary cost is a loss in value which is beyond the control of entrepreneurs, it occurs without regard to decisions whether or not to use equipment and on what scale to employ labor. For the individual business enterprise, net income is the figure which remains after all expenses, including *all* depreciation and obsolescence, have been deducted from proceeds. For the economic system, net income is the aggregate net income (net profits) of all business enterprises plus the payments to

---

2. The total user cost of non-integrated firms also makes allowance for the purchases of the firm from other firms. For the economic system as a whole these interfirm purchases cancel out and do not affect the aggregate user cost.

all other factors of production in the form of wages, interest, and rent. If supplementary cost is represented by V, the aggregate or national *net* income is equal to A — U — V, as compared with the national income, which is equal to A — U.[3]

The importance of net income rather than income in determining how much will be spent on consumption should be obvious. An individual entrepreneur who does not allow for full depreciation before deciding the scale of his consumption is prodigal indeed, even though he would be unwise to determine the scale of his output and employment on this basis. In corporate enterprises, the payment of dividends is limited by law to the amount of net income (net profits), either current or past. Any enterprise which consumed up to the full extent of its income, as defined by Keynes, would not be able to replace its full capital equipment. On the other hand, any practice which understates the amount of net income will tend to retard the amount of consumption and thereby to retard employment. Excessive allowances for depreciation, which are sanctioned and generally practiced by "conservative" accountants, result in an understatement of net income and thereby may contribute to a restriction of consumption and employment (pp. 98-104).

Although the definitions of investment and saving and the equality between them are unaffected by the manner in which income is defined, the magnitudes of saving and investment do depend on the definition of income. Since income is defined as a form of gross income and output as a form of gross output, saving and investment represent a form of gross saving

---

3. If we use lower case letters for individual firms to correspond to upper case letters for the whole economy, the income and *net* income for individual business enterprises are, respectively, a – u – f, and a – u – f – v. An advantage of Keynes' terms is that the firm and national incomes and net incomes are represented by the same symbols except for the obvious fact that the factor cost (f) of the entrepreneur represents the income of the rest of the community and therefore is not to be deducted in arriving at the national income. Wages, for example, are a factor cost to the firm, to be deducted from gross income before arriving at income (profits) or net income (net profits), but to the economic system, wages are a part of the national income.

and gross investment. The excess of gross income over consumption is gross saving and the excess of gross output over consumption is gross investment. Similarly net saving is equal to the excess of net income over consumption and net investment is the excess of net output over consumption. Used without modification, saving means gross saving and investment means gross investment. As with income and net income, Keynes' distinction is between saving and net saving and between investment and net investment. Following his procedure, we shall not use the modifier "gross" when we speak of income, saving, and investment, but it is well to keep in mind how these three important terms are defined.

The Wage-Unit

In order to measure the quantities of output, income, investment, saving, consumption, and demand for the economic system as a whole, Keynes uses two basic units, money and labor. Money is, of course, a basic unit of measurement in any type of economic analysis. Money alone, however, is not enough to enable us to describe the workings of the economic system. In addition to money, there is need for some type of physical unit of production or output. As long as we are dealing with the output of a single enterprise or of a single industry producing a uniform type of product, we may use the physical unit appropriate to each industry. Thus we speak of an individual refinery producing so many million gallons of gasoline, and all the refiners in the petroleum industry producing so many billion gallons of gasoline. The output of every industry can be determined by adding together the appropriate physical units of production of all the firms in the industry. However, if we attempt to add together the output of different industries to arrive at a total output for the entire economic system, we are confronted with an embarrassing situation. The output of the economic system is a combination of gallons of gasoline, tons of coal, pairs of shoes, numbers of automobiles, et cetera. If the number of automobiles produced increases and the number of pairs of shoes decreases, we cannot say whether total output has risen or fallen. Obviously, these non-homogeneous units cannot be added together.

In his *General Theory*, Keynes uses quantities of employment as the index for measuring changes in output of the economic system as a whole. Fluctuations in real output and real income are assumed to correspond to changes in the volume of employment of labor applied to the existing stock of capital equipment. The unit of employment is an hour of labor of ordinary skill, or what is referred to as common labor. One hour of employment of common labor is one labor-unit. The money-unit and the labor-unit are combined to form the wage-unit. The wage-unit is the amount of money received by labor of ordinary skill in one hour of working time. Labor of superior skill is equated to labor of ordinary skill in proportion to its remuneration.[4] For example, if the rate of remuneration of labor of ordinary skill is one dollar per hour, the wage-unit is one dollar. If a bricklayer receives three dollars per hour, then one hour of a bricklayer's labor represents three labor-units and his compensation per hour represents three wage-units.

At any time, total output or total income and other aggregate magnitudes will have a certain value in terms of wage-units. One of the arguments in favor of the wage-unit is the relative stability of the rate of pay to labor of ordinary skill. As long as the hourly money wage of common labor remains unchanged, the wage-unit is constant, and changes in output, measured in terms of wage-units, vary with changes in the amount of labor employed. Keynes does not attempt to use the wage-unit to make comparisons of output over historical time or between different countries or between the output resulting from different quantities of capital equipment. Most of the analysis in the *General Theory* assumes the wage-unit to be constant. Some parts of the analysis,

---

4. For Keynes' defense of this point, see the *General Theory*, pages 41-43.

however, explicitly take into account the influence of changes in the size of the wage-unit. In the theory of prices and inflation, for example, an increase in the hourly wage rate which occurs as employment rises is the basic factor to which a rise in prices is attributed. When hourly wages rise, the wage-unit increases, and when hourly wages fall, the wage-unit decreases. While the wage-unit is not an entirely satisfactory concept, it is important to understand that it is used (1) because changes in output are measured by changes in the amount of employment and (2) because Keynes' general theory of employment deals with the economic system as a whole rather than with individual firms and industries.

References for Further Reading

Keynes, J. M., *The General Theory of Employment, Interest and Money*, Chapters 4, 6, 7, and 8. New York: Harcourt, Brace and Company, 1936.

——, "The Process of Capital Formation," *The Economic Journal*, September, 1939, Vol. XLIX, pages 569-574.

Altman, O. L., *Saving, Investment, and National Income*, Temporary National Economic Committee, Monograph No. 37. Washington: U. S. Government Printing Office, 1941.

Curtis, Myra, "Is Money Saving Equal to Investment?" *The Quarterly Journal of Economics*, August, 1937, Vol. LI, pages 604-625.

Ezekiel, Mordecai, "Saving, Consumption, and Investment," *The American Economic Review*, March and June, 1942, Vol. XXXII, pages 22-49, 272-307.

Gilbert, Milton, and Jaszi, George, "National Product and Income Statistics as an Aid in Economic Problems," *Readings in the Theory of Income Distribution*, selected by a Committee of the American Economic Association. Philadelphia: The Blakiston Company, 1946.

Hansen, A. H., "A Note on Savings and Investment," *The Review of Economic Statistics*, February, 1948, Vol. XXX, pages 30-33.

——, "National Income and Gross National Product," Chapter III in *Economic Policy and Full Employment*. New York: McGraw-Hill Book Company, Inc., 1947.

Hayes, H. Gordon, *Spending, Saving, and Employment*. New York: Alfred A. Knopf, 1945.

Kuznets, Simon, *National Income: A Summary of Findings*. New York: National Bureau of Economic Research, 1946. (Professor Kuznets has done the pioneer work in national income studies of the United States.)

Lerner, A. P., "Saving Equals Investment," *The Quarterly Journal of Economics*, February, 1938, Vol. LII, pages 297-309. Reprinted in *The New Economics*, edited by S. E. Harris. New York: Alfred A. Knopf, 1947.

————, "Saving and Investment: Definitions, Assumptions, Objectives," *The Quarterly Journal of Economics*, August, 1939, Vol. LIII, pages 611-619. Reprinted in *Readings in Business Cycle Theory*, selected by a Committee of the American Economic Association. Philadelphia: The Blakiston Company, 1944; and in *The New Economics*, edited by S. E. Harris. New York: Alfred A. Knopf, 1947.

————, "User Cost and Prime User Cost," *The American Economic Review*, March, 1943, Vol. XXXIII, pages 131-132.

Lutz, F. A., "Outcome of the Saving-Investment Discussion," *The Quarterly Journal of Economics*, August, 1938, Vol. LII, pages 588-614. Reprinted in *Readings in Business Cycle Theory*, selected by a Committee of the American Economic Association. Philadelphia: The Blakiston Company, 1944.

Morgan, Theodore, *Income and Employment*. New York: Prentice, Hall, Inc., 1947.

Ohlin, Bertil, "Some Notes on the Stockholm Theory of Savings and Investment," *The Economic Journal*, March and June, 1937, Vol. XLVII, pages 53-69, 221-240.

Robertson, D. H., "Saving and Hoarding," *The Economic Journal*, September, 1933, Vol. XLIII, pages 399-413. Reprinted in Robertson, D. H., *Essays in Monetary Theory*. London: P. S. King and Son, Ltd., 1940.

Shoup, Carl S., *Principles of National Income Analysis*. Boston: Houghton Mifflin Company, 1947.

U. S. Department of Commerce, *Survey of Current Business, Supplement* on "National Income," July, 1947, Vol. 27. (A valuable statement of the revised basis for computing national income in the United States.)

CHAPTER 5

The Propensity to Consume and the Investment Multiplier

> The psychology of the community is such that when aggregate real income is increased aggregate consumption is increased, but not by so much as income . . . Unless the psychological propensities of the public are different from what we are supposing, we have here established the law that increased employment for investment must necessarily stimulate the industries producing for consumption and thus lead to a total increase of employment which is a multiple of the primary employment required by the investment itself.
>
> J. M. Keynes. *The General Theory of Employment, Interest and Money.**

THE ULTIMATE purpose of Keynes' theory is to explain what determines the volume of employment. The starting point is the principle of effective demand, which states that employment depends on the sum of consumption expenditures and investment expenditures. Consumption depends on the size of consumers' net income and the propensity to consume, and investment depends on the marginal efficiency of capital taken in conjunction with the rate of interest. A high propensity to consume is favorable to employment, and one of

---

* Harcourt, Brace and Co., Inc., 1936, pages 27 and 118.

75

the remedies for unemployment is to be found in measures designed to increase the propensity to consume. When investment increases and causes income to rise, the resulting additions to income are expended largely for consumption. The relationship between increases in investment and increases in consumption, which was discussed in a preliminary fashion in Chapter 3, is explored more fully in the present chapter in terms of the investment multiplier, which is the ratio of an increase of income to a given increase in new investment. In common-sense terms, the investment multiplier means that when investment increases, national income will increase not only by the amount of investment but by some multiple of it. The great practical significance of the multiplier arises in relation to Keynes' advocacy of public investment and other forms of governmental expenditure as a source of effective demand in periods in which private enterprise does not furnish adequate investment to provide full employment of labor and other resources.

The Concept of the Propensity to Consume

The propensity to consume, which is simply the relationship between income and consumption, may be represented by means of a diagram. If values for income (Y) are plotted along the horizontal axis and consumption (C) along the vertical axis, the line which relates these two variables represents the schedule of the propensity to consume, or what is called for the sake of brevity, the propensity to consume. This schedule of the propensity to consume may also be referred to as the "consumption function" because it shows the functional relationship between the two variables, income and consumption. "Propensity to consume" does not mean a mere desire to consume, but the actual consumption that takes place, or is expected to take place, out of varying amounts of income. In this respect it is similar to a demand schedule, which refers not to mere desire to buy but to willingness plus ability to buy. The data on income and consumption in a schedule of the propensity to consume may be either for the community as a whole or for an individual consuming unit. In Keynes' analysis of aggregates, as previously indicated, it is the **national income and national consumption that are significant.** When used without qualification, "propensity to consume" or "consumption function" will mean the community or aggregate concept, and in other cases the adjective "family" or "individual" will be used.

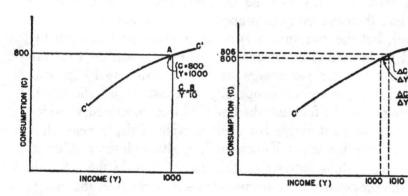

Figure 5a. The Average Propensity to Consume.

Figure 5b. The Marginal Propensity to Consume.

In Figure 5a the *average* propensity to consume at any level of income is represented by the distance along the vertical axis divided by the corresponding distance along the horizontal axis, that is, by $\frac{C}{Y}$. From the line C'C', which represents the schedule of the propensity to consume, the average propensity to consume at any point is easily ascertained. For example, at the point A, consumption is 800 and income is 1000, and the average propensity to consume is thus 800 divided by 1000, or $\frac{8}{10}$. This means that $\frac{8}{10}$, or 80 per cent, of an income of 1000 will be spent for consumption.

The **marginal propensity to consume**, represented in Figure 5b, is the ratio of a small change in consumption to a small change in income. It may be designated by $\frac{\Delta C}{\Delta Y}$, where the symbol $\triangle$ (delta) stands for a small increment.[1] Keynes' fundamental principle that consumption increases less than income when income increases means that the ratio of the increase in consumption to the increase in income is always less than one, that is, $\triangle Y$ is always greater than $\triangle C$. In Figure 5b, if consumption increases by 6 (from 800 to 806) when income increases by 10 (from 1000 to 1010), the marginal propensity to consume is $6/10$, or 60 per cent. This is less than the average propensity to consume, which is 80 per cent. Not only will the marginal propensity to consume be less than the average propensity to consume at any given point, but the marginal propensity to consume will probably fall as income rises because a community will tend to consume a smaller percentage of each addition to its income. The falling marginal propensity to consume is reflected in Figure 5 by the fact that the line $C'C'$ is a smooth curve which flattens out as it moves from left to right. This, in general, is the assumption which Keynes makes, although the validity of his theory does not rest on this assumption. If the schedule of the propensity to consume were a straight line, the marginal propensity to consume would be the same at all points because the ratio of increases in consumption to increases in income would always be the same. The only assumption which is vital to Keynes' theory is that the absolute amount of consumption increases less than the absolute amount of income whenever income increases. This may be expressed

---

1. Although Keynes defines the marginal propensity to consume as $\dfrac{dC}{dY}$ (p. 115), the concept he makes use of is $\dfrac{\triangle C}{\triangle Y}$. In practical application, the distinction is relatively unimportant. $\dfrac{dC}{dY}$ measures the slope of the line $C'C'$ at any point, whereas $\dfrac{\triangle C}{\triangle Y}$ measures the average slope over a small range of the line $C'C'$. In a strict sense $\dfrac{\triangle C}{\triangle Y}$ is really an average of the marginal propensities to consume over a finite range of the line $C'C'$. In the following discussion we shall use the average marginal propensity to consume, but shall refer to it without the qualifying adjective "average." The *average marginal* propensity to consume is not to be confused with the *average* propensity to consume as explained in the text above.

by saying the slope of the line $C'C'$ must be positive and less than one, which merely means that the marginal propensity to consume must be positive and less than one.

Stability of the Propensity to Consume

Let us look more closely at the factors which determine how much will be spent for consumption in a given community at any time. As already indicated, the factor of overwhelming importance is the size of the community's income. As community income rises, consumption also rises; and as community income falls, consumption also falls. The justification for the concept, the propensity to consume, a concept of great practical significance as well as a great simplifier of economic analysis, is the premise that the amounts by which consumption rises and falls as income rises and falls will follow a fairly regular pattern. Only if this is true can the propensity to consume be stable, as Keynes assumes it to be.

We must distinguish clearly between two questions: How much will be spent for consumption, given the propensity to consume? and, How much will be spent for consumption out of a given income? These questions involve a distinction between the amount of consumption and the propensity to consume, that is, between an *amount* and a *schedule*. The amount of consumption is not stable because it depends on income, which in turn is not stable because the inducement to invest is not stable. The (schedule of the) propensity to consume is stable because it is determined by psychological characteristics of human nature and by the general social structure and practices of society, and these do not change readily except under unusual conditions such as social revolution, drastic inflation, or some other abnormal circumstance. In a given community over a short period of time, the subjective and objective factors determining the propensity to consume and to save are relatively fixed. In different communities and over long periods of time, the subjective motives of individuals to refrain from spending will vary with social institutions, education, convention, religion, morals, et cetera. Although the propensity to consume is stable in the short period, it is not absolutely rigid. Changes in government fiscal policy (taxing and spending), substantial changes in the rate of interest, and rapid changes in capital values such as occur during a stock market boom or crash may have some effect on the over-all propensity to consume. Apart from fiscal policy of an unconventional type, however, even these factors are not likely to be very important.

Figure 6 illustrates the distinction between changes in consumption caused by an increase in income (with no change in the propensity to consume) and changes in consumption caused by a change in the propensity to consume (with no change in income).

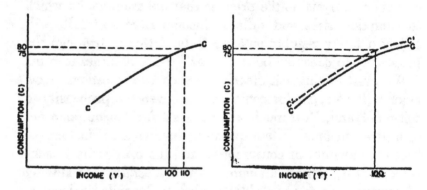

Figure 6a. An Increase in Consumption Caused by an Increase in Income (No Change in the Propensity to Consume).

Figure 6b. An Increase in Consumption Caused by an Increase in the Propensity to Consume (No Change in Income).

In Figure 6a, consumption increases from 75 to 80 as a result of an increase in income from 100 to 110. The propensity to consume, represented by the line CC, does not change. In Figure 6b, consumption increases from 75 to 80 as a result of an increase in the propensity to consume from CC to C′C′. The average propensity to consume at an income of 100 rises from 75 to 80 per cent. Most short-run changes in consumption are of the type represented in 6a, that is, changes in consumption caused by changes in income with the propensity to consume remaining the same. The type represented in 6b is less likely to occur because of the stability of the propensity to consume in the short run. In the simple situation depicted in 6b, there is no change in income. This means that if the average propensity to consume does rise, say from 75 to 80 per cent, the same amount of income can be produced with less investment. However, if investment remains unchanged or increases when the propensity to consume rises, total income and employment will rise.

An important factor determining how much will be spent for consumption out of a given size of community income is the distribution of income. Since individual saving (not-consuming) represents surplus income which is not used for current consumption, saving depends on the presence of people with incomes in excess of their current consumption needs. It is easy for the rich to save but difficult for the poor. One of the chief characteristics of modern capitalistic countries is great inequality in the distribution of income, which results from concentration of the ownership of income-yielding property in the hands of a small fraction of the total population. For the very wealthy, saving is more or less automatic. They may buy everything they need or want and still have income left over for saving. All statistical studies of saving show that a large proportion of total saving is done by a relatively few high-income recipients and that a small part of total saving is done by the great mass of low-income recipients. If total income were more evenly distributed, the total saving out of a given size of community income would tend to be less. Thus widespread inequality of income and wealth tend to lower the propensity to consume. The lower the propensity to consume, the greater the dependence of the economy on investment for maintaining a high level of employment and income. Hence, the fundamental proposition that a high level of employment depends on a large amount of investment is true partly because the inequality of incomes greatly restricts the amount of consumption that will take place at high levels of income. If we were looking at the problem of **unemployment** from the point of view of social structure, we could truthfully say that one of its causes is inequality in the distribution of income. Keynes' theory and policy stress the importance of investment, i.e., of the necessity of having to produce much in excess of current consumption, because he accepts for purposes of most of the analysis of the *General Theory* the existing social structure, including the distribution of income and wealth. Except for occasional digressions with regard to certain long-term secular changes, Keynes' theory is not oriented to changes in the social structure, but is primarily concerned with how to make capitalism work, given the existing social structure. The distribution of income can be changed materially only by far-reaching alterations in the basic fabric of society. To deal adequately with changes of this type would require a different kind of theory from that offered by Keynes. It should, however, be added that his theory, though not oriented to changes in underlying social institutions, throws much light on the consequences of these institutions, including private property in the means of production and the resulting pattern of income distribution.

In an age of progressive taxation, the distinction between the distribution of income before taxation and the distribution of income after taxation is of great significance. Progressive **taxation reduces inequalities of income because it** takes a relatively larger part of the incomes of the wealthy than it does of the poor, and thereby provides some relief from the inadequate demand for consumption in capitalist economies. Keynes advocates progressive taxation as one of the important measures for alleviating unemployment. Without doubt, it is one of the powerful weapons in this connection. Progressive taxation is not, however, a panacea for unemployment. There are distinct limitations to the extent to which progressive taxes are used and can be used to promote high levels of economic activity. The whole tax *system* must be progressive for effective results. While the United States has some highly progressive individual taxes, like the federal income tax and death duties, there are a great number of regressive taxes such as the general sales tax in many states and excise taxes levied by the federal government. An inevitable limitation on the extent to which progressive taxes can be used arises from the fact that the money which is taxed away from the rich can hardly be given directly to the poor, although to some extent this is possible in the form of pensions, relief payments, et cetera. Therefore, the government which collects taxes for purposes of redistribution must either pay subsidies to private citizens or expand the scope of its activities in order to provide social services for lower-income groups. Services like education, medical care, and public recreational facilities are illustrations of such social services. Although services of this type are of great social significance, they do not enable the low-income groups to increase the money income out of which they must feed, clothe, and house themselves. Subsidies for housing, or low-cost government housing, are, of course, possible but tend to be strongly opposed by private interest groups. A further limitation to redistributing income by means of progressive taxation is the danger that high rates on large incomes may discourage private investment, upon which the private capitalist economy primarily depends for filling the gap between income and consumption at high levels of employment. If progressive taxation increases the community's propensity to consume at the expense of weakening the inducement to invest, the losses in employment from the latter may more than cancel the gains from the former. Despite limitations to the use of taxation as a fundamental approach to problems associated with the unequal distribution of income, a fiscal policy in which the amount of money collected and spent by government is highly flexible offers a significant weapon against short-term fluctuations in economic activity. These will be discussed in more detail in the next chapter.

Other factors which make for a low propensity to consume or a high propensity to save in modern communities like the United States are the great magnitudes of life insurance and social insurance and the financial prudence of business corporations in regard to dividend payments and depreciation allowances. The desirability of life insurance and the various forms of social insurance is not to be questioned from the standpoint of the individual or family unit. Nevertheless, it must be recognized that such insurance involves large withdrawals from the income stream which might otherwise be spent for current consumption. The burden on investment for maintaining high levels of employment is increased to the degree to which consumption is restrained. If the amounts paid out in life insurance and social insurance benefits are equal to the premiums paid in (by different sets of persons), there is, of course, no net saving. As long as the total amount of insurance is increasing, however, there is a net withdrawal from consumption demand. The financial prudence that provokes corporation managers to be cautious in paying cash dividends to the full extent of current net profits can hardly be questioned on a business basis, but it is nevertheless a drag on the propensity to consume. Corporations "force" many shareholders to save by withholding from the latter's control income which they would otherwise be free to spend or save as they saw fit. Prudent dividend policy, taken in conjunction with the over-cautious depreciation policy typically followed by American business enterprise, is a major factor tending to lower the propensity to consume.

Over the long run, from decade to decade, we cannot assume that the propensity to consume will remain unchanged. Statistical studies indicate that historically there is a tendency in progressive communities for the consumption function to shift upward in the sense that more is spent for consumption out of incomes of a given size. The upward secular drift of the consumption schedule is reflected in a steady rise in the standard of living of progressive economies like the United States. But in the short run, with which Keynes is primarily concerned, changes in the amount of consumption depend mainly on changes in the amount of income and not on changes in the propensity to consume out of a given income

(p. 110). To repeat for emphasis, this conclusion makes investment the strategic variable in the general theory of employment. The important proposition that employment can increase only if investment increases presupposes a stable propensity to consume. Moreover, the strategic nature of investment is reinforced by the fact that the schedule of the propensity to consume is stable at a relatively low level.

The Marginal Propensity to Consume and the Multiplier

The propensity to consume tells us that there is a fairly definite relationship between consumption and income at all levels of employment. As a further development of this relation, a definite ratio may be established between investment and income. From the marginal propensity to consume, we can tell *how much* income and employment will increase as a result of a given increase in investment. If the propensity to consume is given, a definite ratio will exist between any increase in income ($\triangle Y$) and any given increase in investment ($\triangle I$). This ratio is called the investment multiplier (k) and is equal, subject to certain assumptions, to the employment multiplier (k'). The relation between the marginal propensity to consume ($\frac{\triangle C}{\triangle Y}$) and the investment multiplier ($\frac{\triangle Y}{\triangle I}$) may be illustrated by a simple arithmetical example. Assume a $100 increment in income is derived $90 from consumption and $10 from investment:

$$\triangle Y = \triangle C + \triangle I$$
$$\$100 = \$90 + \$10$$

The marginal propensity to consume, $\frac{\triangle C}{\triangle Y}$, is $90/100$. The multiplier, $\frac{\triangle Y}{\triangle I}$, is $100/10$ or 10. We may generalize and say the multiplier is equal to the reciprocal of one minus the marginal propensity to consume; and the marginal propensity to consume is equal to one minus the reciprocal of the multiplier.[2] In the above illustration, the marginal propensity to consume is ⁹⁄₁₀, one minus ⁹⁄₁₀ is ¹⁄₁₀, and the multiplier is the reciprocal of ¹⁄₁₀ or 10.

The arithmetical relation of the marginal propensity to consume to the investment multiplier may be thought of even more simply: **The multiplier is the reciprocal of the marginal propensity to save,** which is always equal to one minus the marginal propensity to consume. Thus, if the marginal propensity to consume is ⁹⁄₁₀, the marginal propensity to save is ¹⁄₁₀, and the multiplier is 10. If the marginal propensity to consume is ⅘, the marginal propensity to save is ⅕, and the multiplier is 5. If the marginal propensity to consume is ⅔, the marginal propensity to save is ⅓, and the multiplier is 3. The following table lists the values of the multiplier which correspond to certain values of the marginal propensity to consume.

The size of the multiplier varies directly with the size of the marginal propensity to consume. When the latter is high the multiplier is high, and when the marginal propensity to consume is low the multiplier is also low. Theoretically the values of the multiplier can range all the way from one to infinity. However, **it can never fall to one if consumption**

---

2. The investment multiplier may be derived from the marginal propensity to consume in the following manner. Starting with the "fundamental psychological law" that $\triangle Y$ and $\triangle C$ have the same sign but $\triangle Y$ exceeds $\triangle C$, it follows that the marginal propensity to consume is positive and always less than 1. Let us assume it is less than 1 by a fraction $\frac{1}{k}$, where k stands for the multiplier. We then have given:

(1) $\frac{\triangle C}{\triangle Y} = 1 - \frac{1}{k}$, where k is equal to or greater than 1; and

(2) $\triangle Y = \triangle C + \triangle I$. Transposing and dividing through by $\triangle Y$, we get

(3) $\frac{\triangle C}{\triangle Y} = 1 - \frac{\triangle I}{\triangle Y}$. From (1) and (3), it follows that

(4) $\frac{1}{k} = \frac{\triangle I}{\triangle Y}$, or (5) $k = \frac{\triangle Y}{\triangle I}$, which may also be written (6) $\triangle Y = k(\triangle I)$.

By transposing (1) we get (7) $\frac{1}{k} = 1 - \frac{\triangle C}{\triangle Y}$, or (8) $k = \frac{1}{1 - \frac{\triangle C}{\triangle Y}}$, which

may also be written (9) $k = \frac{\triangle Y}{\triangle Y - \triangle C}$. $1 - \frac{\triangle C}{\triangle Y}$ in (8) is, of course, the marginal propensity to save.

TABLE 1

CORRESPONDING VALUES FOR THE
MARGINAL PROPENSITY TO CONSUME AND THE MULTIPLIER

Marginal Propensity to Consume $\left(\dfrac{\Delta C}{\Delta Y}\right)$	Multiplier (k)
0	1
1/3	1 1/2
3/8	1 3/5
2/5	1 2/3
1/2	2
3/5	2 1/2
5/8	2 2/3
7/10	3 1/3
3/4	4
4/5	5
9/10	10
99/100	100
1	Infinity

always increases when income increases because this means the marginal propensity to consume is never zero. At the same time, the multiplier can never be equal to infinity if Keynes' assumption that the marginal propensity to consume is always less than one is valid. The actual value of the marginal propensity to consume is not likely to fall outside the range from ⅛ to ⁹⁄₁₀, and therefore the multiplier will lie somewhere between 1.5 and 10. Keynes estimates the actual value of the multiplier to be about 3, with variations in different phases of the business cycle. Since the multiplier is more than unity but not very great, any new investment will increase income by more than the amount of the investment, but a small increase in investment will not be sufficient to lift the economy from a low level of employment to full employment.

The process whereby new investment brings a multiple increase in income by increasing consumption may be illustrated by an arithmetical example. Assume the marginal propensity to consume is ⅘. The multiplier will then be 5. One million dollars of new investment will lead to a total increase in income of $5,000,000. The initial $1,000,000 outlay for investment increases the incomes of the recipients by $1,000,-000. Since the marginal propensity to consume is ⅘, only 80 per cent of this initial increase in income will be spent for consumption. The $800,000 which is spent for consumption will add, at the second round, to the community's income by that amount, one person's expenditure being another's income. Of the $800,000 addition to income, 80 per cent will again be spent on consumer outlays, and in turn the community's income will increase by $640,000. Out of the further increase in income of $640,000, 80 per cent will go into consumption and income will increase by an additional $512,000. This process whereby consumption increases to the extent of 80 per cent of each addition to income will continue through successive stages toward a definite limit until the aggregate increase in community income is equal to 5 times the original investment. The various stages of expansion or income turn-overs are not to be thought of in terms of a series of time periods, but as cumulative increases that occur simultaneously.

Does this mean that Keynes' theory is invalid since, obviously, the spending and respending of income for consumption cannot possibly take place simultaneously with the new investment? No, it is an assumption which simplifies the exposition and, at the same time, illustrates Keynes' basic contention that in every interval of time the increase in income is equal to the increase in investment multiplied by the multiplier (p. 123). In the first place, investment does not occur simultaneously, but over time. If the consumption industries anticipate the expansion of income that will be available to buy consumers goods, the time lag is greatly reduced. However, the increased demand for consumption may not be foreseen, so that investment will create new income for which no new consumption goods have been produced. In these circumstances, the new demand may be met partly by depletion of stocks (disinvestment) and partly postponed because of resistance to higher prices and also because the type of goods demanded is not available. To the extent that consumption is postponed, the marginal propensity to consume and the multiplier will fall temporarily below their normal size. Later when the goods become available, the marginal propensity to consume may rise above its normal level and "eventually returns to its normal level." (p. 124)

The temporary departure of the marginal propensity to consume from normal is important in explaining how the equality of investment and saving is maintained throughout the expansionary process. If there are no new consumers goods at all to meet the additional demand arising from the income distributed by the new investment, there can be no increase in real consumption, so that, momentarily, income would increase but consumption would not. Hence, added saving (the excess of income over consumption), which is equal to added income, would be equal to added investment. Total saving and total investment are equal, and would remain equal regardless of the time lag. Momentarily, the marginal propensity to consume would be zero and the multiplier equal to one. They would rise gradually and return to normal after an interval of time. The emphasis in Keynes' analysis at this point is as follows: The efforts of consumers to spend their additional income according to their normal marginal propensity to consume will result in more consumption, which in turn will lead to the creation of more income, and out of the larger income more will be saved. When the normal marginal propensity to consume is functioning, the total addition to national income will be equal to the investment multiplied by the normal multiplier. Table 2 shows how the expansion of income takes place when the marginal propensity to consume is at its assumed normal level of 80 per cent. It would be a misrepresentation of Keynes' position to assume that investment originally exceeds saving, and becomes equal to it only after all the stages have been completed, which might be a very long time indeed. Keynes is not unaware of time lags, but for the pure theory of the multiplier, which we are discussing in this chapter, the introduction of time lags would greatly complicate the analysis. In the next chapter, which deals with the application of the multiplier principle, account will be taken of time lags.[3]

The following table presents the first 10 stages of this multiplying process whereby an original investment of $1,000,000 raises total income by $5,000,000 when the marginal propensity to consume is $\frac{8}{10}$, and therefore the multiplier is 5. The data in this table indicate that the formula for the multiplier, the reciprocal of the marginal propensity to

TABLE 2

EFFECT OF INCREASED INVESTMENT ON
INCOME, CONSUMPTION, AND SAVING

Original Increase in Investment ΔI	Induced Increase in Income ΔY	Additional Consumption from Increased Income ($\frac{8}{10}$ of ΔY)	Saving out of Income
$1,000,000	$1,000,000	$800,000	$200,000
	800,000	640,000	160,000
	640,000	512,000	128,000
	512,000	409,600	102,400
	409,600	327,680	81,920
	327,680	262,144	65,536
	262,144	209,715	52,429
	209,715	167,772	41,943
	167,772	134,218	33,554
	134,218	107,375	26,843
	107,375		
	etc.	etc.	etc.
Totals $1,000,000 Investment	$5,000,000 Income	$4,000,000 Consumption	$1,000,000 Saving

3. The above paragraph is based on Keynes' discussion in the *General Theory,* pages 117, 122-125, and upon the clarification of this aspect of Keynes by Professor Alvin Hansen in "A Note on Savings and Investment," *The Review of Economic Statistics,* February, 1948, Vol. XXX, No. 1, pages 30-33. The adaptation of the multiplier to take account of time lags has been worked out by a number of writers, including Professor Hansen, Professor Fritz Machlup, and others.

save, is just a shorthand method for simplifying the arithmetical calculations involved in the table. If the successive
additions were made in the table, the total in the income column would be $5,000,000, or 5 times the original investment, and 5 is the value for k, which is the reciprocal of ⅕,
the marginal propensity to save.

The sum of the consumption column at its mathematical
limit is $4,000,000. The increase in investment of $1,000,000
plus the $4,000,000 increase in consumption equals the total
increase in income of $5,000,000. Thus given the marginal
propensity to consume and the amount of the increment in
investment, we can determine the total resulting increase in
income by finding k and substituting in the equation $\triangle Y =
k \cdot \triangle I$. Thus, $5,000,000 = 5 \cdot $1,000,000.

That part of newly created income which is not re-spent is,
of course, saved. In Table 2 total saving is equal to the investment of $1,000,000, which is as it should be. This
amount of saving results from the propensity of the community to save 20 per cent of the $5,000,000 addition to its
income. Income which is not spent for consumption (shown
in the last column in Table 2) is sometimes spoken of as a
"leakage" in the cumulative income stream. It is this leakage
which limits the extent of the total increase in national income. If there were no leakage, that is, if the marginal propensity to consume were 100 per cent, full employment would
result, and beyond full employment, inflation would set in,
from any small increase in investment because, under the
ideal conditions assumed in Table 2, the second column would
show an infinite number of constant additions to income. Since
these successive additions diminish at each stage, the total
increase in income is a finite amount.

The form which leakages take is determined by what happens to the money received as income but not spent for consumption. It may be used to pay off debts, to add to idle cash
balances, or to purchase bonds, stocks, mortgages, insurance
policies, and similar financial investments. The particular
form of leakage is of no direct consequence as long as we hold

to the assumption that the marginal propensity to consume is 80 per cent, and that total new investment is $1,000,000. These two factors together determine the total effect of new investment on income and employment. Leakages which tend to reduce the size of new, net investment (the multiplicand), rather than the size of the multiplier, will be considered in the chapter on fiscal policy in depression. Foreign trade and corporate saving will also be discussed in this connection.

To take two more very simple cases showing the relation of the marginal propensity to consume to the multiplier: If the marginal propensity to consume is ½, the multiplier is 2 because 1 plus ½ plus ¼ plus ⅛ plus ¹⁄₁₆ etc. add up to 2. With a multiplier of 2, each $1 of additional investment will result in a $2 increase in income. Or if the marginal propensity to consume is ⅔, the multiplier is 3 because 1 plus ⅔ plus ⁴⁄₉ plus ⁸⁄₂₇ etc. add up to 3. In this case each $1 of investment will result in a $3 increase in income.

The multiplier concept is concerned only with original investment as a stimulus to consumption and thereby to income. It is not intended to deal with the question whether additional consumption will induce further investment. The effect of added consumption upon the demand for investment involves the so-called "acceleration" principle, which is not an important part of Keynes' theory.[4]

Amount of investment needed to sustain various levels of income and employment

Keynes' fundamental position is that income and employment can rise only if investment increases, subject to qualifi-

---

4. For studies which integrate the principle of acceleration with Keynes' multiplier analysis, see R. F. Harrod, *The Trade Cycle.* London: Oxford University Press, 1936; A. H. Hansen, *Fiscal Policy and Business Cycles.* New York: W. W. Norton and Company, Inc., 1941, Chapter 12; Paul A. Samuelson, "Interactions between the Multiplier Analysis and the Principle of Acceleration," reprinted from *The Review of Economic Statistics,* 1939, in *Readings in Business Cycle Theory.* Philadelphia: The Blakiston Company, 1944, Chapter 12, and "A Synthesis of the Principle of Acceleration and the Multiplier," *The Journal of Political Economy,* December, 1939, Vol. XLVII, No. 6, pages 786-797.

cations that may be ruled out as of no great practical significance in the short run. The reason why income can increase
only if investment increases is that as income rises, consumption will rise but by less than income, and so a gap is left to
be filled by investment. Consequently, increases in output
above a low level at which aggregate income is equal to
aggregate consumption will have to be divided partly to
consumption goods and partly to investment goods. If the
marginal propensity to consume is $\frac{8}{10}$, for example, an addition to output of a million dollars must be divided $\frac{8}{10}$ to
consumption goods and $\frac{2}{10}$ to investment goods. This means
the multiplier is 5 because an addition to investment of, say,
$2,000,000 will be accompanied by an increase in consump-
tion of $8,000,000 and a total increase in income of
$10,000,000.

In order to ascertain how much investment is necessary to
give full employment, or any other level of employment for
that matter, we may set up a table of income, consumption,
and investment. From this table it is easy to calculate the
amount of investment required to boost income and employment to higher levels. Following is such a table with hypo-
thetical figures. In addition to figures on income, consumption, and investment, data are also given for employment, the
marginal propensity to consume, the multiplier, and the
average propensity to consume.

The range of national income shown in the table is from
$100 billion to $200 billion. The higher figure is assumed to
represent full employment and maximum attainable real
income. At the lower level of $100 billion, consumption is
equal to income, and the average propensity to consume $\left(\frac{C}{Y}\right)$
is unity. No net investment is necessary to maintain a $100
billion flow of income. Supply tends to create its own demand
up to this level, and if income falls below consumption, as it
may temporarily do, there will be a tendency for income to
rise to the level at which it equals consumption because the
effective demand for consumption will call forth an output

TABLE 3
Amount of Investment Needed to Sustain Various Levels of Income and Employment

Employment (millions of workers) N	Income (billions of dollars) Y	*Consumption (billions of dollars) C	**Investment (billions of dollars) I	Marg. Prop. to Consume $\frac{\Delta C}{\Delta Y}$	Multiplier (k)	Average Prop. to Consume $\frac{C}{Y}$
30	100	100	0			1.00
				.90	10	
33	110	109	1			.99
				.80	5	
36	120	117	3			.98
				.75	4	
39	130	124.5	5.5			.96
				.70	$3\frac{1}{3}$	
42	140	131.5	8.5			.94
				.65	$2\frac{6}{7}$	
45	150	138	12			.92
				.60	$2\frac{1}{2}$	
48	160	144	16			.90
				.55	$2\frac{2}{9}$	
51	170	149.5	20.5			.88
				.50	2	
54	180	154.5	25.5			.86
				.45	$1\frac{9}{11}$	
57	190	159	31			.84
				.40	$1\frac{2}{3}$	
60	200	163	37			.82

* Including tax-financed government expenditures.
** Including loan-financed government expenditures.

equal to the entire value of consumption. At income levels below $100 billion there is no gap that needs to be filled by investment. This basic national income, as Professor Hansen aptly calls it, is self-perpetuating. Above the basic income is the dynamic income, which is not self-perpetuating because it depends on investment to maintain itself and there is nothing automatic about investment. At $100 billion the gap begins to develop and income can rise above this level only as a result of deliberate calculations on the part of private businessmen to invest in new capital assets or on the part of governmental authorities to promote public investment. If the margin between basic national income and income at full employment is to be filled at all, it will be filled by investment plus the consumption induced by that investment under the multiplier principle. The concepts of the multiplier and the marginal propensity to consume become of practical significance in the range of incomes, in our example, above $100 billion.

Thus for all levels of income above $100 billion, consumption is less than income, and each addition to new investment will boost the national income by more than the amount of the investment because consumption will rise from the stimulus furnished by investment. The first billion-dollar increase in investment raises the national income by $10 billion, which means that the (average) multiplier between incomes of $100 and.$110 billion is 10, or the average marginal propensity to consume is .9, and this first $10 billion rise in output is divided $9 billion to consumption and $1 billion to investment. The next $10 billion rise in income requires a $2 billion outlay on investment, or twice as much as the first $10 billion rise, because the (average) multiplier has fallen from 10 to 5, or the marginal propensity to consume from .9 to .8. And the third $10 billion rise, from $120 billion to $130 billion, is divided $7.5 billion to consumption and $2.5 billion to investment because the average multiplier is 4 and the average marginal propensity to consume is .75 in this range of income. Finally, the last $10 billion rise to the full-employment income of $200 billion is divided $4 billion to consumption and $6 billion to investment, which means that the multiplier has fallen to 1⅔ and the marginal propensity to consume to .4. These figures show how the marginal propensity to consume indicates the division of additions to output between consumption and investment, and they also indicate that the investment multiplier is just another way of talking about the marginal propensity to consume.[5]

In Table 3 both the marginal and average propensities to consume fall as income rises, and rise as income falls. Over a broad range of the schedule, the decline in the average propensity to consume is a necessary condition of Keynes' analy-

---

5. We have been dealing with the average marginal propensity to consume and the average multiplier. "Marginal" is a mathematical concept which involves small, incremental changes. Obviously, $10 billion in $100 billion or in $200 billion does violence to the concept of small variations. But for the purposes at hand, it is perfectly legitimate to speak of the average marginal propensity to consume and the average value of the multiplier over a given range. See note 1 above. See also *General Theory*, page 121.

sis, and the decline in the marginal propensity to consume is a probable condition of actual experience. At the bottom of a very bad depression the average propensity to consume may be greater than one because consumption may exceed income while the community is depleting stocks of goods and large numbers of people are living off their past savings. However, any fall in income below consumption will tend to be restored by the self-sustaining nature of basic national income. Above the point at which income equals consumption ($100 billion in Table 3), aggregate consumption is less than aggregate income. The average propensity to consume has obviously fallen to less than one.

Keynes accounts for the relative stability of the economic system by this characteristic of a community to increase consumption by a lesser *absolute* amount than income when income rises, and to decrease consumption by less than income when income decreases (pp. 97, 251). Although there is great instability in economic life, it is not so great as to cause fluctuation all the way from zero employment to full employment. Movements upward and movements downward both encounter self-limiting forces. Changes upward are limited by the increasing difficulty of finding investment to fill the widening gap between income and consumption. Changes downward are limited because income falls more rapidly than consumption and therefore catches up with falling consumption long before a point of zero employment is reached. At the point on the downswing where consumption is equal to income—where the average propensity to consume is unity—economic activity reaches its self-sustaining basis. If Keynes' fundamental psychological law did not hold at all, any small increment in investment would set up a cumulative increase in effective demand which would go unchecked until full employment was reached; and any decrease in investment, however small, would set in motion a cumulative decrease in effective demand until everyone was out of a job. However unstable we may think economic life actually is, as compared with what it ought to be or might be, it is not nearly as unstable as it would be if the so-called fundamental psychological law did not obtain.

The actual arithmetical values of the multiplier in experience help to account for the relative stability of our economic system. The multiplier is neither extremely large nor is it so small as unity. If the multiplier were very large, small additions to investment would result in a great cumulative rise in effective demand, income, and employment. But Keynes estimates the actual multiplier to be somewhere between 2½ and 3 in the United States and England, varying, of course, at different levels of employment in different phases of the business cycle. Thus the multiplier is not so large as to lead to wild fluctuations in employment as a result of small changes in the volume of investment, yet it is small enough to require huge amounts of investment to sustain economic activity at high levels of employment in wealthy communities.

Since the marginal propensity to consume and the multiplier will be higher in a poor community than in a wealthy community, it might appear that the poor community would be subject to more violent fluctuations in employment as a result of changes in investment. This, however, is not the case. The degree of instability depends on the average as well as the marginal propensity to consume. While a high marginal propensity to consume makes for large relative changes in income from a given amount of investment, a high average propensity to consume reduces the absolute amount of investment needed to sustain full employment. A poor community which produces little more than enough to sustain itself will have a high average as well as a high marginal propensity to consume. Therefore, its absolute dependence on investment will not be great, even though changes in its small amount of investment may cause large relative fluctuations. A wealthy community, on the other hand, will have a low average as well as a low marginal propensity to consume. There will be a large absolute gap between income and consumption at all high levels of employment, and therefore large absolute amounts of investment are required to fill this gap. While the relative fluctuation in income from a given amount of investment will not be great because of the low value of the marginal propensity to consume and the multiplier, the absolute amount of fluctuation will be great because the low average propensity to consume makes the wealthy community dependent on a large volume of investment, the demand for which is unstable. Instability in the wealthy community is accentuated by the weak inducement to invest that is associated with a large previous accumulation of capital assets.

The Employment Multiplier: Attention is now directed to the first column in Table 3. This column shows the volume of employment which corresponds to various levels of income ranging from the low of 30 million workers to the full-employment level of 60 million. It is assumed that increases in employment are directly proportional to increases in income, so that, for example, a doubling of employment from 30 million to 60 million men is accompanied by a doubling of national income from $100 billion to $200 billion. Obviously this exact relationship will not hold in any rigid fashion, but as a first approximation it may be accepted as valid. Under this assumption, the employment multiplier (k') will be equal to the investment multiplier (k). Since Keynes' work is primarily concerned with the volume of employment, it is important to discuss the multiplier in terms of employment as well as in terms of income and investment. The employment multiplier is the ratio of increase in total employment (N) to the increase in primary employment (N_2), in the same way in which the investment multiplier is the ratio of increase in income to the increase in (primary) investment. Thus the expression for increases in employment, $\triangle N = k' \cdot \triangle N_2$, is analogous to the expression for increases in income, $\triangle Y = k \cdot \triangle I$. The simplifying assumption that the employment multiplier is equal to the investment multiplier does no violence to the general theory of employment. Most of Keynes' analysis is stated in terms of the investment multiplier

because of greater convenience of expression, but the employment multiplier is useful for showing the relation of the foregoing discussion to the problem of primary and secondary
employment from public works.

All discussions of public works recognize that in addition
to the original or "primary" employment directly relating to
the public works there will be a further or "secondary" employment resulting from the public works. The total benefit
of public works as a remedy for unemployment is greater
than the immediate or primary employment. "Secondary"
employment is that which occurs in consumption goods industries as a result of the primary employment in investment
industries. The employment multiplier tells us the number
of men who will be added to employment for every one that
is directly employed. When the multiplier is 5, for example,
every man newly employed in investment goods production
will cause four other men to be newly employed in consumption goods industries, for a total new employment of five men.

From Table 3, we can ascertain what income and employment will be if we know the volume of investment. If we are
able to control the volume of investment, we can make real
income what we want it to be, up to the point of full employment. Above full employment, true inflation sets in and further increases in income will be purely monetary, i.e., inflationary. From earlier discussion, it is clear that the volume
of private investment is highly variable, largely because of
the inherently unstable nature of the marginal efficiency of
private capital. The first object of public policy designed to
work within the private-enterprise economy is to maintain a
high level of private investment. But since this is at best precarious, governmental authorities should be prepared to offset the effects of variations in the volume of private investment by effecting counter-variations in public investment.
The objective is to maintain total investment, private and public, at a level which will fill the gap between the desired level
of income and consumption out of that income. If the volume
of private investment is chronically deficient, the mainte-

nance of a high level of employment calls for permanent supplementary investment in public projects. According to the figures in Table 3, if at a certain time investment is taking place at a rate of $12 billion per year, there will be 45 million people employed and income creation will be at a rate of $150 billion per year. In order to raise employment to 48 million workers and national income to $160 billion, investment must be increased by $4 billion to a total of $16 billion. In order to reach full employment, total investment must be raised to $37 billion. Any other level of activity may be attained by variations in the amount of investment. This illustrates the meaning of Keynes' important proposition that changes in employment depend upon changes in investment, given the propensity to consume.

References for Further Reading

Keynes, J. M., *The General Theory of Employment, Interest and Money*. Chapters 8, 9, and 10. New York: Harcourt, Brace and Company, 1936.

———, *The Means to Prosperity*. New York: Harcourt, Brace and Company, 1933.

———, "Fluctuations in Net Investment in the United States," *The Economic Journal*, September, 1936, Vol. XLVI, pages 540-547.

———, "Mr. Keynes' Consumption Function: Reply," *The Quarterly Journal of Economics*, August, 1938, Vol. LII, pages 708-709. (A reply to an article by G. R. Holden in the same volume, pages 281-296. See a further brief comment by Keynes in the same Journal, November, 1938, Vol. LIII, page 160.)

———, "The Income and Fiscal Potential of Great Britain," *The Economic Journal*, December, 1939, Vol. XLIX, pages 626-635.

———, "The Concept of National Income, A Supplementary Note," *The Economic Journal*, March, 1940, Vol. L, pages 60-65, also page 341.

———, "Mr. Keynes on the Distribution of Incomes and 'Propensity to Consume,' A Reply," *The Review of Economic Statistics*, August, 1939, Vol. XXI, page 129.

Gilboy, E. W., "The Propensity to Consume," *The Quarterly Journal of Economics*, November, 1938, and August, 1939, Vol. LIII, pages 120-140, 633-638. (Pages 633-636 contain an important letter from Keynes to Dr. Gilboy on the propensity to consume.)

Goodwin, R. M., "The Multiplier," *The New Economics*, edited by S. E. Harris, Chapter XXXVI, pages 482-499. New York: Alfred A. Knopf, 1947.

Hansen, A. H., *Fiscal Policy and Business Cycles*, Chapters XI and XII. New York: W. W. Norton and Co., 1941.

Kahn, R. F., "The Relation of Home Investment to Unemployment," *The Economic Journal*, June, 1931, Vol. XLI, pages 173-198. (Keynes credits Mr. Kahn with introducing the conception of the multiplier into economic theory in this well-known article.)

Lange, Oscar, "The Theory of the Multiplier," *Econometrica*, July-October, 1943, Vol. II, pages 227-245. (A mathematical treatment)

Machlup, Fritz, "Period Analysis and Multiplier Theory," *The Quarterly Journal of Economics*, November, 1939, Vol. LIV, pages 1-27. Reprinted in *Readings in Business Cycle Theory*, selected by a Committee of the American Economic Association. Philadelphia: The Blakiston Company, 1944.

Salant, W. S., "The Demand for Money and the Concept of Income Velocity," *The Journal of Political Economy*, June, 1941, Vol. XLIX, pages 395-421.

Samuelson, P. A., "Interactions Between the Multiplier Analysis and the Principle of Acceleration," *The Review of Economic Statistics*, May, 1939, Vol. XXXI, pages 75-78. Reprinted in *Readings in Business Cycle Theory*, selected by a Committee of the American Economic Association. Philadelphia: The Blakiston Co., 1944.

———, "A Synthesis of the Principle of Acceleration and the Multiplier," *The Journal of Political Economy*, December, 1939, Vol. XLVII, pages 786-797.

(See also the items listed for Chapter 6.)

CHAPTER 6

Fiscal Policy in Depression

Thus we are so sensible, have schooled ourselves to so close a semblance of prudent financiers, taking careful thought before we add to the "financial" burdens of posterity by building them houses to live in, that we have no such easy escape from the sufferings of unemployment.

J. M. Keynes, *The General Theory of Employment, Interest and Money.**

KEYNES viewed fiscal policy, that is, government spending, taxing, and borrowing, as the most important weapon against unemployment. His general explanation of the need for positive fiscal policy runs as follows: At a level of income corresponding to full employment, the gap between total income and total consumption is so great in advanced industrial economies that private investment is inadequate to fill it. If unemployment is to be avoided, the gap must be bridged either by filling in with government expenditure or by reducing the size of the gap by increasing the propensity to consume. The problem has both its cyclical and its secular aspects. If the average propensity to consume can be raised through such measures as progressive taxation, the magnitude of cyclical fluctuations can be reduced. Although Keynes has made suggestions in this connection, he emphasizes that in a

---

* Harcourt, Brace and Co., Inc., 1936, page 131.

capitalist economy, characterized by wide inequalities in the distribution of income and other institutional factors which make for a high propensity to save, the propensity to consume cannot easily be raised enough to have a significant effect upon employment. Therefore, the chief burden for maintenance of high levels of employment falls on public expenditures designed to fill in the existing gap between income and consumption at full employment.

Public expenditure for the purpose of relieving unemployment raises two main questions: Is it justified in terms of good economy? and, How effective is it in creating and stimulating employment? The investment multiplier is important in relation to the second issue. The basic case for public works, when there are unemployed resources, does not rest on the validity of the multiplier theory. In the language of common sense, the case for public works, or more generally public investment, rests on the notion that, from the point of view of the whole economic system, it pays to employ workers as long as they produce anything more than nothing. Since unemployed workers contribute nothing to the national income, whatever they produce when employed represents a net gain to society. This idea may be expressed by saying that the marginal cost to society of employing labor which otherwise would be idle is zero or virtually zero. Slight additional social cost may arise, for example, if men eat more, or otherwise consume more, when they work than when they do not. It is better for a man to produce something, however little, while working and maintaining his self-respect, than to remain idle and produce nothing at all. As Keynes says, it is obvious that 100,000 new homes are a national asset and that 1,000,000 unemployed men are a public liability.[1]

As the representative of the entire nation, a national government has the duty to behave in a manner which will increase the national income. The individual, as the representative of his own interests, is expected to behave in a manner

1. *The Means to Prosperity*, page 22. London: Macmillan and Company, Ltd., 1933.

which will increase his individual income. Since individual and social costs and revenues do not always correspond, the government may take action which will benefit the whole economy when no individual is in a position to do so. The theory that government should not participate in economic life rests on the assumption that the national income will be maximized when business profits are maximized. National income must always be the criterion of social welfare. Business profits are only one part, and a relatively small part, of total national income, and cannot provide an adequate criterion of social welfare. Yet the motivation to production derives from the expectation of profit. Business men have the power, the legal right, and often the incentive to withhold from use the means of production to which the labor of the community must be applied in order to produce the goods and services that provide the basis of community welfare. Without equipment, labor cannot produce. When business men decide to let their factories remain idle, they serve their own interest but they do not serve the interest of the community. This is perfectly "natural." It is not in the nature of business accounting to be directly concerned with what happens to the national income when wages and salaries fall because of unemployment. Workers employed by a single business enterprise usually purchase only a relatively small part of the output of the enterprise for which they work, whereas their wages as a rule constitute a major portion of the expenses of their firm. Hence, any firm is in a position to lower its costs more than its returns by reducing its payroll at any time, even though this may prove disastrous to all firms if all act in the same way. To the individual business enterprise, labor is a variable cost that ceases when employment ceases. But to the economy as a whole, labor is an overhead or fixed cost which goes on whether the worker is employed or unemployed. Workers must eat whether or not they have jobs. There is the alternative of letting the unemployed starve, but this is more callous than the proponents of "sound" finance would tolerate, so they advocate supporting the unemployed on relief where they produce nothing rather than giving them useful employment where they will add directly to the national income. It is the divergence between the principles of social and private accounting which holds the clue to the inconsistencies of so-called "sound" finance.

Obviously, it is not very convincing to tell an unemployed man that society cannot afford to burden his future by building him a house in which to live, even though he and his fellow-workers are doing nothing with their time and skill. The staunch advocates of annually balanced budgets are perhaps so accustomed to thinking in terms of the financial principles appropriate to an economy of full employment that they do not see the implications for public finance of an economy with widespread unemployment. When there is full employment, the real cost of hiring a man is what he produced in the job he gives up in order to accept a new position. When there is unemployment, the real cost of hiring an unemployed person is nothing because nothing is sacrificed by the employment of his labor. This fundamental principle is not altered when money is brought into the picture in order to finance the employment.

Having in mind that the basic case for public works and other forms of income-creating expenditures in time of depression does not rest on the multiplier effect but is merely reinforced by this effect, it will be understood that the limitations and qualifications to the multiplier in practice do not invalidate the case for public investment. Even if the multiplier effect were lacking altogether, public works might be desirable as a means for employing otherwise idle resources.

The Multiplier and Public Investment

The present section is concerned with the practical application of the multiplier as contrasted with the "pure" or "logical" theory of the multiplier discussed in the preceding chapter. It is one thing to accept the logical conversion of the marginal propensity to consume into the investment multiplier and quite another to accept the hypothesis that each dollar of public spending in depression will add several dollars to the national income. Responsible statesman called upon to vote large sums of money for public works on the assumption that this will bring recovery will want to know more than that the investment multiplier is equal to the reciprocal of the marginal propensity to save. While support for public expenditure might be secured just because it is better to have men producing something rather than nothing, the possible repercussions of public spending on private spending should be explored. If it can be demonstrated that an increase in government spending will increase national income by more than the original outlay, the case for such expansionary policies will be much more convincing than if there is no multiplying effect. After all, the idea of public works as a remedy for unemployment is very old. The multiplier aspect of it is the modern innovation.

Two preliminary points need to be made. The first concerns the relation of the multiplier to pump-priming, and the second the meaning of the term "public investment" in reference to the multiplier effects of public spending. The multiplier theory is not pump-priming. The latter rests on the assumption that a *temporary* new expenditure will have a lasting tendency to raise the level of economic activity, whereas the multiplier theory assumes that the income-generating effects of new expenditure will continue only as long as the expenditure is present, working with some time lag. Although Keynes did at one time believe in the pump-priming hypothesis, he had passed beyond that stage when he wrote his *General Theory*. Pump-priming implies that the economic system has been in *unstable* equilibrium before the injection of new spending pushes it back on the track from which it has been derailed by some fortuitous event.[2] Keynes' theory is that the economic system is characteristically in stable under-employment equilibrium from which there is no tendency to depart.

2. See Paul A. Samuelson, "The Theory of Pump-Priming Reëxamined," *The American Economic Review*, September, 1940, Vol. XXX, No. 3, page 502.

Therefore, repeated shoves and not just a single shove are required to move the economic machine up the high road to prosperity. In this sense, Keynes' theory is really a repudiation of the pump-priming thesis. Furthermore, the multiplier theory does not imply that public spending will stimulate private investment as a result of the stimulus it gives to private consumption. This may happen, but it is not part of the multiplier doctrine.

The term "public investment," in the sense in which it is relevant to cumulative increases in private consumption under the multiplier influence, means any autonomous increase in net government outlays. Hence, it includes new consumption expenditures as well as public works of the durable type. Consumption expenditures such as relief payments and subsidies to education may be viewed as investments in human beings, which no government can afford to neglect even though private enterprise may do so. More important, however, is the fact that government expenditure, even for consumption, does not depend on the size of the consumers' income in the way that private consumption expenditure does. Private consumption varies in a regular manner with income, but government expenditure, like private investment, results from autonomous decisions. Saving rises automatically with income and requires offsets, which may be in the form of public expenditure just as well as private investment. In Keynes' theory, investment is important because it distributes demand for consumption output without adding immediately to the supply of consumption output that must be sold. Not only is government expenditure capable of acting as an offset to saving, but it has the further, ironical advantage that often it is of such a nature as not to bring forth future consumption output.

With these preliminaries in mind, the following discussion of the effects of government investment may be summarized as follows: (1) If the government spends money that would not otherwise be spent, either because it would not have been in existence or because it would have remained idle, (2) if this spending has no repercussions on existing spending, and (3) if leakages and the multiplier remain unchanged long enough for the effects of successive respendings of the funds to work themselves out, then repeated government expenditures will permanently raise the national income by the multiplier times the expenditure in question.

Method of financing

The increase in income that results from new investment is equal to the multiplier times the new investment (the multiplicand). The increase in income may be affected either by changes in the size of the multiplier or in the amount of investment. Since any government spending will replace some amount of private spending, we cannot assume, for example, that an expenditure of one million dollars when the multiplier is 5 will increase income by $5 million. Keynes estimates that in a community like the United States in depression the marginal propensity to consume is about 80 per cent, indicating a multiplier of 5, but that the actual increase in income will be more nearly 2 or 3 times the amount of government expenditure. We may refer to the latter as the government expenditure multiplier, in contrast with the full value of the multiplier of 5 when the marginal propensity to consume is 80 per cent. Among the factors accounting for this difference is the method of financing public expenditure. If outlays are to be income-generating, they must represent "new" expenditure, and not just a substitution of one expenditure for another. Workers who receive $100 per month on public works and who previously received $40 per month on relief have a net increase in income of $60 and not of $100. Furthermore, the over-all economic effect depends upon how the former relief was financed as compared with how the present public works are financed. The greatest stimulation to employment will result when a public construction program financed by borrowing replaces a public relief program which was paid for out of taxation. Less stimulation is felt when both the former relief and the new public works are financed by loans. Least stimulating would be the case in which both the former relief and the new public works were financed from taxation. The expenditure of funds raised by taxation represents mainly a substitution of one form of expenditure for another, that is, a reduction in private spending and an increase in government spending. The expenditure of funds raised by borrowing represents mainly new expenditure and therefore an addition to total effective demand. In order to have significant expansionary effects, therefore, a program of public investment should be financed by borrowing rather than by taxation. This kind of borrowing or loan expenditure is popularly called "deficit financing," although the term "income-creating finance" is a more appropriate designation. The term "deficit financing" means, of course, simply that the government spends more than it collects in taxes, leaving the budget unbalanced. The belief that deficit financing will bankrupt the government or the economic system arises from a false analogy between the economic system as a whole and the individual business enterprise. An individual who keeps on spending more than he takes in will go bankrupt and, so the argument runs, the same will happen to a government that spends more than it collects in taxes. However, the same tests of "soundness" do not apply to the economy and to the parts which make up the economy. An individual, a business enterprise, or a government can spend more than it receives, but the economic system as a whole cannot spend more than it receives (ignoring for the time being international economic relations or considering the whole world as the economic unit). Therefore, if the government pays out (spends) more money than it takes away from the public in the form of taxes, there must be a net addition to the money income available for spending by the public. This represents a net addition to effective demand. When there is unemployment, this increase in effective demand results in more employment and the creation of a larger real national income. The amount of the increase in effective demand will be at least equal to the amount of the new or additional spending, which is equal to the excess of the amount of money the government spends over the amount which it takes away from the taxpayers in the form of taxes. The deficit results on the books of the government if the government borrows from its citizens in order to get the money to spend. When a government, or anyone else, borrows, it goes into debt. Since the government is a representative of its citizens, this means some people will owe money to others. Taxpayers will owe money to bondholders. However, the government may, if it wishes, issue new money rather than borrow it, in which case there is no loan-deficit. Hence, deficit financing is a consequence of a particular manner of financing income-creating expenditures. The important thing is that the spending should represent new expenditures. New expenditures will increase the national income, and out of the enlarged income saving will increase by an amount equal to the deficit.[3]

In addition to the distinction between loans and taxes, there are significant differences between various types of loans and taxes. Loans from banks are more expansionary than loans from the public because bank loans result in the creation of new deposit money, whereas loans made by the public result merely in the transfer of part of the existing money supply from the public to the government. In the former case, no one need restrict either his consumption or his investment. The bond is purchased with new money created within the banking system in the form of new checkbook money. The total quantity of money is increased by the lending activities of the banking system. There is no transfer or giving up of means of purchase by one party for expenditure by the government; there is merely the creation of additional means of purchase. Selling bonds to banks is not, as a rule, difficult because in depression banks have excess reserves

---

3. The expression saving = investment may be phrased: saving = private investment + the government deficit. Expressed in terms of total government expenditure and taxes, this means that saving + taxes = private investment + government expenditure.

which they are willing to make use of by investing in government bonds, even though the rate of interest paid on government bonds may be quite low. The eagerness of the banks to purchase bonds is subject to the qualification that they feel the rate of interest will not rise in the calculable future to cause a fall in the market value of the bonds they purchased when interest rates were low.

Loan expenditures which are financed by selling government bonds to individuals (the public) are stimulating, but to a lesser extent than expenditures from funds raised by selling bonds to the banking system. When an individual as distinct from a bank buys a bond, a transfer rather than a new creation of means of purchase occurs. The individual buyer transfers his command over purchasing power to the government. No new money is created as a result of this form of borrowing. Such borrowing is a stimulus to economic activity, however, to the extent to which the government spends more readily than did the individual who formerly commanded the funds. Borrowing of this type is sometimes referred to as "tapping the savings stream." Individual savings which might otherwise have found no outlet in investment find an outlet in the form of governmental expenditure. Individual saving which otherwise would have forced a reduction in income to the point where social income exceeds aggregate consumption by the amount of actual investment is offset by public investment. Of course, if the individual who buys a government bond would otherwise have spent his money on either consumption or investment, there will be no net stimulus when he transfers his money to the government for spending. As a rule, however, a considerable proportion of the money used to buy government bonds would not otherwise have been spent, so the effect is generally stimulating. Nevertheless, borrowing from the public, especially on a large scale, is likely to restrict consumption or private investment to some degree, and is therefore less desirable in a deep depression than borrowing from banks. As over-all economic activity expands in a business recovery and the savings stream rises, borrowing from the public becomes both more feasible and more desirable. Once full employment has been attained, inflation will be forestalled by borrowing from the public or by taxation rather than by borrowing from the banks.

Among the different types of taxes, those which are progressive tend to restrict consumption less than those which are regressive. All taxes tend to be deflationary in the sense that money turned over to the government in the form of taxes would have been spent, in some part at least, had it been left in the control of the taxpayer. If public works are financed by funds raised by progressive income taxes or death duties which fall mainly on the wealthy, total consumption from private expenditure probably will not be much reduced because the consumption of wealthy persons tends to be about the same regardless of the amount of taxes they pay. In the case of very high tax rates, this would not be true. To the extent that taxes are paid from funds which would not otherwise be spent during the current period, idle money has been tapped and put to work by government spending. A further disadvantage of steeply progressive taxation is the danger that it may react adversely on the inducement to private investment. Private investment is a process which often does not lend itself to rational calculation. It depends to an important degree upon the state of confidence and spontaneous optimism of the business community. Highly progressive taxation is an element that tends to depress business confidence and inhibit spontaneous optimism.

Least desirable of all methods of financing public expenditure in depression is that by which taxes fall largely upon funds which would have been spent if left in the hands of taxpayers. Consumer sales taxes illustrate this least desirable way of raising funds to finance public investment in periods of depression. Consumer sales taxes reduce expenditure on consumption by nearly the full amount of the tax. Hence, government expenditures financed by regressive taxes are much less effective against unemployment than expenditures financed by progressive taxes, which in turn are less effective than expenditures financed by borrowing.

It is quite consistent for those who advocate loan expenditure, or deficit financing, in depression to advocate balanced budgets in boom periods. The purpose of deficit financing is to create full utilization of resources. Beyond the point of full employment, there is no need for further deficit financing. Keynes' program is one which calls for full employment without inflation or deflation. Monetary expansion through income-creating expenditure which is designed to increase both investment and consumption is the appropriate policy in depression years. High taxes and debt reduction are the fiscal tools for preventing inflation in boom years like those which usually characterize postwar periods.

Interest-free financing

An aspect of fiscal policy which Keynes does not discuss but which naturally arises in view of his position on the nature of interest is the question of interest-free financing of public expenditures which are designed to put idle resources to work. Loan expenditure involves an increase in the public debt and in annual interest payments on the public debt. The nature and significance of the public debt is one of the least understood issues in public life, but the common misconceptions cannot be examined here. However, if a major objection to loan financing is the increase in the principal and in the service charge on the public debt, the question arises as to why society should have to pay interest to banks and others in order to get the money needed to mobilize idle resources. Is there any necessity for subsidizing the commercial banks by paying them huge amounts of interest to create the new money which is required for economic expansion? Is not the creation of new money properly a government function, and if so, what is there to prevent the government from issuing new money directly, without paying interest on bonds to commercial banks?

The answer, in terms of Keynes' theory of interest which

will be discussed more fully later, is that there is no necessity for paying interest under these circumstances. Interest pay· ments are not needed to induce people to save nor to reward them for saving. The banks, which receive most of the inter· est, create new balances on a basis of excess reserves to pay for the bonds they buy, and, therefore, interest payments to them are in no sense an inducement to curb consumption. The interest income received by commercial banks, except for the amount used to defray cost of performing a few clerical services, is a monopoly payment which rewards no genuine sacrifice or function. The risk is very slight on government bonds, which are considered to be the nearest possible ap· proach to a riskless investment. Consequently, there appears to be no valid economic reason why the government should not by-pass the commercial banks and increase the money supply directly without resort to the sale of interest-bearing bonds. The particular technique employed to carry out the increase in money supply would depend on the nature of the central monetary authority. In the United States, the Treasury could issue non-interest bearing notes to the Federal Reserve banks with instructions to increase the government deposits to the extent of the value of the notes. The government could then spend its balances in the usual fashion for public works and other expenditures.

The objection that a policy of interest-free financing is cer· tain to be inflationary is easily answered in terms of the gen· eral theory of employment. As long as there are unemployed resources, the increase in money expenditure will increase em· ployment rather than prices.[4] Beyond the point of full employ· ment there is no necessity for further monetary expansion. If monetary expansion continues after full employment is at· tained, inflation will result. This, however, is a consequence of monetary expansion *per se* and not of the manner of its execution. For example, selling interest-bearing bonds to commercial banks can cause inflation if carried to excess. In

---

4. See Chapter 9, section on the theory of prices, for a fuller statement of what happens to prices as employment and output increase.

fact, any mismanagement of the money supply will cause either inflation or deflation. Objections of this type are not objections to interest-free financing as such but to any type of managed currency. They are objections which indicate a lack of trust in the competence of government monetary authorities to act with wisdom and restraint. For better or for worse, any type of managed currency implies a faith in the wisdom and restraint of the monetary authorities. Since the abandonment of metallic standards, the money systems of the world are almost exclusively managed systems.

Leakages

Foreign Trade: The multiplying force of new expenditures is reduced by leakages which take the form of spending for imported goods and services. If the marginal propensity to consume is $\frac{9}{10}$ of which $\frac{3}{10}$ is for imports, the effective domestic marginal propensity to consume is lowered to $\frac{6}{10}$. A reduction in the marginal propensity to consume from $\frac{8}{10}$ to $\frac{6}{10}$ will cause the multiplier to fall from 5 to 2½. In a nation like Great Britain, where imports are estimated to constitute 20 per cent of consumption, the foreign trade leakage alone is sufficient to explain the discrepancy between a potential multiplier of 5, based on a marginal propensity to consume of 80 per cent, and the empirical estimates of a multiplier of approximately 2½ to 3. In the United States, where the proportion of imports is only about 5 per cent, the effect of foreign trade on the multiplier is much less than in Britain. A fall in the marginal propensity to consume from 80 per cent to 75 per cent will lower the multiplier from 5 to 4. The foreign trade figure which is relevant in these estimates is the proportion of *additional* or new expenditure which is made abroad and not the average proportion of *all* expenditures which are made abroad. In other words, the distinction between the marginal and the average propensity to consume is to be borne in mind.

The foreign trade leakage means that employment at home increases less than it would if all spending were for products produced within the domestic economy. The loss is only a national and not a world loss because benefits will accrue to foreign countries to the extent to which they are lost to the domestic economy. Improved economic conditions in foreign countries will, as a rule, react favorably upon the domestic economy in the form of increased exports. If we reduce the multiplier to allow for imports, any increase in exports should be included as new investment and hence as one of the favorable repercussions. There is no reason to assume, however, that what is lost by way of spending on imports will be gained back in the form of increased exports, especially in the short run. Since there is in any national economy some foreign spending for imports, the world multiplier is always larger than the domestic multiplier for any given primary expenditure. This strengthens the case for world economic co-operation in the form of simultaneous expansionary policies in all national economies.

Taxes and Corporation Saving: The marginal propensity to consume out of national income depends on taxation and corporation dividend policies. When the national income in the United States is at $200 billion, more than $50 billion is collected in taxes (federal, state and local at 1948 tax rates) and the proportion of increases in income taken by taxes is much more than 25 per cent because of the progressive nature of federal income taxes. Hence, the size of the marginal propensity to consume calculated in terms of the total national income is much lower than if calculated in terms of net disposable income (roughly equivalent to "take home" pay). At each stage in the income-generating process, consumption is reduced by the drain of taxation. Of course, not all income paid in taxes would otherwise be spent, but probably a very large part of it would be if the taxpayer were free to dispose of it as he wished.

The national income includes corporation earnings which are not paid out in dividends as well as those which are paid out in dividends. Undistributed profits are not available for consumption spending and represent a factor tending to reduce the propensity to consume out of total national income. When corporate saving is added to taxes, there is a large difference between the total national income and the net disposable income available for consumer spending. Hence, it is not surprising that the marginal propensity to consume calculated on a basis of the total national income is smaller than it might appear to be if the only leakages taken into account were the savings of individual consumers out of their disposable income. Any change in tax rates or dividend policies will affect the size of the marginal propensity to consume and hence the size of the government expenditure multiplier.

Neutralizing factors

Public works in time of depression have as their fundamental purpose an increase in aggregate employment in the economy as a whole, including the private and the public sectors. Any decrease in private investment which results from increases in public investment tends to neutralize the employment- and income-creating effects of public investment. Any increase in private investment that may be induced by the greater amount of consumption tends to increase employment and the income-creating effects of public investment. In accordance with Keynes' theory of the inducement to private investment, any repercussion of public spending can be traced to a change either in the rate of interest or in the marginal efficiency of capital, or both.

The Rate of Interest: In the absence of positive action on the part of the monetary authority to make available a larger supply of money for transactions, the rate of interest will tend to rise as a result of an expansionary program. Any rise in the rate of interest will tend to discourage private investment. There is no necessary reason, however, why a program of large-scale public investment should cause the rate of interest to rise. If the quantity of money is increased sufficiently to prevent a drain on the balances held to satisfy the speculative motive, the interest rate will not rise. The monetary authority may exercise policies which will induce the banks to expand their deposits and to buy large issues of government securities so there will be no necessity to borrow from the public. The state of liquidity preference for the speculative motive, which together with the quantity of money determines the rate of interest, is less manageable and less predictable than the quantity of money itself. If the situation which accompanies a large-scale program of public works is confused and confusing, liquidity preference may rise and cause the rate of interest to increase. Above all, the monetary authority should appear firm in its determination to prevent the long-term rate of interest from rising.

The Marginal Efficiency of Capital: The beneficial effects of public investment financed by loan expenditure may be neutralized by a fall in the marginal efficiency of private capital. These neutralizing effects may work either through an increase in the costs of producing capital goods or through unfavorable expectations of entrepreneurs. Some increase in the costs of capital assets must inevitably occur during the transition from low levels to high levels of investment and employment. In a large-scale public works program, increases in demand are concentrated on building materials and construction workers. Since private and public investment are dependent upon the same type of factors of production, increases in the cost for one represent increases in the cost for the other. As costs of production rise under the impact of increasing demand, the marginal efficiency of private capital tends to fall and this in turn tends to lessen the volume of private investment.

Private investment may also be deterred if public investment creates an unfavorable psychological attitude on the part of business entrepreneurs toward the prospective yields of private investment. In their political outlook, businessmen are characteristically conservative to a degree that renders them highly sensitive to unbalanced budgets and government spending. Fortunately business "confidence" is not so sensitive as to be completely overruled by the political prejudices of the business community. Public investment on a sufficient scale must inevitably increase the sales of business firms and bring dollars rolling into their cash registers and bank accounts. Dr. A. P. Lerner optimistically suggests that "Their pockets will ultimately overcome their prejudices" even though they continue to grumble that the prosperity which is enriching them is "artificial," "illusory," and "unsound."[5]

In so far as large-scale government investment involves the expansion of public enterprise into fields previously restricted to private enterprise, further private investment in these fields may be discouraged by the fear that profits will be lowered by the competition of public enterprise. Such fear on the part of private investors can be offset only partly by limiting public investment to strictly government activity like road-building, reclamation, flood control, and public buildings. Projects like the Tennessee Valley Authority compete with private power companies, and government housing competes with private housing. Under capitalism, private investment is normally much greater than public investment. As long as chief reliance is upon private investment to fill the gap between income and consumption at full employment, it is important to avoid weakening the incentives to private investment.

When there is involuntary unemployment, even wasteful expenditure may enrich the community if the multiplier is greater than one. Let us suppose a million dollars is paid out to men for some activity like leaf-raking which we may assume adds nothing to the real income or real wealth of society. If the multiplier is three, the total addition to money income is three million dollars. Subtracting the one million dollars of money payment for which no corresponding value of output has been produced, the addition to real income and wealth is two million dollars. The original outlay to leaf-rakers results merely in a redistribution of existing real wealth, with the rest of the community losing what the leaf-rakers gain. But when

5. Lerner, A. P., *The Economics of Control*, page 321. New York: The Macmillan Company, 1944.

the two-thirds of a million dollars of effective demand is spent for consumption, it calls forth the production of an equivalent amount of real income and real output. The total indirect effect of the original outlay for a worthless project is to add two million dollars to real income and to real output. Of course, it is better to have useful expenditure, but if this is politically objectionable, wasteful expenditure is better than nothing. Thus, says Keynes, "Pyramid-building, earthquakes, even wars may serve to increase wealth, if the education of our statesmen on the principles of the classical economics stands in the way of anything better." (p. 129) Lest there be any misunderstanding, this statement does not mean that Keynes recommended pyramid-building, earthquakes, and wars.

Even though there may be no actual encroachment by public enterprise into the fields previously limited to private enterprise, the existence of large-scale public works may create the fear of encroachment in the future. Such fear will tend to dampen the expectations of private entrepreneurs. What the actual effect of planned public investment upon the "confidence" of business men will be, and how it will be manifested in their economic behavior with regard to investment decisions, is one of the enigmas of public policy. It is not the kind of issue that can be demonstrated definitively one way or the other. No economic theory is capable of assigning quantitative values to all the variables in such situations.

In concluding the discussion of neutralizing effects of public spending, it is to be noted that the cumulative increase in effective demand stemming from primary public expenditure may induce new private investment. As the demand for consumers goods rises, existing plant capacities in some fields may prove inadequate. Plant expansion in these fields will then be in order. Likewise, investments in inventories are likely to be induced by any cumulative rise in demand even though there is no increase in the demand for new investment in durable plant and equipment. Keynes excludes these considerations from the multiplier theory by the assumption that investment increases only by the original amount. However, this is for theoretical simplification. When the question is that of evaluating the actual prospects and effects of a public spending program, the possibility of induced investment from induced consumption should not be ignored.

Time lags between successive spendings

Keynes' "logical" theory of the multiplier abstracts from time lags. Obviously, however, in judging the practical application of the multiplier, account must be taken of the fact that time elapses between the successive spending and respending of income. If the period between spendings is two months, and the marginal propensity to consume is ½, meaning a multiplier of 2, the initial injection of a new dollar of spending will increase income by one dollar at the time it is first spent by the government. Two months later 50 cents will be spent on consumption and income will rise by a corresponding amount. Four months after the injection, 25 cents will be added, and six months after the injection, 12½ cents will be added to income. In each successive period, the income will be raised by less and less as a result of this initial expenditure of one dollar and will approach a total increase in income of two dollars when the multiplier is 2. If successive spendings are continued long enough, the total income-increasing effect in each period will be approximately two dollars and will continue at this level as long as the rate of injection remains the same, other relevant factors remaining unchanged. This means that some time must elapse after public spending has begun before it will attain its maximum effectiveness. Once the public spending ceases, the income-creating effect will gradually dwindle and finally disappear altogether.

Conclusion

There are many other factors and influences that should be taken into account in analyzing the practical application of the multiplier. Enough has been said to indicate that this is no magic formula which will enable us to predict with any degree of accuracy just what the influence of public investment will be. By assigning different weights to various factors, one might conclude either that public investment will have a tremendous income-creating effect or that it will have, on balance, a negative effect on employment and income. Only actual experience can give an answer to what the over-all influence will be. We may summarize again the chief assumptions and qualifications of the preceding section: Repeated government expenditures will raise permanently the level of national income by the government expenditure multiplier times the expenditure in question if the spending is new spending, if the new spending has no repercussions on existing spending, and if there are no changes in leakages and in the size of the multiplier.

Other Types of Fiscal Policy Designed to Expand Employment

A government which desires to stimulate a higher level of employment may combine spending, borrowing, and taxing in any one of at least three types of fiscal policy. Keynes deals primarily with one method, the case in which government expenditures are increased while tax rates remain unchanged.[6] Instead of altering the propensity to consume, this type of fiscal policy aims at increased investment, which includes in this connection private capital formation plus loan-fianced government expenditure. Consumption increases because added investment causes higher incomes according to the multiplier principle, and out of larger incomes more will be spent for private consumption even though the propensity to consume is unchanged. Since tax rates are unaffected, there is no reason to assume that such a fiscal policy will change the propensity to consume. Before proceeding to the other two methods of fiscal policy which do affect the propensity to con-

---

6. For a discussion of all three methods, see Alvin H. Hansen, "Three Methods of Expansion through Fiscal Policy," and R. A. Musgrave, "Alternative Budget Policies for Full Employment," in *The American Economic Review*, June, 1945, Vol. XXXV, No. 3, pages 382-387 and 387-400.

sume, it should be noted that tax *yields* tend to increase even if tax *rates* are unchanged when income is rising. Unbalanced budgets result because tax yields from higher levels of income do not increase as much as do government expenditures.

As mentioned earlier, in our discussion of the propensity to consume, Keynes recognizes that changes in fiscal policy may alter the propensity to consume even in the short run. If tax rates which are high are cut drastically and government expenditures remain unchanged, the private propensity to consume out of total income (before taxes) rises because the amount of disposable income remaining in the hands of the public after taxes is greater. By reducing the amount of money taken away from the public, the government stimulates private spending for consumption. Private investment also may be stimulated. Disregarding the effect on private investment, if the government spends as much as before and if the public spends more than before on consumption, total effective demand must increase. Employment and income will therefore increase. The resulting government deficit is income-generating in the same sense as a deficit which occurs when tax rates remain unchanged and government expenditures are increased.

The tax-remission type of fiscal policy has some advantages over methods which involve increases in expenditures. A sudden increase in government expenditure tends to be used for make-work projects like leaf-raking because there is usually insufficient time to plan and execute more worthwhile types of projects. Make-work projects are better than none in time of severe depression, but they involve an inefficient allocation of community resources. The tax-reduction approach to expansion avoids the need for enlarged government activity. It relies instead on the willingness of private citizens to spend some or all of their added income remaining after (lower) taxes are paid. Individual freedom of choice by consumers to spend their remitted tax money for whatever they want is likely to increase welfare more than an equivalent amount of spending by government on improvised projects. There are, of course, many types of government outlays which need to be expanded in the social interest. Education, health, and slum clearance are a few of the most obvious examples. These government activities can be pursued more rationally in terms of a careully planned, long-range program which is free from improvisation and sudden expansion and contraction. Whether tax remissions would provide a significant stimulus to employment depends on the extent and the nature of tax reductions. As an ultimate but unlikely limit, taxes may be reduced to zero.[7] With the high levels of government taxation and expenditures which seem to be a more or less permanent part of the legacy of the second world war, the possibilities of significant tax reductions have come within the range of practical consideration as a stimulus to employment. In the United States, such a program could be rendered more effective by a change which would permit the President or some other official body to adjust tax rates without having to await action by Congress as a whole.

A third type of fiscal policy which can expand employment and income when there is a deficiency of regular effective demand operates through an increase in government expenditure financed entirely by taxation. Under this policy, taxation must be increased as much as government outlay and therefore the budget is always balanced. While it is true that all forms of taxation are to an extent deflationary in that they restrict private consumption, tax money spent by the government is in itself expansionary. Although higher tax rates reduce private consumption, they also reduce private saving and thus reduce the dependence of the economic system on effective demand from private investment. Ultimately the private propensity to save will be lowered by heavy taxation to the point where private investment equals private saving out of the income corresponding to full employment. Even if private investment should fall to zero, full employment could be

---

7. It would be theoretically possible to have negative taxes in the form of subsidies or bounties to taxpayers, but this seems hardly deserving of practical consideration.

attained under this type of fiscal policy because private saving also would ultimately be reduced to zero with sufficiently high tax rates.

The objection to such a fiscal policy is obvious. To be an effective weapon against unemployment, this policy must involve a much greater amount of government expenditure than either of the other two forms of fiscal policy, both of which result in deficits in the government's budget. About the only time such a program would be practicable is in war, when government outlays are necessarily very large. When purchases of the federal government in the United States approximate $100 billion, as they did in 1944, no deficit is required in the government budget so far as full employment is concerned. This amount of expenditure, and even a much smaller amount, would be great enough to yield full employment even if taxes of an equivalent amount were to be levied. In peace time, however, the federal government would have to expand its activities beyond acceptable limits to spend even half as much as it did in 1944. Therefore, if in peace time there is a sizable deficiency in regular effective demand, government deficits are desirable because the same degree of expansion of employment can be achieved with a much smaller amount of government expenditure if the people are permitted to spend their money instead of having it taken away from them in the form of taxes for the purpose of balancing the budget.[8]

What Experience Proves About Public Works

What does experience prove with regard to the validity of Keynes' thesis that public works financed by loan expenditures will increase employment in depression, and what is Keynes' interpretation of this experience? Obviously, there are no simple answers to either of these two questions, but nevertheless, recent economic developments give some basis

8. For some estimates of the relative amounts of expenditure and taxes under the various types of budget policies, see Musgrave, *op. cit.*, pages 393-400.

for answers. The best testing ground for Keynes' thesis is the experience of the United States between 1933 and 1945. During the depression of the 'thirties the Conservative Government of Keynes' native Britain rejected the spending philosophy whereas the "New Deal" in the United States subscribed to Keynes' general philosophy.

The broad contours of economic development in the United States between 1929 and 1945 may be summarized briefly as follows. The great depression which began in 1929 reached a low point in the winter of 1932; a rapid expansion followed between 1933 and 1937; in 1937, with approximately eight million still unemployed, a sharp recession occurred; expansion began again in 1938 and continued into the defense period beginning in 1940, and the defense period soon developed into the tremendous war expansion which carried production and employment in the United States to an all-time high of income, output, and employment. The decade from 1929 to 1939 represents the longest and deepest depression which the United States has ever experienced, and the failure to achieve anything approaching full recovery has led to the thesis that private capitalism has entered a new phase of economic development, the era of secular stagnation. Secular stagnation means chronic, mass unemployment resulting from the lack of sufficient private investment to fill the gap between income and consumption at full employment.

During the period between 1933 and 1940, Keynes' ideas concerning the role of public spending underwent an important change. In 1933 he believed in the pump-priming thesis that temporary injections of government spending would set the wheels of private enterprise in motion and, once private enterprise was back on its feet, the government expenditures could be withdrawn without causing any relapse in total economic activity. As previously indicated, by the time he was writing the *General Theory* in 1935 Keynes had abandoned the pump-priming thesis. Meanwhile, his belief in the multiplier was reinforced by the experience of the early 'thirties.

Recovery in the United States in the spring of 1933 was

followed by a relapse in the latter half of that year. Keynes attributed this relapse to the failure of the New Deal to organize loan expenditure on an adequate scale. At the beginning of 1934, he said that a resumption of the recovery that had begun in early 1933 would depend almost entirely upon larger loan expenditures in the ensuing months. During the early months of 1934, loan expenditure did increase from about $100 million monthly to approximately $300 million monthly. The resumption of recovery predicted by Keynes did result. In what was a remarkable achievement for so short a time, income, output, and employment increased by about 15 per cent in the first half of 1934. The total increase in national income exceeded the additional loan expenditure three- or four-fold, suggesting an empirical multiplier of 3 or 4.

On the occasion of a visit to the United States by Keynes in June, 1934, the volume of federal emergency expenditure was declining below the $300 million per month level of the preceding months. Keynes predicted that if the volume of emergency spending were permitted to fall as low as $200 million per month, much of the ground already gained would be lost in declining business activity. On the other hand, if the volume of emergency expenditure were increased from $300 to $400 million monthly, he predicted a strong business recovery would result, since the multiplier effect would increase total economic activity by three or four times the amount of the increase in primary loan expenditure.[9] The still-lingering belief in pump-priming is seen in Keynes' further prediction in June, 1934, that outlays of $400 million per month for twelve months might bring a return to normal business activity, or at least give private business enterprise enough time to carry on without emergency government financing.

The economic expansion between 1933 and 1937, despite occasional minor relapses, was one of the most rapid in the history of American business cycles. The speed of this recovery was undoubtedly conditioned by the depths to which

9. *New York Times*, June 10, 1934, page 1E.

activity had plummeted in 1932. It was, nevertheless, a remarkable recovery which was nurtured by fairly large-scale
government loan expenditure. Although the volume of spending was large, it never attained a magnitude sufficient to stimulate private investment to a significant degree. On the other
hand, a much larger volume of public loan-expenditure might
have induced a significant increase in private investment. In
any event, the level of private investment throughout the
'thirties remained abnormally low as compared with the
'twenties. Income-creating expenditures were drastically curtailed by the federal government in the spring of 1937, presumably because a very considerable recovery had already
been achieved and because the administration was sensitive to
criticisms of its unbalanced budgets. Almost simultaneously
with the decline in loan expenditures, there ensued the sharp-
est decline in economic activity ever experienced in the United
States, not excluding even the rapid declines of 1920 and
1929. There seems little doubt that curtailment of government loan expenditures was a major factor in this downturn,
although other factors contributed. Among the other factors
were the curtailment of consumer credit, raising the minimum
reserve requirements of the member banks of the Federal
Reserve System, and the abnormal accumulation of inventories.[10] The most unprecedented and shocking aspect of the
1937 recession was that it occurred when there were approximately eight million men still out of work. No major recovery
had ever before stopped so far short of full employment.

The 1937 recession began in the fall and lasted well into
1938. Seven or eight months after the downturn, another
large-scale federal spending program was begun and once
again economic conditions improved. A strong recovery was
getting under way by June, 1938, and continued, with a
minor relapse in 1939, on into the defense period which began in 1940.

The concomitance of increases in loan expenditure with in-

---

10. See Sherwood M. Fine, *Public Spending and Postwar Economic Policy*,
pages 107-115. New York: Columbia University Press, 1944.

creases in economic activity at nearly every turn between 1933 and 1940 seems to be more than a mere coincidence. Experience of this period seems to verify the thesis that economic expansion can be promoted by government expenditures, and that the total increase in income will exceed the amount of primary expenditure (the multiplier effect). Certainly Keynes thought there was verification of his loan expenditure and his multiplier theories in this experience. The failure of private investment to regain the level of the 'twenties gives some plausibility to the thesis that public spending and unbalanced budgets tend to discourage new private investment in durable capital assets. The failure to achieve full recovery and full employment throughout the decade of the 'thirties clearly indicates the inadequacies, if not the inherent weaknesses, of New Deal spending policies. Keynes' chief criticisms of the New Deal loan-expenditure program were that it was on too small a scale to achieve full recovery and that it was inadequately planned and poorly executed. At the end of the 'thirties, there had been no test of how large the loan expenditure would have to be to lift the economy to full employment.

In 1940, at the beginning of the American defense program, Keynes expressed the hope that at last a situation had arisen which would prove his case and make the "grand experiment" that would demonstrate "what level of total output accompanied by what level of consumption is needed to bring a free, modern community having the intense development of the United States within sight of the optimum employment of its resources."[11] In summarizing the experience of the 'thirties, Keynes wrote: "The conclusion is that at all recent times investment expenditure has been on a scale which was hopelessly inadequate to the problem. . . . It appears to be politically impossible for a capitalistic democracy to organize expenditure on a scale necessary to make the grand experiment

---

11. "The United States and the Keynes Plan," *The New Republic,* July 29, 1940, Vol. CIII, No. 3—Part 2, page 159.

which would prove my case except in war conditions."[12] Keynes recognized that the vast productive capacity of the United States required a very high level of effective demand at full employment. Instead of outlays by the federal government of a few billion dollars per year, it would have required perhaps 10 to 15 billion in the late 'thirties to achieve full employment.

To some extent, the defense expenditures of 1940 and 1941 provided the evidence necessary to indicate the amount of expenditure needed to lift the American economy to full employment. The outlays were sufficiently large to put the economy on the high road to full utilization of resources. The chief difficulty was that the expenditures soon became much greater than necessary for full employment. Inflation replaced unemployment as the threat to economic stability. A net increase in federal governmental expenditures of less than $12 billion in 1941 as compared with 1939 was accompanied by an increase of approximately $32 billion in national income.[13] It seems quite probable that expenditures continued on this scale would have resulted in continuing full employment. When federal government purchases of goods and services rose to $52 billion, $81 billion, and $89 billion in 1942, 1943, and 1944, respectively, the necessity for restricting consumption rather than stimulating it with the aid of the multiplier effect became the order of the day. Whatever else it may have proved, the war experience demonstrated beyond a shadow of a doubt that government expenditure on a sufficiently large scale can bring the economic system swiftly to a point of full utilization. It did not, of course, indicate that it was the only way or the best way to achieve this objective.

Conclusion

The experience with public spending in the United States

---

12. *Loc. cit.*

13. National income, as measured by the Department of Commerce, increased from $72.5 to $103.8 billion from 1939 to 1941; gross national product increased from $90.4 to $125.3 billion from 1939 to 1941.

between 1933 and 1945 seems to (1) repudiate the pump-priming thesis, (2) verify the multiplier theory, (3) indicate that a very great volume of loan expenditure is necessary to bring a modern industrial economy to full employment, and (4) demonstrate conclusively that public spending on a sufficient scale will raise output and income quickly to a level corresponding to full employment. The pump-priming thesis that a temporary priming of the economic system by government expenditure will set the private enterprise system going on its own power proved illusory during the 'thirties. Total economic activity suffered a relapse at each withdrawal of government loan expenditure. As long as loan expenditure continued, however, it appears to have acted as a quick stimulant to total economic activity. National income increased not only by the amount of government spending but by several times that amount, the amount of this multiple being the (empirical) multiplier. Failure of the economic system to attain a high level of employment at any time during the 'thirties despite the multiplying effect of government loan expenditure indicates that full employment can be attained only with a much larger volume of loan expenditure than was forthcoming under the New Deal program of that period. When the amount of federal loan expenditure skyrocketed in the defense and war periods beginning in 1940, unemployment disappeared rapidly. Full employment became merely a question of how long a time was required to remedy technological obstacles to expanded output. We shall have more to say about the inflation of the war and postwar periods in Chapters 9 and 10.

References for Further Reading

Keynes, J. M., *The General Theory of Employment, Interest and Money*, Chapter 10. New York: Harcourt, Brace and Company, 1936.

Clark, Colin, "Determination of the Multiplier from National Income Statistics," *The Economic Journal*, September, 1938, Vol. XLVIII, pages 435-448.

Clark, J. M., *Economics of Planning Public Works*. Washington: U. S. Government Printing Office, 1935.

——, "An Appraisal of the Workability of Compensatory Devices," *The American Economic Review, Papers and Proceedings*, March, 1939, Vol. XXIX, pages 194-208. Reprinted in *Readings in Business Cycle Theory*, selected by a Committee of the American Economic Association. Philadelphia: The Blakiston Company, 1944.

Colm, Gerhard, "Fiscal Policy," *The New Economics*, edited by S. E. Harris. Chapter XXXIV, pages 450-467. New York: Alfred A. Knopf, 1947.

Fine, S. M., *Public Spending and Postwar Economic Policy*. New York: Columbia Univ. Press, 1944.

Hagen, E. E., "The Problem of Timing Fiscal Policy," *The American Economic Review, Papers and Proceedings*, May, 1948, Vol. XXXVIII, pages 417-429.

Hansen, A. H., *Fiscal Policy and Business Cycles*, especially Chapters I, IV, VI, IX, XI, XII, XIII, XVII, and XX. New York: W. W. Norton and Co., 1941.

Harris, S. E., *The National Debt and the New Economics*. New York: McGraw-Hill Book Company, Inc., 1947.

Higgins, Benjamin, *Public Investment and Full Employment*. Montreal: International Labour Office, 1946.

——, "Keynesian Economics and Public Investment Policy," *The New Economics*, edited by S. E. Harris, Chapter XXXV, pages 468-481. New York: Alfred A. Knopf, 1947.

Machlup, Fritz, *International Trade and the National Income Multiplier*. Philadelphia: The Blakiston Company, 1943.

Samuelson, Paul A., "The Theory of Pump-Priming Reëxamined," *The American Economic Review*, September, 1940, Vol. XXX, pages 492-506.

——, "Fiscal Policy and Income Determination," *The Quarterly Journal of Economics*, August, 1942, Vol. LVI, pages 575-605.

Smithies, Arthur, "The Multiplier," *The American Economic Review, Papers and Proceedings*, May, 1948, Vol. XXXVIII, pages 299-305.

Somers, H. M., "The Impact of Fiscal Policy on National Income," *The Canadian Journal of Economics and Political Science*, August, 1942, Vol. VIII, pages 364-385.

Stone, R. and Stone, W. M., "The Marginal Propensity to Consume and the Multiplier, A Statistical Investigation," *The Review of Economic Studies*, October, 1938, Vol. VI, pages 1-21.

Villard, H. H., *Deficit Spending and the National Income*. New York: Farrar and Rinehart, 1941.

Wallich, H. C., "Income-Generating Effects of a Balanced Budget," *The Quarterly Journal of Economics*, November, 1944, Vol. LIX, pages 78-91.

CHAPTER 7

The Marginal Efficiency of Capital

> Speculators may do no harm as bubbles on a steady
> stream of enterprise. But the position is serious when
> enterprise becomes the bubble on a whirlpool of specula-
> tion. When the capital development of a country becomes
> a by-product of the activities of a casino, the job is likely
> to be ill-done.
>
> J. M. Keynes, *The General Theory of Employment, Interest
> and Money.**

THE MARGINAL efficiency of capital in conjunction with the
rate of interest determines the amount of new investment,
which in turn determines the volume of employment, given
the propensity to consume. In this chapter the marginal efficiency of capital is discussed, with special attention to the
prospective yields of capital assets, and in the next chapter
the rate of interest is considered.

As indicated in Chapter 3, the marginal efficiency of capital
is equivalent to what is ordinarily called the rate of profit, or
better, the *expected* rate of profit. The word "efficiency" as
used in the term "marginal efficiency of capital" refers to
the effectiveness, or rate of return over cost, or profitability,
of a capital asset. The efficiency or earning power of any capital asset is its rate of return over cost. The *marginal* effi-

---

* Harcourt, Brace and Co., Inc., 1936, page 159.

ciency of a particular type of capital asset is the highest rate of return over cost expected from an additional, or marginal, unit of that type of asset. The marginal efficiency of capital *in general* is the highest rate of return over cost expected from producing an additional, or marginal, unit of the most profitable of *all* types of capital assets.[1]

Any investment opportunity which is as yet unutilized will be carried out as long as the expected rate of return over cost exceeds the rate of interest. This fundamental principle that new investment will be carried to the point at which the marginal efficiency of capital is equal to the rate of interest (on money) rests on the assumption that business men and other wealth-holders will attempt to maximize the returns from their investments. People with money in excess of that which is used for current consumption, will invest it, lend it, or hoard it, according to the relative advantages offered by these various alternatives. The advantages of storing wealth in the form of money, that is, of hoarding, are discussed in the following chapter. Here we may approach the concept of the marginal efficiency of capital in terms of the advantages of constructing a new capital asset rather than buying an old one or of lending money at interest.

The Concept

The marginal efficiency of capital is a rate or ratio of two elements, (1) the expected yields or returns from an income-yielding asset, and (2) the supply price or replacement cost of the asset which is the source of the prospective yields. Prospective yield is what a business firm expects to obtain from selling the output of its capital assets. These yields take the form of a flow of money income over a period of time. For example, when a factory is built and equipped, the investor

---

1. Keynes says that the concept "marginal efficiency of capital" was first introduced into economic theory by Irving Fisher under the name of "rate of return over cost" in his *Theory of Interest* (1930). See *The Lessons of Monetary Experience—Essays in Honor of Irving Fisher*, edited by A. D. Gayer, page 145. New York: Farrar and Rinehart, Inc., 1937. See also *General Theory*, pages 140, 141.

expects to get back his original investment plus a surplus in the form of a continuing series of receipts from sales of the output of the factory. If we divide the total expected life of the factory into a series of periods, say years, we may refer to the annual returns as a series of annuities represented by $Q_1, Q_2, Q_3, \ldots Q_n$, the subscripts referring to the years of the respective annuities. If we estimate the values of the Q's and if we know what it will cost to produce the necessary capital assets which will be the source of these yields, then a comparison of the expected returns with the cost gives the rate or ratio known as the marginal efficiency of capital. Keynes defines the marginal efficiency of capital in this manner: "More precisely, I define the marginal efficiency of capital as being equal to that rate of discount which would make the present value of the series of annuities given by the returns expected from the capital-asset during its life just equal to its supply price." (p. 135)[2] This definition may be expressed in the following terms:

$$\text{Supply Price} = \text{Discounted Prospective Yields}$$

$$\text{or, Supply Price} = \frac{Q_1}{(1+r_m)} + \frac{Q_2}{(1+r_m)^2} + \frac{Q_3}{(1+r_m)^3} + \cdots \frac{Q_n}{(1+r_m)^n}$$

The Q's are the prospective yields in the various years 1, 2, 3, and n; and r_m is the marginal efficiency of capital, or the rate of discount. The values of the Q's are not necessarily the same for each year, and the presumption in a dynamic world is that only by the rarest accident would any of them turn out to be identical. There will be some unique value of the marginal efficiency of this particular investment which will bring the two sides of the equation into equality. The term $\frac{Q_1}{(1+r_m)}$ represents the present value of the yield or annuity to be received at the end of the first year discounted at the rate r_m. If the rate of discount is 10 per cent, each dollar due or expected one year hence is worth 90.91 cents ($1.00 divided by

---

2. *The General Theory of Employment, Interest and Money.* New York: Harcourt, Brace and Co., Inc., 1936.

1.10). This means each 90.91 cents invested at 10 per cent will grow to $1.00 in one year. The term $\dfrac{Q_2}{(1+r_m)^2}$ represents the present value of the expected yield at the end of the second year discounted also at the rate r_m. At 10 per cent, each dollar due or expected two years hence is worth 82.65 cents ($1.00 divided by $(1.10)^2$, or $1.00 divided by 1.21), which means that 82.65 cents invested now at 10 per cent will grow to $1.00 in two years. Regardless of the number of annuities, the present value of each would be discounted in the same way to bring the aggregate of all the annuities into equality with the current supply price or replacement cost of their source.

A simple arithmetical example will illustrate the meaning of the efficiency of capital as a rate of discount. Suppose we are contemplating the construction of an asset which is expected to yield $1100 at the end of one year and $2420 at the end of two years, after which time it will cease to have any economic value. If the supply price, or cost of constructing this capital asset is $3000, its efficiency is 10 per cent, because this is the rate of discount which will equate the value of the future yields to the current supply price. At 10 per cent, the present value of $1100 discounted for one year plus $2420 discounted for two years gives a total sum of $3000, the current supply price.

$$\text{Supply Price} = \text{Discounted Prospective Yields}$$

$$\$3000 = \frac{\$1100}{1.10} + \frac{\$2420}{(1.10)^2}$$

$$\$3000 = \$1000 + \$2000$$

If the yields were less than those used in the above calculation, the rate of discount which would equate the two sides of the equation would be lower than 10 per cent. Naturally, a fall in the amount of expected yield will lower the rate of expected yield. Likewise, if the supply price were more than $3000, the rate of discount would be lower. The more costly the construction of a capital asset, the lower will be its rate of return if the amounts of the yields remain the same. The rate of return over cost may change either because the cost changes or because the amount of return changes.

If 10 per cent is the highest rate of return that can be secured from any capital asset newly produced, it is the *marginal* efficiency of capital in general. Since the marginal efficiency is expressed as a per cent per year, it can be compared directly with the rate of interest. In the above example, if the rate of interest on money is less than 10 per cent, the construction of a new capital asset of the type in question would be worthwhile. People with money to invest can get more by building the new capital asset than by lending their money at interest, or by buying an old capital asset of the type in question. People who have access to money at less than 10 per cent will profit by borrowing in order to build this capital asset. The market value of an asset which promises to yield $1100 at the end of one year and $2420 at the end of two years will be greater than $3000 when the interest rate is less than 10 per cent. For example, if the market rate of interest is 5 per cent, the capital asset will have a present value of:

$$\frac{\$1100}{1.05} + \frac{\$2420}{(1.05)^2} = \$1047.62 + \$2195.01 = \$3242.63$$

This is what Keynes calls the demand price, in contrast with the supply price, of a capital asset. **The demand price of any asset is defined as the sum of the expected** future yields discounted at the *current rate of interest*. Thus defined, the demand price of an asset is its true present value, what it is worth in the market. The demand price and the supply price are determined respectively:

Demand Price = Sum of prospective yields discounted at the *rate of interest*.

Supply Price = Sum of prospective yields discounted by the *marginal efficiency of capital*.

The demand price is greater the lower the rate of interest at which it is discounted. Hence, the lower the rate of interest, the greater will be the number of capital assets for which the demand price will exceed the supply price, and the greater the pace of investment in new capital assets. The marginal efficiency of capital will exceed the rate of interest, and therefore new investment in capital assets will prove profitable as long as the supply price or cost of production remains less than the demand price.

Since investors in income-yielding wealth desire to maximize their prospective yields, they will naturally buy the source of these prospective yields as cheaply as possible. When it is cheaper to create a new source of prospective yields than to buy an already existing source, the former course of action will be followed. If, and only if, these conditions prevail, will new capital assets be produced by private investors. The existence of such circumstances is the essential condition for the successful functioning of an economic system in which private profit is the stimulus to enterprise.

It is to be noted that the market value of an asset, whether it be a capital asset or a claim upon capital assets in the form of marketable securities, cannot be determined from a knowledge of the marginal efficiency of capital. Nor can the rate of interest be deduced from the prospective yields or the marginal efficiency of capital. Before the present market value of an asset can be ascertained, the rate of interest must be determined independently from a knowledge of the quantity of money and the state of liquidity preference. The rate of interest as well as the marginal efficiency of capital must be known before the volume of investment is determined. These two rates are determined independently of one another, the marginal efficiency being the resultant of the supply price and the prospective yields of assets, and the rate of interest the resultant of the schedule of liquidity preference and the quantity of money. The fact that investment will be carried to the point at which the marginal efficiency of capital is reduced to equality with the rate of interest does not mean that these two rates depend upon the same things or that they depend upon each other. They are independent variables, and investment is dependent upon them. There is a sense, however, in which the marginal efficiency adjusts to the rate of interest rather than the other way around. For changes in the volume of investment directly influence the marginal efficiency of capital but not the rate of interest, and it is changes in the volume of investment which bring the two rates to equality. As long as the marginal efficiency of capital exceeds the rate of interest, investment will continue, and when there are no more investments for which the marginal efficiency exceeds the rate of interest, investment will come to a halt. When it is recalled that employment cannot increase without an increase in investment, the propensity to consume being unchanged, the importance of the relationship of the marginal efficiency to the rate of interest for the problem of employment will be appreciated as being of the most fundamental significance.

The marginal efficiencies of all types of capital assets which may be made during a given period of time represent the *schedule* of the marginal efficiency of capital, or the investment-demand schedule. A diagram representing the schedule of the marginal efficiency of capital of all types would take the general shape of an ordinary demand curve, slanting down toward the right as the quantity of investment for the period increases. It will show how much investment can be carried out in a given period of time at 10 per cent, at 8 per cent, at 7½, at 7, 6½, 6, 5½, 5 per cent, etc. The larger the amount of investment per unit of time, the lower the marginal efficiency of capital will fall.

The position and shape of this investment-demand schedule is of great significance in determining the volume of employment because it will indicate the extent to which the amount of investment will change in response to changes in the rate of interest. The more elastic the schedule of the marginal efficiency of capital, the greater will be the increase in investment in response to a given fall in the rate of interest. The more inelastic the schedule of the marginal efficiency of capital, the less will be the increase in investment in response to a given fall in the rate of interest. Figures 7a and 7b contrast a relatively elastic and a relatively inelastic schedule of the marginal efficiency of capital.

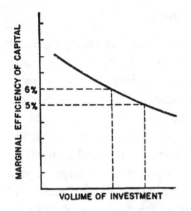

Figure 7a. A Relatively Elastic Schedule of the Marginal Efficiency of Capital, or Investment Demand Schedule.

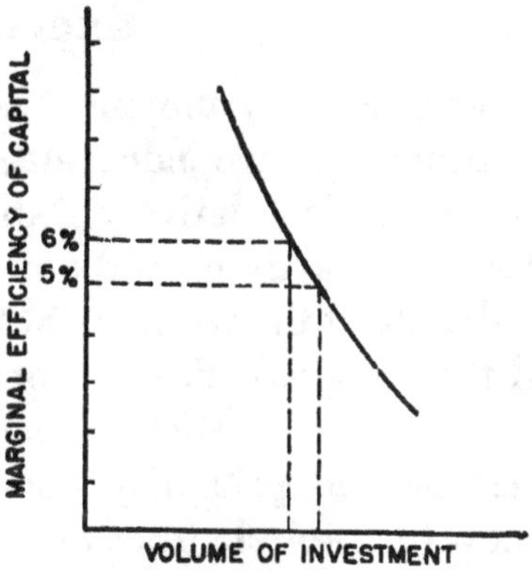

Figure 7b. A Relatively Inelastic Schedule of the Marginal Efficiency of Capital, or Investment Demand Schedule.

In 7a the schedule is relatively elastic so that a fall of one per cent in the rate of interest will result in a relatively large increase in the volume of investment, whereas in 7b a fall of one per cent in the rate of interest will result in a much smaller increase in the volume of investment. What the actual position and shape of this curve will be depends upon many complex factors which are subject to different estimation by each entrepreneur and to frequent revision, but it is not impossible to draw an approximate schedule of the marginal efficiency for particular industries and for the economy as a whole at any given time. Experience indicates that the schedule of the marginal efficiency of capital tends to be inelastic (7b) rather than elastic (7a). Therefore, changes in the rate of interest only slightly influence the flow of new investment. More important than decreases in the rate of interest are the dynamic forces of growth and technological progress which are constantly lifting the schedule of the marginal efficiency of capital. When these dynamic forces weaken, the rate of

investment per period of time decreases causing unemployment, and in the absence of such growth factors, opportunities
for profitable new investment would soon disappear altogether.

Expectations

The volume of employment is determined by the propensity
to consume and the inducement to invest. Since the propensity
to consume is relatively stable, fluctuations in employment
depend primarily upon the inducement to invest. The two determinants of the inducement to invest are the rate of interest
and the marginal efficiency of capital. Since the rate of interest is relatively "sticky," fluctuations in the inducement to
invest depend primarily upon changes in the marginal efficiency of capital. The two determinants of the marginal
efficiency of capital are the supply price or cost and the prospective yield or return. It is the prospective yield which gives
the marginal efficiency of capital its most important characteristic, its instability. Hence, a great part of the instability
of economic life under capitalism is attributable to the unstable character of prospective yields from capital assets.
Since it is important to account for instability of employment, and because of the role played by prospective yields
in this connection, it becomes important to explore the nature
of the forces which determine prospective yields.

These yields which figure so prominently in determining
the volume of employment are *prospective* yields because at
the time an investment is made they are nothing but expectations on the part of the investor. The expectations may never
be realized at all, and an entrepreneur does not really believe
that everything will turn out just as he predicts when the investment is made. In other words, the investor expects to be
"surprised," either favorably or unfavorably, because he
cannot honestly hope that events will actually unfold in exactly the way he foresees as most probable. Thus investment
decisions are governed by expectations of yield and not by
actual yields. Because of the nature of capital assets, espe-

cially those of a durable type, large immediate outlays are required before any actual returns can begin to flow back to the investor. Capital assets are a link between the present and the uncertain future.

A prospective yield is what an entrepreneur expects to obtain from selling the output of his capital assets. There are two types of expectations regarding the yields of assets: (1) short-term expectations and (2) long-term expectations. Short-term expectations concern the sales proceeds from the output of existing plant. Long-term expectations concern the sales proceeds which an entrepreneur can hope to earn with variations in the size of his plant or from the building of entirely new plant. In short-term expectations, the plant is assumed to be of a fixed size; only the output from that given sized plant is variable. In long-term expectations, the size of the plant as well as the amount of output from plant is variable.

Short-term Expectations: Short-term expectations are more stable than long-term expectations because the *realized* results of the recent past are a relatively safe guide to what will happen in the near future, whereas there exists no past experience which will serve as a comparably safe guide to what will happen in the distant future. Realized results of past activity are important only in so far as they influence current expectations about the future. It is always the current expectations concerning prospective future yields that are relevant to current investment and therefore to current employment. In the case of short-term expectations, most of the circumstances which influence current output remain substantially the same from day to day or from week to week or month to month. In economic life, as in other areas of experience, there is a high degree of continuity over short periods. In the absence of definite evidence for expecting a change, the most recent events may be expected to continue in the near future. By their very nature, short-term expectations are subject to frequent check in the light of realized results. Since realized results are a satisfactory guide to the near future, it is relatively safe to substitute these realized results for expectations relating to the near future. Short-term ex-expectations are relatively stable. Hence, it may be concluded that short-term expectations are less important than they would be if realized results of the recent past were not a relatively safe guide to what to expect in the near future. It is not necessary to try to predict the future when only short-term plans are in question. It is safe to rely upon past results.

Long-term Expectations: In contrast with short-term expectations, long-term expectations regarding the probable yields of new investments in durable plant and equipment are highly unstable and therefore more important in explaining the fluctuations in aggregate investment and aggregate employment in the economic system. While we may safely assume that economic activity next week will be approximately what it was during the past week, experience tells us that we cannot safely assume the next five years will be approximately like the past five years as concerns events which will determine the yields to be received from current investments. Realized results of past years are not a trustworthy guide to future years. It is not possible in the case of durable assets to check expectations against realized results at short intervals as can be done in the case of short-term expectations.

There are some considerations affecting long-term expectations which do not rest upon the shifting sands of a precarious future. Decisions to invest are partly based upon facts regarding the existing stock of capital assets. Especially relevant are the types of assets which will be available to compete with the projected new investment. For example, a decision to build a new steel plant depends partly upon the amount of existing steel capacity. Steel capacity is a fact that can be ascertained with more or less certainty. Likewise, the ability of the existing capacity to meet the existing demand at the prices being paid for current output are data of a more or less definite nature. But as we begin to look ahead, the horizon becomes more clouded. The probable life and maintenance of the plant the construction of which is being contemplated cannot be accurately predicted. Still less predictable are such considerations as possible changes in technology in the steel industry which would influence the rate of obsolescence of the projected plant. In the precarious zone are considerations of the general level of effective demand 10 or 20 years hence, the amount of new competition, the prices which can be realized from year to year, the prospect of war, the size of the export market, changes in tax burdens, conditions in the labor market including the level of wages and freedom from strikes, and finally, the political climate of future decades which will influence the extent of social control over industry. Concerning these latter events, there is no probability calculus upon which to base scientific judgments.

Our general ignorance of the future and the precariousness of the basis of what we think we do know about the future stand out above all other aspects of long-term expectations in an unplanned economy. The distant future is never clearly foreseen and this is especially true when entrepreneurial decisions are made by a large number of private entrepreneurs whose decisions are uncoordinated. Nevertheless, mere social survival, not to speak of economic progress, requires that decisions be made no matter how precarious the basis upon which they rest. The upshot of the extreme precariousness of the circumstances in which long-term expectations are formed is the great instability which characterizes these expectations and the consequent instability of economic life in general. Long-term expectations are subject to sudden revisions. Periods of feverish investment activity tend to be followed by periods of extreme pessimism and depression in which investment in durable capital assets falls to an extremely low level.

In making a most probable forecast as to what will happen to a long-term investment, not much weight is or can be attached to matters which are very uncertain. We cannot act in any positive fashion upon what we do not know. Hence, there is a tendency for long-term expectations to be influenced to a disproportionate degree by the ascertainable facts of the current situation and to assume that the existing summing up of the future is correct and that things will continue as they are in the absence of specific reasons for changing our expectations. Nevertheless, the things we do not know exert a powerful influence upon investment activity. For the degree of confidence with which most probable forecasts are made is affected by what we do not know. It is lack of confidence in the most probable forecasts which renders investment decisions so subject to sudden shifts. Furthermore, when there is great uncertainty about which of several alternative investment opportunities offers the highest return, there is a tendency to postpone a positive decision in the hope that the view of the future will become clearer at a later date. Thus, even when there is confidence that profitable investment opportunities do exist, the lack of confidence in ability to determine which is most profitable will tend to depress the marginal efficiency of capital and reduce the volume of investment and employment. Investors with limited resources cannot exploit all investment opportunities they believe will turn out to be profitable, and therefore they will try to make certain that their limited resources are placed where the returns are maximized. The belief that knowledge will improve is a cause of apathy in the investment market. If for some reason the vista seems to become clearer to a significant degree, apathy will give way to a wave of new investment. This bunching of positive decisions to invest following a period of apathy is one of the causes of fluctuations in employment.[3]

Influence of the Stock Market Upon Prospective Yields: The prevailing state of long-term expectations in modern capitalistic societies is reflected in the activities of the stock exchange. When prospective yields are viewed favorably, stock prices tend to be high; and when prospective yields are viewed unfavorably, stock prices tend to be depressed. A purchase of securities does not, of course, represent real invest-

3. G. L. S. Shackle, "Expectations and Employment," *The Economic Journal,* September, 1939, Vol. XLIX, No. 195, pages 442-452.

ment. It is purely a financial transaction involving the transfer of titles to existing wealth and does not involve the production of new wealth or of social income. Securities traded on the stock exchange are "old stocks" already outstanding in the hands of the public. When one party purchases such stocks, representing claims to existing capital assets, he increases his individual investment. But at the same time someone else disinvests to the same extent when he sells the securities. The sale is equal to the purchase and the disinvestment is equal to the investment. Aggregate social investment, as well as aggregate financial investment, remains unchanged as a result of stock exchange transactions. What matters for employment is the use of men and materials to build new factories and other forms of capital assets. When real investments of this type are made, new securities may be floated through investment banking channels and thereafter the securities may be traded on the stock exchange.

How then does stock market activity affect real investment and employment? The prices of "old" securities traded on the stock exchange influence the prices at which "new" securities can be floated in the new investment market. When the price of old securities is high, the price of new securities will tend to be high also. Ability to float new securities at high prices will encourage investment in new projects on a scale which might seem extravagant in other circumstances. High quotations for existing stocks mean that the marginal efficiency of capital for this type of enterprise is high in relation to the rate of interest and consequently the inducement to invest is strong. It is cheaper to build new capital assets of a given variety than to buy the claims to existing capital assets of the same variety. On the other hand, when the prices of securities on the stock exchange are low, it will be cheaper to buy claims to existing enterprises than to build new capital assets; the supply price (cost of building new capital assets) exceeds the demand price (present value of existing capital assets discounted at the current rate of interest); or, to express the same idea in still another way, the marginal efficiency of capital is below the rate of interest. This condition is unfavorable to the inducement to invest. In general, new investment in many types of capital assets is governed by quotations in the stock market.

In highly organized markets like the stock exchange, existing investments are revalued daily, even hourly. The chief basis for changes in valuations are changes in current expectations concerning future events which will influence future yields. Such markets are links between the present and the future. Any event that is expected to happen in the future is taken into account ("discounted") in the present prices of securities. When an event actually occurs, it will influence the prices of securities only in so far as it is "unexpected" in the sense that it has not been foreseen, or has been "uncertain" in the sense that the event confirms views previously held with less than complete confidence. For example, several commercial airplane crashes occurring over a week-end are likely to depress the prices of commercial airline stocks when the exchange opens on Monday morning because these crashes will not have been foreseen. Presidential veto of a bill to reduce business taxes, which veto has been generally expected but concerning which there has been some doubt, may tend to depress the prices of securities because what was previously uncertain becomes certain. However, in the latter case the effect will probably not be great since the veto will have been largely discounted in advance.

Speculative activity in the stock exchange contributes to the instability of the marginal efficiency of capital. If "speculation" is defined as the attempt to forecast the psychology of the market, and "enterprise" as the attempt to forecast the yield of assets over their entire life, Keynes concludes that the state of long-term expectations which governs the quotations of securities in the stock exchange is more the result of speculation than of enterprise. The tendency for speculation to outrun enterprise arises from various psychological and institutional factors connected with the precarious basis of knowledge regarding the future. Investors are aware that their individual judgments about the long-term future are practically worthless and they tend to rely upon the judgment of others who may be better informed. This is especially true of the mass of amateur investors who do not possess even the technical and business knowledge which is utilized by professionals. The main concern is what other people think. It is assumed that existing quotations accurately reflect the future, so that in the absence of specific reasons for expecting a change it is further assumed that there will be no major shifts in the market in the near future. Therefore, the only major risk lies in a change of news and views in the near future. Even the amateur may feel capable of judging the significance of new knowledge in relation to changes in stock prices. Since the market is "liquid," i.e., since anyone can sell out on a moment's notice if something drastic should happen, the investor need not worry about the long-term prospects of the enterprise in which he invests because there is no need to continue to hold these securities for a long time. Thus, in practice, long-term expectations rest upon the acceptance of a conventional judgment, i.e., the acceptance of the unique correctness of the existing estimate of the future and the assumption that only genuine new knowledge will cause a significant change. The widespread acceptance of this convention gives a certain stability to the market *so long as the convention is maintained.*

The separation of ownership from management in modern corporate business enterprise has fostered reliance upon conventional judgments. The ignorance of most shareholders in regard to the organization and functioning of the business enterprise of which they are part owners diminishes the profitability of professional attempts to judge long-term prospective yields. Instead of trying to estimate the probable yields of capital assets over their entire life, investors are guided under modern institutional arrangements by forecasts of the psychology of the market over the relatively short run. The quotations which will exist at any time reflect the dominant opinion of the mass of participants. If the dominant opinion three months hence is optimistic, the market will be good; and if dominant opinion three months hence is pessimistic, the market will be bad. One who wishes to make money in the stock market should then try to forecast what the predominant opinion will be three months hence. Since the dominant opinion is largely a conventional matter, those who make the most money in the stock market will be those who are most successful in forecasting what average opinion thinks average opinion will be three months from now. Investment becomes a psychological game which can be played by amateur and professional alike.

The investor who wishes to base his behavior upon more genuine and scientific forecasts of long-term yields is confronted with at least two major obstacles. First, the intrinsic difficulty of accurately judging the long-term future makes all such forecasts extremely precarious. There exists hardly any basis for being "scientific" in judging the prospects of a transoceanic steamship line 20 years hence. Think of the great French liner, *Normandie*, in the year 1935. Within less than ten years she had been the victim of war, fire, and scrapping. Second, the long-term yield is largely irrelevant in relation to what the price of an asset will be next week or next month. If a security now selling at 100 is expected to be down to 50 ten years hence but up to 120 next month, it is more profitable to buy the security now and sell it next month than to sell now merely because the long-term future is gloomy. The most profitable occupation for even the skilled forecaster is to anticipate market psychology, to rationalize the irrational activities of the mob of less skilled participants in the market. Hence "speculation" tends to dominate "enterprise" in the stock market.

A conventional judgment which rests on the mass psychology of a group of investors who are without knowledge or conviction about real market forces affecting long-term yields is a highly unstable basis upon which to build the capital development of a country. Resting as it does upon the assumption that things will continue as they now are unless there is reason to expect a change, the conventional judgment is stable only as long as the convention holds, i.e., as long as there is no reason to expect things to change. Ignorant investors are in no position to judge what kind of factors will make a real difference and so they may be provoked into a chain reaction of pessimism or optimism by superficial events which bear no relation to the actual long-term yield of an enterprise. Doubt as to the significance of some new event may lead to further doubt as to whether the present state of the market does sum up accurately the future. In the event of a con-sensus that present security prices do not accurately reflect the future, stability, based on a convention that no longer holds, gives way to erratic fluctuations. Like all speculation based on ignorance, the market is subject to unreasonable spurts and irrational collapses. "Speculators may do no harm as bubbles on a steady stream of enterprise. But the position is serious when enterprise becomes the bubble on a whirlpool of speculation. When the capital development of a country becomes a by-product of the activities of a casino, the job is likely to be ill-done."[4]

New investment is facilitated on the one hand and impeded on the other by markets organized with a view to individual liquidity. In highly organized markets like the stock ex-change, the individual wealth-owner holds his assets in a form which can readily be converted into cash. Investment is facilitated because the stock exchange enables the investor, as an individual, to liquidate his holdings at any time. This encourages individual investors to contribute to the risk-taking involved in new enterprises. On the other hand, the separation of ownership from control, the general ignorance of the majority of investors, the mass psychology which dominates the market, and the undue weight given to super-ficial occurrences, render the market supersensitive to slight disturbances and make the individual prone to convert his holdings into money upon relatively slight provocation, lead-

---

4. Keynes, *The General Theory of Employment, Interest and Money.* New York: Harcourt, Brace and Co., Inc., 1936, page 159.

ing to easy breakdown and to a dampening of prospective yields which weaken the inducement to invest. Liquidity exists for the individual investor but not for the community as a whole. Individuals may dispose of their holdings in enterprises with specialized plant and equipment, but there is no way by which the community as a whole can liquidate these fixed assets. But in their desire to liquidate, individuals who make up the community depress the marginal efficiency of capital, weakening the inducement to invest and increasing unemployment for the community as a whole. Prior to the separation of ownership from management and the emergence of organized stock exchanges, decisions to invest in enterprise were irrevocable for the individual as well as for the community as a whole. A major contribution of the stock market is the ease with which capital can be mobilized for the development of new productive wealth, but a great disadvantage is the associated instability arising from a speculative liquidity which can lead to a paralyzing collapse of the existing productive capacity of society.

It would be misleading to suppose that instability of investment decisions is entirely the outcome of rational calculations and speculative conventions within the framework of an irrational institutional setting. The non-rational aspect of human behavior finds an outlet in the investment market. In fact, much long-term investment would never occur if investors depended upon mathematical calculation or even psychological convention. In a practical sense, the basis for scientific calculation often does not exist. The propensity of human nature toward spontaneous optimism, the human urge to action rather than inaction, the tendency for positive activity to depend upon a sort of animal spirit or *élan vital*—all these are nurtured by and at the same time contribute to the extreme uncertainty of long-term expectations. Even in the market place, human behavior is not always guided by an "irrational passion for dispassionate rationality." Even in the money market, "the heart knows reasons that reason cannot know."

The foregoing discussion indicates clearly that instability is the outstanding short-run characteristic of the marginal efficiency of capital. Over historical time, there are upward and downward movements in the expected rates of return from new investment. Since the rate of interest does not fluctuate in a comparable manner, the rate of investment, which is determined by these two forces, must also fluctuate and in turn cause the total volume of employment and output to fluctuate. These variations in over-all economic activity follow a cyclical pattern familiarly known as the business cycle. In a later discussion we shall see that the essence of the business cycle is to be found in the more or less rhythmic fluctuations in the marginal efficiency of capital.

Secular Decline in the Marginal Efficiency of Capital

In the secular long run, the significant characteristic of the marginal efficiency of capital is its tendency to fall. The diminishing marginal efficiency of capital is a new name for the old idea of the falling rate of profit. Many of the great economists, including Adam Smith, David Ricardo, Karl Marx, and John Stuart Mill, accepted the tendency for the rate of profit to fall as one of the basic phenomena of long-term development of the capitalistic economy. Despite wide acceptance of the tendency of the rate of profit to fall, there has been scant agreement as to why it falls. Adam Smith attributed the falling rate of profit to the mere fact that capital becomes more abundant in a progressive society. Ricardo and Mill saw the basic cause for falling profits in the niggardliness of nature in the sense that the food supply for an increasing population had to be grown from land of ever-diminishing productivity. Marx's theory of the falling tendency of the rate of profit is associated with the nature of capital itself rather than with the niggardliness of nature. Keynes' theory of the declining marginal efficiency of capital differs from all of these others but has most in common with Smith's explanation. Keynes' theory has something in common with that of Marx and is most unlike that of Ricardo and Mill.

Keynes' explanation of the decline of the marginal efficiency of capital, like other secular aspects of his theory, is not fully developed. The general idea is that diminution results in the long run from decreased prospective yields associated with a growing stock of capital assets. The marginal efficiency of capital is determined by the supply price or cost of production and the prospective yields. It may fall either from a rise in the supply price or from a decrease in prospective yields. In the short run, the more important factor is the increase in supply price. The longer the period becomes, the less important is the increase in supply price and the more important the diminution in prospective yields. Thus the secular decline in the marginal efficiency of capital is almost entirely the result of a fall in prospective yields.

Prospective yields fall because capital assets become more abundant. The returns from capital assets over their life exceed their cost only because they are scarce. Every increase in investment brings an increase in output which competes with the output of existing capital. The greater abundance of output tends to lower prices and hence to lower also the expected yields from further plant capacity. The process of creating more capital assets to compete with existing capital assets continues as long as the marginal efficiency exceeds the rate of interest. If the rate of interest were permitted to fall to zero, the unimpeded accumulation of real capital would lower the prospective yields to the point where there would be no return in excess of cost. Capital assets would cease to be scarce; they would yield a return just equal to their cost of production; the marginal efficiency of capital would be zero. With uninterrupted production, Keynes suggests that capital assets might cease to be scarce within one or two generations.

The decline in the marginal efficiency of capital arising from the fall in prospective yields is a tendency which may be offset by dynamic growth factors such as increase of population, territorial expansion, and certain types of technological change. During the nineteenth century, these growth factors and the frequency of war were sufficient to forestall the *tendency* from becoming an actuality. Even though the rate of interest did not decline, the marginal efficiency of capital was maintained at a level sufficiently high to prevent chronic unemployment of an amount so intolerable as to provoke revolutionary changes in the economic system. Unemployment in the nineteenth century manifested itself primarily in the form of periodic depressions sandwiched between spurts of feverish investment activity. In the twentieth century, the rate of growth of population has slowed down and territorial expansion has virtually ceased. Changes in technology have been increasingly of the capital-saving type, which means there has been no marked rise in the ratio of capital assets to output. Under these circumstances, brief periods of capital accumulation like that between 1922 and 1929 in the United States are sufficient to lower the marginal efficiency of capital to equality with the rate of interest. Hence, the inducement to invest is weakened, and with capital accumulation at a virtual standstill, chronic mass unemployment like that of the 1930's results. Secular stagnation is the end result of the slowing down in the dynamic growth factors. Although Keynes makes no dogmatic assertions concerning the inevitability of secular stagnation, his hypothesis that wealthy capitalist economies cannot hope to maintain full employment without social control of investment rests on the view that investment opportunities in the present stage of capitalist development are less than they were in the earlier centuries of capitalism. The concept of secular stagnation, which pervades Keynes' *General Theory*, has been more fully developed by Professor Alvin Hansen.[5]

---

5. See especially Alvin H. Hansen, *Full Recovery or Stagnation?* New York: W. W. Norton and Company, Inc., 1938, and *Fiscal Policy and Business Cycles,* New York: W. W. Norton and Company, Inc., 1941.

Some Practical Conclusions

Keynes' analysis of the characteristics of the marginal efficiency of capital leads him to the practical conclusion that the control of investment in capital assets cannot safely be left in private hands (p. 164). The precarious nature of long-term expectations which finds its objectification in the violent fluctuations of the stock market leads to an instability in the marginal efficiency of capital so great that it cannot be offset by any practicable changes in the rate of interest. The secular decline caused by uninterrupted production of new capital assets would soon (within one or two decades) push the rate of return down so low that a securities market organized according to the principles of private profit could not provide adequately for the development of society's future productive power. The state, which is in a better position than private enterprise to calculate long-run needs in terms of general social advantage, should assume greater responsibility for directly organizing investment. The practical counterpart, or the operational meaning, of the theoretical concept of the marginal efficiency of capital is referred to by Keynes as the "socialisation of investment."

Although the *General Theory* contains numerous references to the socialization of investment, it is nowhere elaborated. In the broadest sense, it may be taken to include a policy of investment control to offset cyclical fluctuations in private investment, and to overcome the obstacles in the way of, and the difficulties arising in connection with, the secular decline in the marginal efficiency of capital. In regard to cyclical control, Keynes' ideas about public works and other forms of public investment have been referred to in connection with the multiplier. Keynes first advocated public investment as a recovery measure in the British election campaign of 1929, and he became during the 'thirties the leading scientific authority for this type of "spending" policy. When little came of public works in Great Britain, Keynes turned his attention to the New Deal in the United States, where he praised the principle of the public-works program of President Roosevelt. However, he was critical of the lack of planning in American public works, and used the shortcomings of the New Deal policy to reinforce his demands for a well-ordered public-expenditures program. In 1938 Keynes recommended that the British government set up a Board of Public Investment, whose function would be to make plans for increases in public investment to supplement private investment whenever an economic recession threatened. To critics of this plan, Keynes replied that such a program had never been given a fair trial. President Roosevelt's program, although useful in saving the United States from a more complete economic collapse, was largely improvised as a system of work relief. Plans for increased public investment on housing, public utilities, and railroads, to mention a few of the potential outlets, were still in a stage of preparation when the 1937 recession wiped out most of the recovery gains made in the United States up to that time. Keynes saw in this lack of preparedness for public investment the main cause of the recession of 1937 and 1938.[6] The Board of Public Investment was to be organized as a permanent agency of the government, although Keynes did not believe it necessary to carry out new projects continuously at that juncture of his country's economic development. The Board should, however, stand in readiness with plans to be executed at the first sign of a slump.

Keynes' suggestions for implementing the long-term secular aspects of the socialization of investment are less satisfactorily discussed by him than the short-term, public works phase. The secular policy involves government control over the entire investment process, private as well as public. Keynes held some such idea for state control over aggregate investment and saving at least as early as 1926, when he questioned the desirability of leaving to private judgment and private profit the allocation of resources going into investment.[7] This idea becomes more prominent in the *General*

6. *The Times*, London, January 3, 1938, page 13.
7. *Laissez-faire and Communism*, page 69. New York: New Republic, 1926.

Theory, but even here it is left undeveloped. Presumably this long-range control over investment would be placed in the hands of a governmental agency resembling the Board of Public Investment suggested for Great Britain in 1937. Through the appropriate agency, the government would determine the total volume of resources to be allocated to investment. The basis for deciding what proportion this should be would, of course, have to be related to total consumption as determined by the propensity to consume at full employment. State authority would also determine the basic rate of return to the owners of the instruments of production, as long as such rewards were paid. Even after the average rate of return on capital assets has fallen to zero, and mere ownership ceases to be a basis for income, there will remain functional capitalists who can make income from superior skill in calculating risks on alternative forms of investment. Keynes apparently did not intend that state authority should control the allocation of resources among various forms of investment even though state authority did determine the total quantity of investment. He states explicitly that socialized investment does not mean that the instruments of production would be owned or operated by the government, although, of course, there would be some expansion of the amount of actual public investment as a result of an enlarged public-works program.

Beyond these few principles, Keynes does not set forth the principles and procedures for allocating investment funds. This failure may be attributed to the undeveloped nature of his secular analysis. Just how investment could be "socialized" while management and ownership remained in private hands requires explanation that Keynes fails to supply. The suggestion may be ventured, however, that if Keynes had followed out his secular analysis for the elimination of rewards for ownership in a private-property economy, his proposal for socializing investment might have led to the necessity for over-all economic planning, and this in turn to the fundamental question whether over-all planning is possible under private ownership of the means of production. Keynes advocated neither general planning nor the nationalization of industry.

Some further implications of Keynes' social philosophy will be considered in the concluding chapter. It should be clear from what has already been said that the fulfillment of his program, involving as it does the elimination of income from mere ownership of property, would constitute a minor revolution in the social structure of the traditional private-enterprise system. Yet this "euthanasia of the rentier," as Keynes calls it, would be achieved peacefully and gradually as a result of the accumulation of so much productive wealth that capital assets would cease to be scarce. Before the marginal efficiency of capital could fall so low, however, the rate of interest would have to be correspondingly reduced. Otherwise, wealth-holders would universally prefer to own "debts" or money rather than productive assets. Real investment occurs only as long as the marginal efficiency of capital exceeds the rate of interest. The nature of the problem of reducing the rate of interest in order to stimulate the inducement to invest requires further investigation of interest and money.

References for Further Reading

Keynes, J. M., *The General Theory of Employment, Interest and Money*, Chapters 11, 12, and 5. New York: Harcourt, Brace and Co., 1936.

———, "Some Consequences of a Declining Population," *Eugenics Review*, April, 1937, Vol. XXIX, pages 13-17.

Fisher, Irving, *The Theory of Interest*, Chapter VII, pages 150-177. New York: The Macmillan Company, 1930. (Fisher discusses the "rate of return over cost" and the "marginal rate of return over cost.")

Hansen, A. H., "Economic Progress and Declining Population Growth," *The American Economic Review*, March, 1939, Vol. XXIX, pages 1-15. Reprinted in *Readings in Business Cycle Theory*, selected by a Committee of the American Economic Association. Philadelphia: The Blakiston Company, 1944.

———, *Full Recovery or Stagnation?* especially Chapter XIX,

"Investment Outlets and Secular Stagnation." New York: W. W. Norton and Co., 1938.

Hart, A. G., "Keynes' Analysis of Expectations and Uncertainty," in *The New Economics*, edited by S. E. Harris, Chapter XXXI, pages 415-424. New York: Alfred A. Knopf, 1947.

———, *Anticipations, Uncertainty and Dynamic Planning*. Chicago: University of Chicago Press, 1940.

———, "Uncertainty and Inducements to Invest," *The Review of Economic Studies*, October, 1940, Vol. VIII, pages 49-53.

Kaldor, Nicholas, "Speculation and Economic Stability," *The Review of Economic Studies*, October, 1939, Vol. VII, pages 1-27.

Shackle, G. L. S., *Expectations, Investment, and Income*. London: Oxford, 1938.

———, "Expectations and Employment," *The Economic Journal*, September, 1939, Vol. XLIX, pages 442-452.

———, "The Nature of the Inducement to Invest," *The Review of Economic Studies*, October, 1940, Vol. VIII, pages 44-48, 54-57.

Strachey, John, "Mr. J. M. Keynes and the Falling Rate of Profit," *The Modern Quarterly*, October, 1938, Vol. I, pages 337-347. (A Marxist interpretation of Keynes' declining marginal efficiency of capital)

Swanson, E. W., and Schmidt, E. P., *Economic Stagnation or Progress*. New York: The McGraw-Hill Book Company, 1946. (Severely critical of the "Keynes-Hansen School")

Sweezy, A. R., "Population Growth and Investment Opportunities," *The Quarterly Journal of Economics*, November, 1940, Vol. LV, pages 64-79.

———, "Secular Stagnation?" in *Postwar Economic Problems*, edited by S. E. Harris, Chapter IV, pages 67-82. New York: McGraw-Hill Book Company, Inc., 1943.

———, "Declining Investment Opportunity," *The New Economics*, edited by S. E. Harris, Chapter XXXII, pages 425-435. New York: Alfred A. Knopf, 1947.

Terborgh, George W., *The Bogy of Economic Maturity*. Chicago, Illinois: Machinery and Allied Products Institute, 1945. (Severely critical of Keynes and Hansen)

CHAPTER 8

Interest and Money

For the importance of money essentially flows from its being a link between the present and the future.

J. M. Keynes, *The General Theory of Employment, Interest and Money*, page 293.*

The possession of actual money lulls our disquietude; and the premium which we require to make us part with money is the measure of the degree of our disquietude.

J. M. Keynes, *The Quarterly Journal of Economics*, February, 1937, page 216.

INTEREST is a payment for the use of money. Since this is just what the arithmetic books say it is, it would be unnecessary to make much of the point if traditional economic theory had not viewed interest as something quite different, as a payment for "waiting," for "saving," for "abstinence," or for "time preference."

The difference between the traditional theory of interest and Keynes' money theory of interest is a fundamental aspect of the difference between the economics of full employment and the economics of less than full employment. By the economics of full employment is meant an economic analysis which assumes that no resources are involuntarily unem-

---
* Harcourt, Brace and Co., Inc., 1936.

161

ployed so that an increase in the production of one thing necessarily involves the withdrawal of resources from some other employment. If investment is to be increased, for example, this can only be done if resources are withdrawn from employment in the consumers goods industries. If people can be induced to wait a while for some of their consumption, resources can be shifted out of consumers-goods production into investment-goods production to an extent corresponding to the reduction in spending for consumers goods. The inducement which is paid to get people to forego present consumption is interest, the payment for waiting. Within the framework of a system of theory built on the assumption of full employment, the notion of interest as a reward for waiting or abstinence is highly plausible. It is the premise that resources are typically fully employed that lacks plausibility in the contemporary world.

If unemployed resources are present on a large scale, there is no obvious necessity for paying people to abstain from consumption, i.e., to wait, in order that more resources may be devoted to the production of capital goods (investment). The obvious way to produce more capital goods is to put the idle resources to work and not to withdraw resources already employed from the production of consumers goods. Up to the point where full or approximately full employment is reached, it would be foolish to try to force or even to try to induce people to forego consuming in order to free resources so that more capital assets could be produced. In fact, a reduction in the demand for consumers goods is likely to lessen the incentive to produce capital goods if the reduction in consumer demand represents a permanent change of habit on the part of the consuming public. Something other than a theory of "waiting" or "time preference" is needed to explain why interest is paid.

Keynes' explanation is that interest is a purely monetary phenomenon, a payment for the use of money. This view of interest gives at the same time an explanation of the role of money in the economic system. The main tradition in economic theory since the time of eighteenth century mercantilism has banished money as a significant factor in the main body of principles of economics, but Keynes' monetary theory of interest reintegrates money into the theory of output and employment for the economy as a whole. While technical monetary theory falls into the background, the essential role of money is explained in relation to the theory of interest. The rate of interest is vital in relation to investment, and investment is the strategic determinant of the volume of employment since, according to the principle of effective demand, employment cannot increase unless there is an increase in investment. Thus monetary theory becomes an essential part of general economic theory through its relation to the theory of interest, and monetary policy becomes a vital part of general economic policy.

At every step in the following discussion of the theory of interest, it is helpful to bear in mind the close connection between Keynes' theory and the policy which he advocates. The theory of interest is at the same time part of the theory of money, and control of the rate of interest is to be attained through control of the supply of money. Control of the supply of money is one of the most effective and least objectionable methods of controlling output and employment. This is the operational meaning of Keynes' theory of interest and money referred to in Chapter 3. The agency of control of the money supply is the monetary authority, in particular the central banking system.

Banking policy in the past has all too frequently resulted in a shortage of money when more money was needed and an oversupply when less money was needed. The former contributes to unemployment and the latter to inflation. Since the long-term trend under private capitalism in its present stage of development is probably toward unemployment rather than inflation, Keynes gives special attention to the necessity of an "easy money" policy. He recognizes at the same time the dangers of inflation in war and postwar periods and has made outstanding proposals for coping with such situations. Keynes' theory of interest and money has its operational or practical meaning in the thesis that the banking system holds the key to the expansion of employment. With this in mind, the meaning and significance of interest rates will easily be understood. In a period of expanding output, a bank policy which does not permit a sufficient increase in the supply of money will cause a rise in the rate of interest and in this manner choke off the incipient expansion. An energetic policy by the monetary authority can do much to lower the long-term rate of interest to a level which will stimulate enough investment to fill the ever-threatening gap between income and consumption.

Statement of the Theory of Interest

The proposition that interest is a monetary phenomenon does not, of course, in itself constitute a theory of money or of interest. However, it does provide a point of departure for a theory of interest which differs fundamentally from the traditional view of interest as a reward for "waiting." Interest is a monetary phenomenon in the sense that the rate of interest is determined by the demand for and the supply of money. Money is demanded because it is the only perfectly liquid asset. People who need money for personal and business reasons and do not possess it are willing to pay a price for its use. Before a holder of money will surrender the advantages that attach to the ownership of the only perfectly liquid asset, he must be paid a reward. Interest is the reward paid for parting with liquidity, or in slightly different terms, the reward for not-hoarding. The rate at which interest will be paid depends on the strength of the preference for liquidity in relation to the total quantity of money available to satisfy the desire for liquidity. The stronger the liquidity preference, the higher is the rate of interest; and the greater the quantity of money, the lower is the rate of interest. A decrease in liquidity preference will tend to lower the rate of interest and a decrease in the quantity of money will tend to raise the rate of interest. The rate of interest, like any price in a free mar-

ket, is established at a level at which the demand will be
equilibrated with the supply available to meet the demand.
At any time, an increase in the desire of the public to hold
cash—that is, an increase in its liquidity preference—may be
met either by an increase in the price paid (interest) or by
an increase in the quantity available. Since money cannot
be produced by the public, the direct result of an increase in
its desire for money will not be to increase the quantity available but to increase the premium paid to those who give up
their cash holdings. An increase in the rate of interest means
a larger reward is paid for not-hoarding, and people who
otherwise would not be satisfied except to increase their cash
holdings will be satisfied as a result of the higher premium
they receive for not holding cash. If the rate of interest did
not rise when liquidity preference increased, the total amount
of cash the public would wish to hold at the existing rate of
interest would exceed the available supply. If the rate of
interest did not fall when liquidity preference decreased,
there would be a surplus of cash which no one would be willing to hold. Thus, if the rate of interest tends to be too high
or too low, an adjustment takes place whereby the demand is
equated to the available supply.

Since the quantity of money is the other factor which, along
with the state of liquidity preference, determines the rate of
interest, it is possible for the monetary authority to meet an
increase in the desire on the part of the public to hold money
with an actual increase in the supply of money. If people
want to hold more money, the monetary authority, and only
the monetary authority, can give them what they want. If
the quantity of money is increased in proportion to the increase in liquidity preference, the rate of interest will not rise
as it does when the quantity of money remains unchanged and
liquidity preference increases. Since the rate of interest is
one of the co-determinants of investment, and investment is the
main determinant of employment, the importance of monetary policy in determining the volume of employment is
easily seen.

The relationship between the rate of interest, the quantity of money, and liquidity preference may be represented by means of a diagram. In Figure 8, the quantity of money is shown along the horizontal axis and the rate of interest along the vertical axis. The liquidity-preference schedule will then appear as a smooth curve which decreases toward the right as the quantity of money increases. It is obvious from the

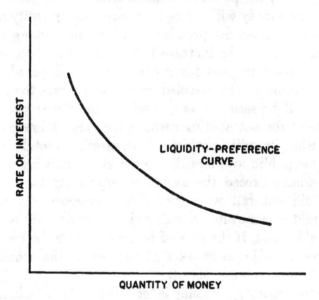

Figure 8. Liquidity-Preference Schedule.

diagram that larger quantities of money will be associated with lower rates of interest as long as the liquidity-preference schedule remains unchanged.

Interest appears in the market in the form of a reward paid to a wealth-holder who parts with control of money in exchange for a debt, e.g., for a bond or note or mortgage, for a stated period of time. The *rate* of reward per unit of time differs for debts of varying lengths. Thus there will be one rate of interest on call loans, another rate on three-day loans, and still other rates on six-month, one-year, five-year, ten-year and longer loans. While these rates differ in amount, they are all of the same specie. It is convenient in discussions of the theory of interest to speak of *the* rate of interest without reference to debts of any particular maturity. This simplification should not cover the fact that what really exists in the money market is a complex of rates of interest. Sometimes it is convenient to distinguish the short-term rate of interest paid on commercial bank loans from the long-term rate paid on bonds. In Keynes' general theory of employment, the important role played by real investment in durable capital assets makes the long-term rate of interest on loans used to finance such investments of prime significance. Fluctuations in the long-term rate of interest are reflected in changes in the price of bonds in the securities markets. As the price of bonds already outstanding in the market rises, the effective rate of interest falls; and as the price of bonds falls, the rate of interest rises. Thus, if a bond paying $50 per year sells at $1000 in the market, the prevailing rate of interest on that type of security is 5 per cent. If the price of the bond in the market rises above $1000, this means the effective rate of interest falls below 5 per cent because more than $1000 is now required to purchase an annual income of $50. Thus, references to changes in the rate of interest arising from changes in the state of liquidity preference or from changes in the supply of money may be visualized as taking the form of fluctuations in the price of bonds in the organized securities markets. A decrease in liquidity preference is reflected in an eagerness on the part of the public to purchase bonds at current prices, thus pushing up the prices of bonds and lowering the rate of interest. An increase in liquidity preference is reflected in an eagerness by the public to sell bonds in order to get cash. On a seller's market, the price of bonds falls and the rate of interest rises. The monetary authority may increase the supply of money and thus prevent the rise in the rate of interest by purchasing securities which the public wishes to sell at the current market price. When the monetary authority pays for its purchases with "new" money, it increases the supply of money and forestalls a rise in the rate of interest.

Liquidity Preference

The demand for money is a demand for liquidity. Liquidity may be analyzed in more detail by distinguishing three separate motives which lead to liquidity preference: (1) the transactions motive, (2) the precautionary motive, and (3) the speculative motive. Although interest is peculiarly related to the speculative motive, the other two motives cannot be ignored because money held for one purpose is a perfect substitute for money held for other purposes. A cash balance is, as a rule, held in a single pool the size of which is determined by a combination of the motives for liquidity preference. Part of the total may be held primarily for one purpose and secondarily for another purpose so that even the possessor does not have clearly in mind how much he holds for each separate motive (p. 195). In the total economy, an increase in the demand for money, e.g., for transactions, may be met by drawing upon the amount held for the speculative motive, in which case the rate of interest would tend to rise even though there were no change in the strength of the speculative motive and no change in the aggregate supply of money. Therefore, consideration is given to the transactions and the precautionary as well as to the speculative motive. But it is the last named which calls for the most attention in connection with the theory of interest.

Transactions motive

The quantity of money required to satisfy liquidity preference for the transactions motive is closely related to the volume of income and employment, that is, to the general level of business activity. As total output and employment rise and as prices and wages rise, the transactions demand for money also rises. A cash balance is required to bridge the interval between the receipt of income and its outlay for expenditures. The size of the cash balance will be related to the size of the income received and also to the frequency of income payment and the frequency of expenditure. If everyone received income in cash and simultaneously paid their expenses in cash, there would be little necessity for holding money balances for transactions purposes. There would be no interval to bridge. In the case of personal accounts, the cash balance actually held will be greater in proportion to the length of interval between paydays. A person who is paid monthly will have need for a larger average cash balance than an individual who is paid daily, assuming that there is some similarity in their expenditure habits. For example, a man who receives his entire income of $300 per month in a single payment and spends it in constant outlays of $10 per day will have a $300 balance the first day and a balance which decreases by $10 per day until at the end of the month he has a zero balance. The average cash balance for the month would be $150. But if this same individual were to be paid weekly, he would require an average balance of only $37.50, or one-half of his weekly $75 pay check.

Business firms, like individuals, find it necessary to hold bank balances to bridge the gap between outlays for expenses and the receipt of cash from sales of finished products. Again as with individuals, the size of the balance will vary directly with the length of the interval. The business motive for holding cash will rise as business activity increases. Payments from one entrepreneur to another will vary with the number of stages through which goods pass on their way to final completion, that is, with the degree of integration in the economy as a whole. Increasing integration will, other things being equal, diminish the demand for money. However, factors like the degree of business integration change relatively slowly, and, except for fluctuations in the level of business activity, there is no major factor causing changes in the demand for cash for transactions in the short run.

Precautionary motive

The second motive for liquidity preference—the precautionary motive—arises because individuals and business firms find it good practice to hold a reserve of cash in addition to what is needed for transactions. An individual who goes shopping will normally take more money than just the amount he thinks he will need for planned purchases. Plans may change, or opportunities may arise to make especially advantageous purchases if they are transacted on the spot without delay. In business the need for immediate cash may arise in order to meet contingent liabilities or unforeseen opportunities to make advantageous purchases. The quantity of money held to satisfy the precautionary motive will vary widely with individuals and businesses, according to their degree of financial conservatism, the nature of their enterprise, their access to the credit market, and the stage of development of organized markets for quick conversion of earning assets such as stocks and bonds into cash. Danger of being cut off from the credit market, say as a result of business losses, will be an especially important factor tending to increase the size of precautionary holdings by business firms. As long as individuals and businesses feel assured of ready access to extra cash by temporary borrowing, the precautionary motive to hold money will be relatively weak.

Although organized markets in which securities can be converted quickly and cheaply into cash tend to reduce the size of precautionary holdings, the possibility of forced liquidation under highly unfavorable conditions serves as a precautionary basis for preferring cash to securities. Precautionary balances may be held in savings deposits, where they will earn a low rate of return but where there is no danger, apart from failure of the bank, that the money value of the investment will depreciate. If, however, a notice of thirty days or so is required before funds may be withdrawn, the savings account lacks the advantage of perfect liquidity. Savings deposits are useful as a form of asset with a value fixed in terms of money which can be used to meet a subsequent liability fixed in terms of money. The cash reserves of a bank are themselves money held by the bank to protect itself against outstanding liabilities, the payment date of which cannot be predicted with certainty.

Speculative motive

Despite some important differences between the demand for money for transactions and that for precautionary motives, Keynes lumps these two together in discussing the relation of money to the rate of interest. While cash for transactions will be kept to a minimum, there is an obvious point where the convenience of holding cash to pay for regular expenditures will not be much affected by changes in the rate of interest. Likewise precautionary holdings, which depend mainly on the nature of the contingencies that are envisaged, are unlikely to be much affected by small changes in the rate of interest. Thus the significant type of liquidity preference in relation to the rate of interest is that arising from the so-called speculative motive, because speculative holdings are especially sensitive to changes in the rate of interest. If the total supply of money is designated by M, we may refer to that part of M held for transactions and precautionary motives as M_1, and to that part held for the speculative motive as M_2. Thus $M = M_1 + M_2$. The rate of interest is primarily determined by the propensity of the public to hold money for the speculative motive in relation to the quantity of money available for that purpose, i.e., M_2. The quantity of money which will be held to satisfy the speculative (M_2) is a function (L_2) of the rate of interest (r), or reward paid for giving up temporary control over money. A convenient shorthand expression for this relationship between money held for the speculative motive and the rate of interest is $M_2 = L_2(r)$. Since the amount of money held for the transactions and precautionary motive (M_1) depends primarily upon the general level of business activity, which may be measured by income (Y), the shorthand for this is $M_1 = L_1(Y)$. Then the equation $M = M_1 + M_2$ may be expressed, $M = L_1(Y) + L_2(r)$.

In connection with liquidity preference for the speculative motive (the desire for money as a store of wealth), the fundamental issues of modern monetary theory are raised. Why should anyone with a surplus of wealth choose to store it in the form of money and thus sacrifice the interest income which could be earned by exchanging money for a debt in the form of a bond or mortgage, et cetera? According to Keynes, the one essential condition in the absence of which liquidity preference for money as a store of value could not exist is the *uncertainty as to the future of the rate of interest*, by which is meant uncertainty as to the future of the complex of interest rates on debts of varying lengths which will prevail in the future. A wealth-holder who does not know on what terms he may be able to convert debts into money in the future has reason to believe that a postponed purchase may be preferable to a present purchase of a debt. For example, a man who contemplates paying $1000 for a bond yielding $30 per year when the rate of interest on this type of bond is 3 per cent will hesitate to do so if he thinks the rate of interest on this same type of security may later rise, say to 4 per cent. At 4 per cent it is necessary to invest only $750 to get a return of $30 per year. Therefore, the price of the security will fall to approximately $750, which will mean a virtual loss of $250, less whatever interest is received in the interval, to anyone who paid $1000 for such a bond.

At any moment of time, the *current* rates of interest on debts of different maturities are known with certainty because there are actual quotations in the market. The rates of interest that will prevail in the future are not known with certainty. The current rates of interest do, however, take into account estimates or guesses concerning what the future rates will be. Market quotations represent the predominant, but not the universal, opinion as to what the future rates of interest will be. An individual who thinks he knows better than the market, i.e., better than the predominant opinion, what the future will bring, is in a position to profit if his guesses actually turn out to be better than the predominant opinion. In the absence of uncertainty about the future rates of interest, the rates at which debts of varying maturities could be converted into money at any future date would also be known with certainty now because present rates would be perfectly adjusted to future prices. Under these circumstances, which would exist if there were no uncertainty, there would always be clear economic advantage in owning interest-bearing securities as compared with holding non-income-earning cash. There would exist no basis for liquidity preference for the speculative motive. This helps to explain why in the classical theory, which rests upon generally static assumptions, no significance is attached to the speculative motive and therefore M_2 is equal to zero. Under static theory there may be change, but since the direction and extent of the change is assumed to be known now, the future changes are subject to rational discounting which incorporates them into current calculations. Hence, uncertainty in any significant sense is ruled out of the theory. It is precisely at this point that Keynes' theory differs fundamentally from the classical theory of interest. Wealth-holders lull their disquietude about the future by storing wealth in the form of money just because the actual world is highly dynamic and the future is above all uncertain. The degree of disquietude is measured by the rate of interest. Of course the nature of the real world is not changed by making assumptions which differ from reality. The upshot of oversimplified assumptions is to render theory irrelevant for many types of problems. By assuming a kind of knowledge about the future which we do not and cannot possess, the classical theory rules out liquidity preference for the speculative motive, and with this, out goes the basis for a theory of interest. " 'Interest' has really no business to turn up at all in Marshall's *Principles of Economics*,—" says Keynes, "it belongs to another branch of the subject." (p. 189)

The speculative motive for liquidity preference is thus defined as attempting to secure a profit from knowing better than the market what the future will bring (p. 170). Purchases of bonds will be postponed if the rate of interest is expected to rise.[1] If and when the rate of interest does rise, the price of bonds will fall. The person who has speculated by holding money can now buy at the lower price and realize a profit. An individual who expects the price of bonds to rise (the rate of interest to fall) more than predominant opinion, as expressed in market quotations, expects them to rise, is in a position to profit by borrowing money on short term in order to buy securities now and then sell them at a profit later when and if the price does in fact rise. In the language of the market, a "bear" position leads to a holding of cash in anticipation of a fall in the price of bonds (a rise in interest rates) and a "bull" position leads to the purchase of securities in anticipation of a rise in bond prices (a fall in interest rates). As either the "bear" or the "bull" position predominates in the market, there is an alternate rise and fall in the desire to hold cash. In the absence of changes in the total quantity of money (M), these speculative fluctuations impinge on output and employment by changing the rate of interest and thus reacting upon the volume of current real investment.

The difference of opinion among "bears" and "bulls" is in itself a stabilizing influence and contributes to the feasibility of monetary control of the economic system. Differences of opinion prevent, or at least reduce, the extent of shifts in the rate of interest. An increase in the desire on the part of some wealth-holders to hold money is offset by a decrease in the desires of others so that changing events often result in a redistribution of cash holdings rather than a mass rush into cash or out of cash. If the banking authority, through open market operations, is able to purchase bonds by bidding up the price by slight amounts, it does so by causing some "bull" (a person holding securities) to exchange his bonds for the new cash and thus become a "bear." The rise in the price of bonds represents a fall in the rate of interest which, other things being the same, stimulates real investment and em-

---

1. The word "bond" is used as representative of debts of all types. "Debts" would be technically more accurate.

ployment. If everyone reacted in the same way to changing events, the fluctuations in the rate of interest would be much more violent and the stability of the system would be lessened. As Keynes says: "It is interesting that the stability of the system and its sensitiveness to changes in the quantity of money should be so dependent on the existence of a *variety* of opinion about what is uncertain. Best of all that we should know the future. But if not, then, if we are to control the activity of the economic system by changing the quantity of money, it is important that opinions should differ." (p. 172) [2] Since the transactions and the precautionary motives are both relatively insensitive to changes in the rate of interest, the effect of changes in the quantity of money upon the speculative motive is the substantial basis upon which monetary management rests its case for control of interest rates.

Although monetary management by the central monetary authority offers distinct possibilities for social control of employment, it is subject to important limitations which arise from the nature of the speculative motive. For while an increase in the quantity of money will, other things remaining unchanged, lower the rate of interest, it will not do so if liquidity preference is increasing more than the quantity of money (p. 173). In this connection, it is important to distinguish between two points on the same liquidity-preference curve and two different liquidity-preference curves. Figures 9a and 9b are similar to Figure 8 except that the horizontal axis measures only the quantity of money available to satisfy the speculative motive. This is represented by M_2. Corresponding to M_2, the liquidity function for the speculative motive is L_2. As already noted, this function may be written $M_2 = L_2(r)$, meaning the quantity of money held for the speculative motive is a function of the rate of interest. In Figure 9a, A and B represent two points on the same liquidity-preference curve, and in 9b, A and C represent points on two different liquidity-preference curves. This distinction is analo-

2. *The General Theory of Employment, Interest and Money.* New York: Harcourt, Brace and Co., Inc., 1936.

gous to that between two points on the same demand curve and a shift in an entire demand curve.

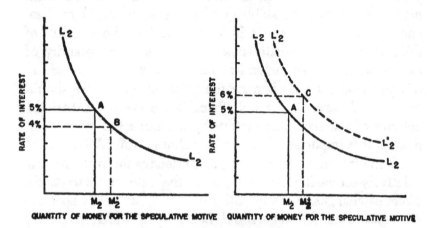

Figure 9a. Two Points on the Same Liquidity-Preference Schedule.

Figure 9b. A Change in Liquidity Preference.

In Figure 9a an increase in the quantity of money from M_2 to M_2' is accompanied by a fall in the interest rate from 5 per cent to 4 per cent. The assumption behind this lowering of the interest rate is that the action of the monetary authority in increasing the supply of money did not affect the expectations of wealth-holders. The additional supply of money was absorbed by the sale of securities to the banking authority with a resultant rise in security prices and a fall in the interest rate.

In Figure 9b the increase in the quantity of money from M_2 to M_2' is accompanied by a revision of expectations in the market such that the entire liquidity-preference schedule shifts upward to an extent that more than offsets the effect of the increase in the quantity of money for satisfying the speculative motive. Hence, instead of falling as in 9a, the interest rate rises from 5 per cent to 6 per cent. This means that central bank policy or some event accompanying it has led wealth-holders to increase their preference for holding money. Such an upward shift could be caused by many factors and might take place independently of a change in bank policy. When such shifts in liquidity preference occur, a considerable fluctuation in the rate of interest, i.e., in the prices of bonds, may take place with very little activity in the bond market. Shifts in the liquidity function may be either downward or upward depending on the way in which the public interprets a change in events. In so far as different individuals react differently to the new situation, movements will be less marked. On the other hand, if everyone interprets the new situation in the same way, the change in interest rate may take place without any buying or selling of bonds and therefore without any redistribution of cash holdings.

As previously indicated, the total quantity of money (M) consists of two parts, money held to satisfy the transactions and precautionary motives (M_1) and money held to satisfy the speculative motive (M_2). Demand for the former varies primarily with changes in income (Y), or in terms of the equation $M_1 = L_1(Y)$. Demand for the latter (M_2) varies primarily with changes in the rate of interest, such that $M_2 = L_2(r)$. However, income (Y) depends partly on the rate of interest (r) and therefore changes in either r or M_1 will affect the other indirectly. This relationship becomes important for monetary policy in periods of expanding output. If income (Y) is rising, the demand for M_1 is also rising. If there is no increase in the total quantity of money (M), the increase in M_1 will take place by a transfer of funds from M_2. The decrease in funds available to satisfy the speculative motive will tend to increase the rate of interest, which in turn will react adversely on investment, and hence upon income. This rise in the rate of interest, which will tend to place a brake on expansion, can be offset by increasing the total quantity of money (M) so that the increase in funds needed to satisfy the growing transactions demand will not be met at the expense of money needed to satisfy the speculative motive (M_2). Here the banking authority is called upon to act in a way which will not allow a shortage of money to lead to a premature brake on expanding output and employment.

We are now in a position to see the practical implications of Keynes' theory of money and interest. The banking authority may be called upon to stimulate employment by increasing the supply of money. The theory behind the idea that an easy-money policy can stimulate expansion is as follows: An increase in the total supply of money (M) operates by increasing the amount of money available for the speculative motive (M_2), which will cause the rate of interest to fall. A fall in the rate of interest will increase investment, and an increase in investment will lead to a multiple increase in income. As income rises, the amount of money required for transactions (M_1) will increase so that the total increase in money (M) will be divided in some fashion between M_1 and M_2. How effective monetary stimulation will be depends on how much the rate of interest falls in response to an increase in M_2 (upon the elasticity of the L_2 function); how responsive investment is to a fall in the rate of interest (the elasticity of the schedule of the marginal efficiency of capital); and how much a given increase in investment will increase income (the size of the investment multiplier).

The pitfalls which may beset monetary policy will be recognized as very great. We have already noted that an increase in the quantity of money will not lower the rate of interest if liquidity preference is increasing more than the quantity of money. Although a fall in the rate of interest will, other things being equal, increase investment and employment, it will not do so if the marginal efficiency of capital is falling more rapidly than the rate of interest. In a bad depression when the preference for liquidity is high and the expectations of entrepreneurs for profitable investment are low, monetary policy may be helpless to break the economic deadlock.

It is much easier to bring down short-term than long-term interest rates. The reason for this is obvious. The chief barrier to a fall in interest rates is the expectation that they may rise later to an extent that makes it worth while to hold cash in anticipation of buying on better terms at a later date. If the banking authority launches a large-scale open-market policy to lower the interest rates, it is logical to assume that this policy will probably be pursued for some time. There will be little reason to expect a rise in the rate of interest in the near future and therefore little incentive to remain liquid in order to buy on better terms later. Furthermore, commitments to debts on short-term cannot involve very great losses even if expectations prove wrong. Securities may be held a short while until maturity when they will be redeemed at face value. It is well known that short-term interest rates have been extremely low in the United States and Britain in recent years.

The long-term rate of interest is more difficult to lower and it becomes increasingly resistant to further reductions at every step on its downward path; at some level, say about 2 per cent, no further reductions may be attainable. To illustrate, let us compare the consequences of a rise from 5 to 6 per cent with the consequences of a rise of from 2 to 3 per cent. To simplify the example, let us assume that the securities bought are perpetual bonds, that is, have no maturity date, like British consols or French rentes. When the rate of interest is 5 per cent, a bond paying $50 per year is purchased at $1000. Three years later the rate of interest on this type of security rises to 6 per cent as a result of which the price of the bond falls to $833 (at 6 per cent $833 will purchase an income of $50 per year). The capital loss is $167 but, during the three-year period, interest income amounting to $150 has been collected. Hence the net loss is negligible. In contrast, when the rate of interest is 2 per cent, a bond paying $20 can be purchased for $1000. Three years later the rate of interest rises to 3 per cent, as a result of which the price of the bond falls to $667 (at 3 per cent $667 will purchase an income of $20 per year). The capital loss of $333 is offset only to the extent of $60 in interest income received in the three-year period. Thus the loss from a rise in the interest rate from 2 to 3 per cent is much greater than from 5 to 6 per cent, first, because the loss in capital value is greater and, second, because the interest income is less at the lower level.

The increasing risk of loss at lower rates of interest will be reflected in the liquidity-preference schedule by a flattening out of the liquidity curve. This flattening of the curve indicates a growing elasticity of the liquidity-preference function. Translated into monetary policy, this means a point will be reached below which it is extremely difficult to lower the interest rate any further. At about 2 per cent, Keynes suggests the liquidity curve may become horizontal, indicating perfect elasticity, and meaning that no further reduction in the rate can be attained merely by increasing the quantity of money. When this point is reached, the demand for money has become absolute in the sense that everyone prefers to hold money rather than long-term securities yielding a return of 2 per cent or less.

When Keynes wrote the *General Theory*, he no longer believed in the adequacy of mere monetary policy, but nevertheless he thought the full possibilities of interest rate control had never been tested. Central bank purchases in the open market had been too limited in amount and confined mainly to short-term securities to the neglect of long-term securities bearing directly upon the much more important long-term rate of interest. The interest rate is a highly psychological or conventional phenomenon and investors who have become accustomed to high rates as "normal" will continue to harbor the hope of a return to "normalcy" unless and until bold monetary policy by the banking authorities breaks through conventional beliefs to convince the public that low long-term rates are both sound and certain to continue. Any monetary policy that appears experimental is self-defeating. The chief hope of lowering the long-term interest rate to a point consistent with full employment rests upon the ability of the monetary authority to convince the community that it should accept as a permanent fact lower rates of return on long-term debts. Such a policy should not be neglected just because it will ultimately reach a limit where it will no longer be effective because of the flattening out of the liquidity curve.

Hoarding and liquidity preference

There is a relationship but not an identity between Keynes' concept of liquidity preference for the speculative motive and the common-sense notion of hoarding. Unemployment and depression are sometimes attributed to "hoarding" although the exact meaning of this term is usually not clear. "Hoarding" in the sense of an actual increase in cash balances in the hands of the public is an incomplete and misleading notion. Since the total quantity of money cannot be altered by the public, but only by the banking system, the public can merely *try* to hold more money. It may increase its liquidity *preference*. At any given time, the total supply of money (M) is, by definition, held by someone. If one individual comes into possession of more money as a result of his increased desire for liquidity, someone else in the economy must decrease his cash holdings, as long as there is no change in the total supply of money as determined by the banking system. The distribution of cash holdings among the public may be changed but no alteration in the aggregate holdings can occur as a result of initiative taken by the public.

Nevertheless, the anxiety on the part of the public to hoard more money has very important consequences for the economic system, since, as will be evident, it is nothing more than an expression of increased liquidity preference. Liquidity preference may be defined as the propensity to hoard. When liquidity preference or the propensity to hoard rises, the rate of interest will also rise, unless the banking system meets the increase in liquidity preference by enlarging the quantity of money available to wealth-holders. An increase in the desire to hoard money can be overcome by paying higher interest to potential hoarders. A rise in the rate of interest chokes off investment and leads to a decrease in income and employment. Thus the notion of "hoarding," rightly viewed, is the heart of Keynes' analysis of unemployment. Unemployment may be caused by "hoarding," in this sense, even if no actual wealth is transferred into money, because hoarding money and not-hoarding it are not simple alternatives. Liquidity preference is always liquidity at a price. The price is the rate of interest. The rate of interest will always be high enough to overcome the liquidity preference of all those who want cash somewhat less intensely than those who actually hold the limited supply available. The rate of interest will be determined immediately by the liquidity preferences of those who are marginal between holding money and purchasing an interest-bearing security. An increase in the desire to shift wealth from securities into money is what causes a rise in the price that must be paid to marginal hoarders to induce them not to hoard. Only those most insistent on having cash will be able to get it. The doubts and fears of others will be lulled by interest payments. This view of the economic process has led Keynes to a sympathetic understanding with those reformers who have suggested that a special levy be placed upon money in order to make it "unhoardable." He praises the proposal of Silvio Gesell, the stamped-money reformer, who wanted to impose a tax upon money to encourage people to spend it before the tax came due. Money held in an inactive balance for an extended period of time would, under Gesell's plan, gradually lose its entire value.

Changes in the Quantity of Money

The rate of interest depends upon the state of liquidity preference taken in conjunction with the quantity of money. If liquidity preference remains unchanged, increases in the quantity of money will lower the rate of interest, and decreases in the quantity of money will raise the rate of interest. It is important to say something more about how changes in the quantity of money occur in modern economic societies.

The total supply of money consists of bank deposits, paper money, and metallic coins. In highly developed capitalistic economies like the United States, the supply of money con-

sists overwhelmingly of bank deposits, which represent liabilities of banks to pay money to depositors. No matter of
principle is involved in determining whether savings deposits
should be included under the category of money. If money is
defined as the perfectly liquid asset, the presumption is
against including savings deposits because banks have the
right to require a certain number of days' notice before they
will convert a savings or time deposit into legal money. On
the other hand, savings accounts differ from debts in that their
value in terms of money is not subject to change. In some
countries the statistical data do not permit a breakdown of
total deposits between demand and time deposits. Even
though a bank has the legal right to require, say, thirty days'
notice on savings accounts, this requirement is not always
strictly followed. Keynes does, in general, include as money
time deposits in banks. What matters most for the present
discussion, however, is not what makes up the total quantity
of money (M), but how changes in this total come about.
These changes arise mainly from the lending and borrowing
activities of the banking system. Therefore demand deposits,
or what may be called check-book money, are the significant
element of the money supply so far as the interest rate and
Keynes' theory of money are concerned.

Banks add to the total supply of money by the creation of
bank credit, that is, by increasing the liquid claims against
themselves in favor of their customers whose additional
money takes the form of increased balances. Balances which
add to the total quantity of money arise when loans are made
or when a security, like a bond, is purchased by a bank as an
investment. For example, when a bank advances a loan to a
business man for $1000, the total supply of money (M) is
increased by $1000. The only physical evidence of this trans-
action is a bookkeeping entry in the accounts of the bank,
debiting "Loans and Discounts" and crediting "Deposits."
Loans and discounts represent an asset of the bank because
they are rights or claims of the bank against its borrowers
to be collected at some specific date in the future, the date

depending upon the length of the loan. "Deposits" are a liability of the bank, representing its obligation to pay money on demand to the borrower-depositor. What matters from the money side is that an increase in total bank loans represents an increase in liquid claims, that is, in bank credit, which is just as good as money for most types of transactions and therefore is part of the supply of money.

When a bank loan is repaid, the quantity of money is reduced, unless of course a new loan of corresponding amount is made at the same time. The physical evidence of this destruction of money is again merely a bookkeeping entry in the accounting records of the bank. The "Loans and Discounts" account is credited to indicate a decrease in this asset, and the "Deposits" account is debited to indicate a decrease in the liability to pay money. If the loan is repaid in cash, the "Cash" account will be debited. As a result of the loan, the bank will have added to its income in the form of interest charged the borrower.

These deposits which result directly from the lending and investing activities of individual banks with individuals, firms, and the government, are called "derivative" deposits, as distinguished from "primary" deposits which result from the actual deposit of cash or its equivalent.[3] Derivative deposits create additional bank credit whereas primary deposits do not. Since bank credit is included in our definition of money, derivative deposits increase the total supply of money outstanding in the economic system. In contrast, if a man deposits metallic or paper money, he exchanges one type of money for another. The structure of the money supply outside the banking system is changed; bank deposits have increased and the metallic or paper money in the hands of the public has decreased, but the total quantity of money (M) is not altered. Likewise, a man who deposits his pay check or any other check with his bank does not increase the total

---

3. See Keynes, *Treatise on Money*, Vol. I, Chapter 2. New York: Harcourt, Brace and Company, Inc., 1930, also C. A. Phillips, *Bank Credit*, page 40. New York: The Macmillan Company, 1921.

supply of money, but merely increases his claims against the bank at the expense of someone else whose claims are decreased. Hence, changes in the total supply of money come about primarily as a result of the lending and investing activities of the banking system associated with derivative deposits. If the public desires to become more liquid, only the banking system can permit it to do so.

There are, of course, limits to the extent to which the banking system is able to increase the liquid claims against itself. In any nation the power of the banking system to alter the quantity of deposit money is limited by legal requirements or business customs. In the United States the central monetary authority, the Board of Governors of the Federal Reserve System, is authorized under law to control the quantity of liquid claims which member banks are permitted to have outstanding by (1) varying the reserve requirements of the member banks, (2) altering the rediscount rate at which member banks may borrow from the Federal Reserve Banks, and (3) engaging in open market operations in order to make rediscount rates effective and in order to influence directly the prices of securities and thereby the rate of interest. When the central banking authority lowers the ratio of legal reserves to deposits which the member banks must hold, it gives the member banks an incentive to increase the claims outstanding since cash for a bank, as for any wealth-holder, is not an earning asset and excess cash reserves represent a basis for potential earning power that is not being utilized. More loans will tend to increase bank profits. Whether the member banks will actually lend more as a result of lowered reserve requirements depends partly on their willingness to lower the rate of interest which they charge and partly on the rate which business men and other borrowers are willing to pay. In any event, it may be supposed that more will be borrowed at lower than at higher interest rates, other things remaining the same. The extent of demand for bank loans will depend upon profit expectations, that is, upon the marginal efficiency of capital. If the marginal efficiency of capital is very low, as it is in time of depression, no fall in the interest rate will have much effect upon the quantity of borrowing. In this respect the initiative for expansion must come from outside the banking system.

When the central banking authorities lower the rediscount rate, they make it cheaper for member banks to add to their cash reserves by selling (rediscounting) commercial paper to the Federal Reserve Banks. In the United States it is customary for member banks to borrow from the Federal Reserve Banks because the rediscount rate is lower than the discount rate charged by the member banks. This means that member banks may be able to add to their reserves at, say, 2 per cent and advance loans to business men at 4 per cent. It will therefore be more profitable to borrow from the central banks when the rediscount rate charged by the central bank is lowered. Here again there are barriers to increasing the quantity of money or liquid claims against member banks. If the member banks already have excess reserves, there will be no incentive which did not already exist to lower their interest rates nor for them to add still more to excess reserves by borrowing from the central bank. Again, the initiative must come from outside the banking system if the quantity of liquid claims is to be increased.

A more positive weapon of monetary control in the hands of the central banking authority is open-market operations. Here the central authority can take the initiative to change the quantity of liquid claims outstanding against the banking system. Open-market operations represent the purchase and sale of securities by the central banks in the open market. "Open market" refers to transactions which are not exclusively with banks and includes especially the bond markets of great financial centers like New York City. The purchase and sale of securities by banks differ from those between two private persons in that the quantity of money in the economy is changed when a bank buys or sells. The purchase of a bond by one person from another person involves only a *transfer* of money and no change in the total quantity of

money and also no change in the money-creating capacity of
the banking system as represented by the extent of its reserves.
When a central bank buys a bond, it pays with funds which
it creates for the purpose. If, for example, an individual sells
a bond to the central bank, the individual receives in payment from the central bank a check which, when deposited
with the individual's (member) bank, represents a net increase in the supply of money in the economy outside the
banking system. What is potentially more important for
monetary expansion arises when the member bank presents
the check for payment from the central bank. The central
bank makes payment to the member bank by increasing the
balance of the member bank. Since balances held by member banks with central banks represent reserves, the capacity
of the member bank to expand its loans is increased by an
amount which depends upon the reserve ratio. If the ratio
is $1 of reserve for each $5 of deposits, an increase in reserves of $1000 means that total deposits in the banking
system may be increased by $5000. Open-market operations
thus bring about changes in the reserves of member banks.
Frequently, open-market operations are used to bring pressure upon the member banks to change their discount rates
in accordance with changes in the central bank rediscount
rates. In depression a lowering of the rediscount rate coupled
with an increase in member bank reserves resulting from
open-market purchases by the central bank will presumably
give the member banks incentive to expand their loans to
customers. In expansion, an increase in the rediscount rate
may be ineffective if the member banks have excess reserves,
but if these reserves are reduced through open-market sales
by the central bank, the member banks will be forced either
to replenish their reserves by rediscounting commercial paper
at the higher rediscount rates or to restrict the volume of
their loans to customers, which is the objective of the central
bank policy.

Open-market operations affect not only the short-term rate
of interest on bank loans but also the long-term rate of inter-

est through the prices of securities. Even the purchase of short-term securities will react upon the longer-term rates of interest, but a more direct effect on long-term rates of interest results from dealings in long-term securities. Keynes criticizes the Federal Reserve authorities for confining their open-market purchases during 1933 and 1934 to very short-dated securities with the result that the effect was confined mainly, though not exclusively, to the very short-term rate of interest. Keynes suggests the most important practical improvement which can be made in the technique of monetary management would be "a complex offer by the central bank to buy and sell at stated prices gilt-edged bonds of all maturities." (p. 206)

Some limitations to monetary control have already been indicated. In general, the limitations of monetary management in controlling the level of employment are limitations of interest rate control. Although proper management of the supply of money is a necessary condition for a stable economy, it is not a sufficient condition. Mismanagement of money may in itself be sufficiently disturbing to lead to economic breakdown. But the best monetary policy in the world can do little to lift an economy out of the depths of a secondary deflation like that experienced in the United States in the early 1930's. What this means in terms of Keynes' principal variables is that if the marginal efficiency of capital has fallen to a very low or even negative position, there is nothing the central banking authority can do to bring about revival through lowering the rate of interest. There might be no demand for investment loans even if the rate of interest were reduced to zero. As long as loans have to be repaid and are not automatically renewable, any borrower runs the risk of being unable to repay his loans. Where the private marginal efficiency of capital has collapsed to a point where no one wants to borrow even at a zero rate of interest, it becomes necessary for a government which wishes to stimulate economic activity to take more direct action to increase the vol-

ume of investment and thus to lift the level of income and
employment.

The Classical Theory of Interest

The contrast between Keynes' *general* theory of interest and
the special theory of interest of the classical school is analogous to the contrast between his general theory of employment and the special theory of employment of the classical
school. Both distinctions between the general theory and a
special theory arise from the difference between fluctuating
levels of employment and income in contrast with the fixed
level of full employment and a corresponding fixed level of
income. By neglecting the all-important changes in the level
of income, the classical school is led into the error of viewing
the rate of interest as the factor which brings about the equality of saving and investment, that is, the equality of demand
for investible funds and the supply of funds provided by
saving. This may be represented by a diagram showing the
rate of interest along the vertical axis and saving and investment along the horizontal axis. The rate of interest is thus

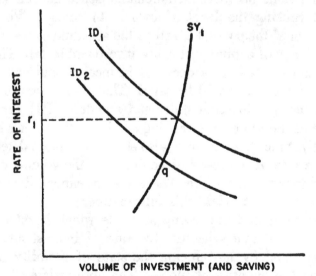

VOLUME OF INVESTMENT (AND SAVING)

Figure 10. The Classical Theory of the Rate of
Interest.

determined by the point of intersection of the investment-demand schedule, ID_1, and the supply of saving line, SY_1. The investment-demand schedule is Keynes' schedule of the marginal efficiency of capital. The line SY_1 represents the amount of saving out of a level of income Y_1 which, under classical assumptions, presumably would be the level of income corresponding to full employment.

Keynes accepts the classical position of equality of saving and investment but attributes this equality to changes in the level of income rather than to the rate of interest. Keynes also would agree with the classical theory that *if the level of income is assumed to be given,* the current rate of interest lies at the point of intersection of the investment-demand schedule and the schedule of saving which will be made at varying rates of interest out of that level of income. Keynes parts company with the classicists when they go a step further and assume that if the investment-demand schedule shifts to the position ID_2, the intersection of this new investment-demand schedule and the old SY_1 at the point q in Figure 10 will determine the new rate of interest. The classical error lies in assuming that the investment-demand schedule can change without causing the level of income to change. We know from Keynes' theory that a fall in the schedule of the marginal efficiency of capital will cause investment to fall. The fall in investment leads to a decrease in income, and out of the reduced income less will be saved. Thus, it is inconsistent to assume that the investment-demand schedule (ID) can shift without at the same time causing a shift in the saving schedule (SY). Since the SY curve also shifts, we cannot determine what the rate of interest will be nor what the volume of saving and investment will be. There are not enough data in the classical scheme to yield this information.

In order to find the saving schedule which is relevant to the new investment schedule, the rate of interest must first be determined by introducing the state of liquidity preference and the quantity of money. The appropriate SY curve will be that which intersects ID_2 immediately opposite the new rate of interest, whatever it may be. If the new rate of interest is r_2, the relevant saving schedule is SY_2 in Figure 11. The amount of investment (and saving) is now determined on the horizontal axis immediately below the point of intersection of the ID_2 line and the SY_2 line. If the rate of interest remains unchanged at r_1—because the state of liquidity preference and the quantity of money for the speculative motive remain the same—the relevant saving-out-of-income schedule will be SY_2', and the point at which this line intersects the ID_2 line will indicate the amount of saving and investment. The point q in Figure 11 corresponds to the same point in Figure 10. It indicates the solution given by the classical theory, which assumes that income and saving-out-of-income remain unchanged when the rate of investment changes, and on a basis of this special assumption, views the rate of interest as the balancing factor which equates the volume of saving to the volume of investment.

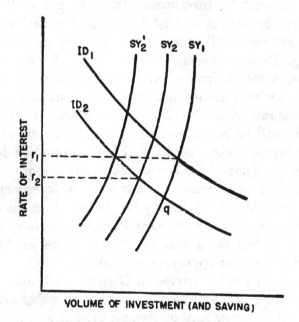

Figure 11. The Rate of Interest and Changing Levels of Income.

The distinctive aspect of Keynes' theory is represented in the diagram by the SY curves. There is a different SY curve for each level of income. In assuming continuous full employment, the classical theory deals only with the SY_1 curve, and in this manner escapes the necessity of having to discover a general explanation for interest. By assuming that the investment-demand schedule (ID) can shift without affecting the level of income, and therefore the schedule of saving out of income (SY), the classical school is led to view interest as the "price" which equates the demand for investment to the supply of saving. This, however, is not an explanation of interest, but a special condition which follows from the special assumption of full employment and a fixed level of income. Nevertheless, the classical school goes on to work out a view of the interest rate as an automatic, self-regulating mechanism for equating saving to investment. When the demand for investment falls, the rate of interest is supposed to fall and lessen the supply of saving to correspond to the reduced demand for investment. Or, if the public decides to save more, the rate of interest is supposed to fall to a point where investment will increase to take care of the increase in saving. Thus, a decrease in the demand for consumption (increase in the desire to save) is supposed to be compensated for by an increase in investment through the mechanism of the rate of interest. This is just another way of saying that there will be no changes in aggregate income or aggregate employment when the demand for consumption declines. A fall in the demand for consumers goods is more likely to diminish than to increase the demand for investment. Empirical verification for this may be gleaned from the statistical fact that, except in war and other rare periods of strained resources, consumption and investment move in the same direction and not in opposite directions.

A glance at the SY curves in Diagrams 10 and 11 indicates that Keynes is willing to accept the view that more will be saved at a higher rate of interest than at a lower rate of interest out of a given income, although saving is not very sensitive to changes in the rate of interest (the SY curves are steep, or interest-inelastic). This is not to be interpreted to mean that more will be saved at a higher rate of interest than at a lower rate of interest when changes in income related to changes in the rate of interest are brought into the picture, as Keynes insists they must be. A rise in the rate of interest will actually lead to a decrease in the amount of saving. For when the interest rate rises, investment falls, and a fall in investment causes a decline in income, and out of a smaller income less will be saved. The fall in saving will be just equal to the fall in investment since the two were equal before income fell and must be equal after income falls. Just as surely as a rise in the rate of interest leads to a decrease in investment so must it also lead to a decrease in saving. This divergence of views between Keynes and the classical school boils down once again to the differences between the logic of an economics of full employment and the logic of an economics of less than full employment.

Observations on the Nature of Capital and Interest

Interest is so universally linked to capital in discussions of economic science that it is useful to ask the question: What view of capital is associated with Keynes' theory of interest? Capital is not an unambiguous concept, but probably it is most commonly defined as produced means of production, in contrast with natural means of production, referred to as "land," and meaning all natural resources used in production. Capital is man-made and land is nature-given. Keynes does not quarrel with this definition of real capital nor with the distinction between land and capital. But the rate or ratio which relates the income yields from real capital to its total value is called by Keynes the (marginal) efficiency of capital, which is quite separate and distinct from the rate of interest as a payment for the use of money. Traditional theory does not distinguish clearly, and from Keynes' point of view con-

fuses, the marginal efficiency of capital as a reward or income derived from the ownership of scarce capital assets and
interest as a reward or income for not-hoarding money. The
arithmetical equality of the rate of interest and the marginal
efficiency of capital in equilibrium has probably been a major
cause of the failure to distinguish between the two phenomena.

The size of the reward paid as interest is traditionally
viewed as a matter of the (marginal) *productivity of capital.*
Interest is said to be the reward for saving, or for waiting
until a later date for consumption which could be enjoyed
now but which is foregone, as a result of which resources can
be diverted from consumption to investment activity with a
consequent increase in the total productiveness of capital.
However, if interest, like the rent of land, is a scarcity payment which rewards no genuine sacrifice, there is little point
in speaking of capital as "productive." Capital assets yield
over their life a return in excess of their original cost only
because they are scarce. As the scarcity of capital diminishes,
the rate of return to owners will fall "without its having become less productive—at least in the physical sense." (p.
213) The main reason capital assets are kept scarce is because the rate of interest on money offers an alternative to
wealth-holders which is more remunerative than the prospective yield (expressed as a rate) from newly-created
capital assets. The rate of interest on money is a kind of
institutional monopoly which leads to an artificial scarcity of
capital assets.

In rejecting the idea that capital is productive, Keynes
sympathizes with the labor theory of value that everything is
produced by labor. Labor, working in an environment of
technology, natural resources, and the assets produced by
past labor, is capable of making capital assets less scarce.
Capital is the product of past labor embodied in assets. Labor,
of course, is used in a broad sense to include mental as well
as manual labor, and the services of entrepreneurs as well
as the services of those who work for wages. Labor working
with machines is more productive than labor working with-

out machines, just as labor working on fertile land is more productive than labor working on infertile land. Acceptance of the human agent as the sole creative force in production does not involve belittling the importance of machinery for increasing productivity. But it does involve an unorthodox way of looking at the economic process. One might view it as a revolutionary doctrine were it not for the fact that Adam Smith and Ricardo and practically all their contemporaries looked at the economic process in much the same manner. Only after the socialists took over the labor theory of value did it lose its respectability among academic economists. The labor theory of value is after all a very humanistic doctrine, which attributes production and productivity only to persons and never to things. It views machines as a mere extension of man's power over his economic environment rather than as co-ordinate partners that labor along with man. It imputes the added productivity that manifests itself in machinery back to the human agent which created the machinery. There is no really serious issue here, however, because it is largely a matter of terminology. Nevertheless, it is important to explain Keynes' departure from the classical (post-Ricardian) terminology and his preference for this way of speaking about the nature of interest and money.

There is implicit in Keynes' views of capital and interest a fundamental criticism of the existing social order. If interest is a payment for money and as such rewards no genuine sacrifice, it is unearned income. It is a form of income that would not need to be paid, at least not for long, under different institutional arrangements. Yet interest is, in a sense, inevitable under laissez-faire capitalism. The implication of Keynes' theory is that income received from not-hoarding money represents an institutional monopoly whereby the possessors of money enjoy the fruits of an unearned income snatched from an economic community so arranged that those who hold surplus money must be bribed before they will surrender it to those who will put it to a socially beneficial use, that is, will use the money as a device for mobilizing labor, material, and machines for the production of goods and services. Those who receive interest income are performing no socially necessary function. The propensity to hoard money impedes full employment and prevents greater production of capital and consumers goods, and denies to the public the full enjoyment of potential consumption. It creates an unnecessary and anti-social scarcity of productive equipment. Operationally, this is an appeal for an easy-money policy as a means to fuller and more abundant production.

Relation of the Marginal Efficiency of Capital to the Rate of Interest

In this chapter and the preceding one, the two basic determinants of the inducement to invest, the marginal efficiency of capital and the rate of interest, have been examined independently of each other. Since each concept is an independent variable and quite distinct, this procedure of separate discussion is justified. The analysis would be incomplete, however, without an examination of the way in which the two variables are related to each other. Traditional economics does not follow Keynes in his clear-cut distinction between the rate of interest and the marginal efficiency of capital. Interest has frequently been viewed as the reward for capital assets and the *rate* of interest as the measure of the marginal productivity of capital assets. Obviously, economists are aware that interest is paid on money borrowed from banks and from other sources. But the classical tradition has been to view the bank rate as the "money side" of the "real rate" of interest. In this strictly classical theory, the real and money rates of interest cannot get out of line because automatic market forces are always at work to prevent any divergence.

Some economists have developed the idea of interest somewhat further by distinguishing between the "market" or "money" rate and the "natural" rate, and have recognized that a divergence between the two might have important consequences. In this setting, economists like Wicksell, Hayek, and Keynes in his *Treatise on Money*, begin to give money a significant role in economic theory. We may identify this as the neo-classical theory of interest. When the market rate set by the banking system is equal to the natural rate, the economic system is in equilibrium according to this neo-classical version. If the banking system permits the market rate to diverge from the natural rate, a disequilibrium of some sort will result. Keynes' distinction between the rate of interest on money and the marginal efficiency of real capital is a further development of the neo-classical distinction between the market rate and the natural rate of interest. However, there is a fundamental difference between Keynes' earlier and later views. First, the natural rate of interest as used, for example, in Keynes' *Treatise*, although cognate with the marginal efficiency of capital, differs in that the natural rate is a unique rate which will prevail under conditions of full employment. The equilibrium which is attained when the market rate of interest is equal to the natural rate of interest is a full-employment equilibrium. But in the perspective of the *General Theory*, there is a different natural rate (or marginal efficiency of capital) for every level of employment. The earlier theory does not allow for the possibility of equilibrium at less than full employment. In brief, it is not a general theory. Second, in the classical and neo-classical views, the money rate of interest adjusts to the real or natural rate and in this sense the real or natural rate determines the money rate of interest or at least determines what it should be. But in Keynes' *General Theory* it is the marginal efficiency of capital that adjusts to the money rate of interest rather than the other way around. It is more correct to say that the rate of interest on money determines the marginal efficiency of (real) capital than it is to say that the marginal efficiency of capital determines the money rate of interest.[4]

---

4. On this very important point Keynes' words are: "Thus, instead of the marginal efficiency of capital determining the rate of interest, it is true (though not a full statement of the case) to say that it is the rate of interest which determines the marginal efficiency of capital." *Quarterly Journal of Economics*, February, 1937, Vol. LI, No. 2, page 223.

In equilibrium, the marginal efficiency of capital is equal to the rate of interest on money. These two rates are brought to equality by the efforts of wealth-holders to maximize the advantages of owning various forms of wealth. Persons who decide to give up immediate command over money still have the alternatives of owning debts (like bonds) or owning capital assets (which may be in the form of equity claims, i.e., stocks). The significant thing here, so far as employment is concerned, is that capital assets are capable of being newly produced. Producing new capital assets is another expression for investment. Preference will be given to building new capital assets rather than buying claims to old ones when it is cheaper to build than to buy, that is, when the supply price or replacement cost is less than the demand price or present value, which is found by discounting the prospective yields by the current rate of interest (see above p. 138). If the prospective yields discounted at the current rate of interest place the demand price or present value of capital assets above their replacement cost or supply price, new capital assets will be produced, i.e., investment will occur. New capital assets will continue to be produced until the marginal efficiency of capital falls to a level at which there is no longer any advantage in building more capital assets as compared with buying old ones or buying debts (bonds).

The marginal efficiency of capital is flexible and will fall under the impact of new investment. Since the marginal efficiency of capital varies with the volume of investment, and since income changes as investment changes, the marginal efficiency is not determined unless the level of income is also determined. Unless the level of income is assumed to be given or unless the rate of interest is determined independently of both the marginal efficiency of capital and the level of income, we do not know at what level the marginal efficiency will be equal to the rate of interest, as it must be in equilibrium. In an economy of fluctuating income, the marginal efficiency of capital is indeterminate as long as the rate of interest is not determined. Keynes solves the equilibrium by determining the rate of interest independently of the level of income.[5] The rate of interest depends upon the quantity of money and the state of liquidity preference. In this sense, the rate of interest sets the pace by fixing the level to which the marginal efficiency will fall. Between them, these two determine the volume of investment, and income falls into line as a truly dependent variable.

The classical theory in which the marginal efficiency of capital sets the pace to which the rate of interest is supposed to adjust is determinate only if the level of income is assumed to be given in order that the marginal efficiency can be found independently of the rate of interest. The classical theory assumes that income is given at the point corresponding to full employment. In a world characterized by wide and almost continuous fluctuations in income below the level of full employment, such a special theory is not very relevant. Thus the fatal flaw in classical economics is the lack of an adequate theory of interest. There are not enough data in the classical scheme to make the system solvable except under special, limiting assumptions. In mathematical language, the

5. This statement that the rate of interest is determined independently of income is subject to the following qualification. The rate of interest depends on the quantity of money available for satisfying the speculative motive (M_2) and this is related to the quantity of money available for the transactions motive (M_1), the demand for which depends on income. Therefore, indirectly the rate of interest depends on income. This is the main reference to "a full statement of the case" in the quotation from Keynes given in the preceding note. If Keynes' recommendation that the total quantity of money be increased to meet the rising transactions demand were followed, the rate of interest would not rise. In this practical sense then, if not in a strict theoretical sense, the rate of interest is determined by bank policy independently of income. Default in banking policy is of course always possible. The purpose of this section on the relation of the rate of interest to the marginal efficiency of capital is to indicate why Keynes thought his theory of interest and money was the distinctive contribution of the *General Theory*. Lest there be some doubt of this, the title of his book is the best *prima facie* evidence. This is not the same thing as saying that the rate of interest is most important in the policy sense, although Keynes seems never to have completely escaped this idea. What it probably does indicate, on a fundamental philosophical level, is an inconsistency between Keynes' theoretical and practical emphasis. However, since the purpose of this book is to give an exposition and not a critique of Keynes, this issue would carry us far afield. See, however, the last chapter below.

classical theory is one equation short of a determinate solution. This is the equation which gives a general theory of interest in which the rate of interest is fixed by the quantity of money and the state of liquidity preference. In Keynes' general theory of employment and income, the money theory of the rate of interest is the linchpin of the system, lacking which no determinate solution can be reached. In contrast, in the classical theory the rate of interest is subsidiary to the marginal efficiency (productivity) of capital, and money has no independent significance in relation to output and employment. It is money's function as a store of value which sets Keynes' theory apart from the classical theory because the holding of money is a crucial alternative both to the ownership of debts and the ownership of durable capital assets. Classical theory is led into a mistaken theory of investment by a false rationalization concerning the type of knowledge which we have about the future. In a world of a calculable future, there is no place for money as a store of value. It would always be preferable to own a debt rather than to hold money. Under these conditions, the rate of interest would fall and investment would increase until all resources were employed. The chief fault of the classical theory lies in its assumptions rather than in its logic.

The preceding analysis shows that the marginal efficiency of capital is more flexible than the rate of interest on money. The former changes fairly readily in response to changes in the quantity of capital assets, whereas the rate of interest is "sticky." The level at which the two rates are equal is dependent more upon the rate of interest than upon the marginal efficiency of capital in the sense that new capital assets are built until their marginal efficiency is reduced to the level of the rate of interest on money. Investment stops and unemployment exists because of the barrier set by the money rate of interest. In the absence of money, or any commodity with the characteristics of money, the marginal efficiency of capital would fall under the impact of increasing investment until full employment were reached.

What are the peculiar characteristics of money that prevent its rate of interest from falling in a manner similar to the fall of the marginal efficiency of all other types of assets? The answer to this important question involves a subtle analysis of the properties of money and interest which may, however, be summarized in fairly simple terms. The properties of money which make the rate of interest "sticky" are found in (1) the zero or negligible elasticity of production of money, (2) the zero or negligible elasticity of substitution of other factors for money, and (3) the high elasticity of demand for money as a store of value.

(1) *Negligible elasticity of production:* Unlike most other commodities, the output of money cannot be increased readily by private enterprise, as distinct from the monetary authority. When the demand for money increases relative to the demand for other things, labor cannot be employed by private enterprise to increase the production of money. If this were the case, the courses of depressions would be different, as indeed they are to some extent in gold-producing countries. With a fall in the demand for things other than money and a rise in the demand for money, men who lost their jobs in producing the former could be put to work in the latter, and unemployment would be avoided or at least mitigated. Modern money, however, is predominantly bank money, and is not produced according to the principles which govern the employment of labor by private enterprise for the production of real goods and services. In so far as gold is still a part of the money supply, there is some mitigation of unemployment. In depression when prices fall and the value of money, including gold, rises, gold mining tends to employ more labor than in prosperity. In gold-mining countries, this may be of some practical significance in offsetting unemployment in other industries, but for the world as a whole it is of minor significance.

Since money cannot be produced by labor, the rate of interest does not decline in the way that the prices of other commodities fall as a result of the increase in their output.

Here the monetary authority can play a part by increasing the quantity of money in an attempt to lower the rate of interest. While this does not result in any increase in employment to produce money, it may lower the rate of interest and permit more labor to be employed in producing other forms of (real) wealth which are now relatively more desirable because the value of money has fallen.

(2) *Negligible elasticity of substitution:* There is no efficient substitute for money as a medium of exchange. When the demand for money increases relative to other things, there is no tendency to substitute other things for money as in the case of other commodities. In the case of land, for example, the elasticity of production is negligible, which means that no more land can be produced as demand for it increases, but nevertheless other factors of production will be substituted for land as its price rises. More machinery and more labor may be used in place of land to produce more output when the price (rent) of land rises. But since there is no other factor capable of performing money's function nearly as efficiently as does money, no substitution of other factors for money takes place.

(3) *High elasticity of demand for money as a store of value:* Even when the quantity of money is made elastic by action of the banking authority, or when the quantity of money available as a store of value (M_2) is increased by virtue of a release from the quantity used for transactions (M_1), the demand for money as a store of wealth is such as to be unresponsive to changes in the proportion which money bears to other forms of wealth. In other words, when M_2 is increased, the rate of interest will not fall readily, and below a certain level of, say, 2 per cent, the rate of interest will not fall at all because the preference for holding wealth in the form of money rather than in the form of debts (like bonds) becomes relatively absolute. (See above p. 180.) This means that the rate of interest does not fall in response to an increase in the quantity of money in the same manner that

the marginal efficiency of capital assets falls in response to increases in their quantity. If the number of houses were to be greatly increased, the marginal efficiency of houses would fall quite rapidly; but great increases in the quantity of money do not lead to marked decreases in the rate of interest, especially after the latter has fallen to a certain level. The demand for money as a store of wealth is relatively insatiable (so long as there is no flight from the currency), whereas the demand for other forms of wealth is quite satiable. One important reason for the willingness to increase ownership of wealth in the money form is the low or negligible carrying cost of money.

Keynes' basic contention is that these properties of money are responsible for unemployment in the sense that in the absence of a form of wealth with the characteristics of money, the ordinary forces of the market would cause the economic system to be self-adjusting at full employment. In the absence of the barrier set by the money rate of interest, the marginal efficiencies of all types of capital assets would be free to fall to a level at which the amount of investment would be sufficient to result in full employment. Actually, however, the level of the money rate of interest sets a limit below which the marginal efficiency of capital cannot fall. Production of new wealth stops at this point because further increases would reduce the marginal efficiency to a level at which the return from new investment would be less than the return from buying existing assets or from buying debts (like bonds). In this explanation of why the special properties of money set the limits to the fall in the rate of interest, we gain insight into why, after all, Keynes' work is called a general theory of employment, *interest and money*. The equilibrium level of employment is reached when the advantages of holding money, owning debts, buying capital assets, and building new assets are equalized. The form of wealth ownership is a matter of indifference to marginal investors. But to the economy as a whole, a preponderant desire to store wealth in the form of money means unemployment and depression which, far from being a matter of indifference, may point the way to revolution.

References for Further Reading

Keynes, J. M., *The General Theory of Employment, Interest and Money*, Chapters 13, 14, 15, 16 and 17. New York: Harcourt, Brace and Company, 1936.

——, *Monetary Reform*. New York: Harcourt, Brace and Company, 1924.

——, *A Treatise on Money*. New York: Harcourt, Brace and Company, 1930.

——, "The Theory of the Rate of Interest," in *The Lessons of Monetary Experience*, edited by A. D. Gayer, pages 145-152. New York: Farrar and Rinehart, Inc., 1937. Reprinted in *Readings in the Theory of Income Distribution*, selected by a Committee of the American Economic Association. Philadelphia: The Blakiston Company, 1946.

——, "Alternative Theories of the Rate of Interest," *The Economic Journal*, June, 1937, Vol. XLVII, pages 241-252.

——, "The 'Ex-Ante' Theory of the Rate of Interest," *The Economic Journal*, December, 1937, Vol. XLVII, pages 663-669.

——, "Mr. Keynes and 'Finance,'" *The Economic Journal*, June, 1938, Vol. XLVIII, pages 318-322.

Ellsworth, P. T., "Mr. Keynes on the Rate of Interest and the Marginal Efficiency of Capital," *The Journal of Political Economy*, December, 1936, Vol. XLIV, pages 767-790.

Hawtrey, R. G., "Alternative Theories of the Rate of Interest," *The Economic Journal*, September, 1937, Vol. XLVII, pages 436-443.

Lerner, A. P., "Alternative Formulations of the Theory of Interest," *The Economic Journal*, June, 1938, Vol. XLVIII, pages 211-230.

Lusher, D. W., "The Structure of Interest Rates and the Keynesian Theory of Interest," *The Journal of Political Economy*, April, 1942, Vol. L, pages 272-279.

Ohlin, Bertil, "Alternative Theories of the Rate of Interest," *The Economic Journal*, September, 1937, Vol. XLVII, pages 423-427.

Phillips, C. A., *Bank Credit*, especially Chapter III, "The Philosophy of Bank Credit." New York: The Macmillan Company, 1921.

Robertson, D. H., "Mr. Keynes and the Rate of Interest." *Essays in Monetary Theory*, Chapter I, pages 1-38. London: P. S. King and Son, Ltd., 1940. Reprinted in *Readings in the Theory of*

Income Distribution, selected by a Committee of the American Economic Association. Philadelphia: The Blakiston Company, 1946.

———, "Alternative Theories of the Rate of Interest," *The Economic Journal,* September, 1937, Vol. XLVII, pages 428-436.

Robinson, Joan, "The Concept of Hoarding," *The Economic Journal,* June, 1938, Vol. XLVIII, pages 231-236.

Smithies, Arthur, "The Quantity of Money and the Rate of Interest," *The Review of Economic Statistics,* February, 1943, Vol. XXV, pages 69-76.

Somers, H. M., "Monetary Policy and the Theory of Interest," *The Quarterly Journal of Economics,* May, 1941, Vol. LV, pages 488-507. Reprinted in the *Theory of Income Distribution,* selected by a Committee of the American Economic Association. Philadelphia: The Blakiston Company, 1946.

Wallich, H. C., "The Current Significance of Liquidity Preference," *The Quarterly Journal of Economics,* August, 1947, Vol. LXI pages 490-512.

CHAPTER 9

Money Wages and Prices

There is, perhaps, something a little perplexing in the apparent asymmetry between Inflation and Deflation. For whilst a deflation of effective demand below the level required for full employment will diminish employment as well as prices, an inflation of it above this level will merely affect prices.

J. M. Keynes, *The General Theory of Employment, Interest and Money*, page 291.

Introduction

In the first four books of the *General Theory*, Keynes states the essence of his theory of employment in terms of the assumption that money wages and prices are constant, i.e., that they do not change as employment and output rise and fall. In contending that employment as a whole is not determined by the wage bargains between workers and employers, Keynes argues that employment depends on effective demand rather than upon the level of money wages. However, all increases in effective demand are not consistent with further increases in employment. Above a certain level, further additions to aggregate effective demand will result in inflation. This point where aggregate employment becomes inelastic in response to further increases in effective demand is the point of full employment. Prices and money wages rise

206

sharply without increasing output and employment. In contrast to Keynes' position is the classical theory that employment depends upon the level of wages, both money and real wages, arrived at through bargaining between workers and employers. If there is unemployment, it is because wages are too high; unemployment can be eliminated if wage earners are willing to accept lower money wages and, in the classical view, lower real wages. In the absence of rigidities, workers will prefer to accept lower wages rather than remain unemployed.

In Book V on "Money Wages and Prices," Keynes drops the simplifying assumption of constant money wages in order to take account of the influence of wage rates on employment. For while wage rates are not a central consideration in Keynes' analysis, they can hardly be ignored in a complete theory of employment. Changes in money wages are capable of influencing employment and output through the repercussions which they exert on the principal determinants of employment—the rate of interest, the marginal efficiency of capital, and the propensity to consume. Since changes in money wages do react upon employment in a roundabout manner involving the principal determinants, it has been necessary to postpone a full discussion of the repercussions until after the main body of the general theory has been presented.

In the following discussion, the term "wages" or "wage rates," used without a qualifying adjective, refers to basic hourly wages. The term "real wages" refers to hourly money wages adjusted for a cost of living index. Where reference is made to the amount of wages received per week, or for any other period longer than an hour, the appropriate modifiers will be used, as "weekly wages," "annual wages," et cetera.

Money Wages and Employment

The classical argument

Although there is no doubt about the conclusion reached by the classical theory of the relation of wage-rate reductions to employment, there is some doubt as to the reasoning by which the classical economists arrive at their conclusion, which is, of course, that wage cuts will reduce unemployment and if pursued with vigor, will restore full employment. In its crudest form, the argument that wage cuts can eliminate unemployment runs as follows: In a competitive system, lower wages mean lower prices and lower prices result in an increase in sales. As more is sold, more will have to be produced and more workers employed. This increase in employment is assumed to be worthwhile because lower money wages are supposed to result in lower real wages, which in turn mean increased profits to entrepreneurs. Profits increase because the fall in wages is assumed to be greater than the drop in prices. This process of falling wages and prices accompanied by rising profits and employment continues until equilibrium is reached at full employment. Thus the classical equilibrium is a full employment equilibrium.

The main flaw in this argument that unemployment can be remedied by cutting wages arises from neglect of effective demand. It assumes that money wages can be reduced and leave aggregate effective demand unchanged. While it is almost certain that a reduction in the money wages of workers in a single industry, say the shoe industry, will increase employment in the shoe industry if there is no fall in the demand for shoes, it cannot safely be assumed that the demand for shoes will remain unaffected by a reduction in the wages of all workers throughout the economy. If the wages of shoe workers only are reduced, the costs of production of shoes will be reduced much more than the demand for shoes will decrease. For while workers in the shoe industry will have less money to spend for things in general, including shoes, workers in all other industries will be able to spend just as much for shoes as before, and if the price of shoes is reduced to correspond to the diminution in their costs of production, there will be a greater quantity of sales than before. Therefore, more employment will be needed to produce the added output of shoes. At the same time, the real income of shoe workers will be lowered as a result of the lessened money wage and the unchanged prices which shoe workers must pay for the things they buy (except for the negligible element of shoes).

So far we have dealt with a wage cut in a single industry only. The demand for shoes has not fallen because wages have been cut only in the shoe industry. However, the wage cut which is proposed by the classical analysis is a general wage cut affecting all workers. If all wages are reduced in the same proportion, the demand for shoes will be affected materially because a lesser volume of effective demand will be forthcoming out of the lowered money incomes. The demand curve for any one commodity like shoes depends upon the incomes received by workers in all industries, e.g., textiles, steel, automobiles, et cetera. Thus, the reasoning which is valid with respect to a single industry cannot be applied to the economy as a whole. Although a reduction of wages in a single industry will not materially reduce the demand for the product of that industry, neither will the increased employment in that industry do much toward relieving unemployment. In fact, increased employment in the shoe industry, for example, will tend to be offset, or may be more than offset, by decreased employment in all other industries resulting from less demand from shoe workers for all the things that shoe workers buy. Any benefits to employment that might result from lowered costs will be offset by reduced effective demand. Since one man's expenditure is another man's income, money incomes fall to the extent of the decrease in expenditure resulting from the economy-wide reduction in money wages. Costs may fall but so does effective demand. Money wages have fallen but there is no assurance that real wages have fallen since the general fall in prices resulting from the general cut in wages may be just sufficient for the two to offset each other. Real wages are left then about as they were before. Keynes does assume that prices fall in the same proportion as wage rates. On this assumption real wage rates will not fall, and if real wages do not

fall, profits cannot rise. Unless profits rise there is no incentive for entrepreneurs to increase output. We are brought
back once again to the conclusion that the classical analysis
suffers from the lack of a theory of effective demand. This
lack is revealed here in an attempt to apply to the economy
as a whole the logic of a theory designed to apply to a particular industry.

Another version or aspect of the classical theory of the
relation between wage cuts and employment rests upon the
belief that the demand for labor is elastic. Although each
worker previously employed will receive less per hour, the
total amount of wages paid will increase because the added
quantity of employment will more than offset the reduction
in hourly wage rates. As a result, total demand will be
greater, and more employment can be sustained at lower
than at higher wage rates. Even if profit per unit of output
does not increase, the total amount of profit is believed to
increase. This version of the wage-cut argument suffers from
the same basic weakness as all the other versions. It assumes
that supply creates its own demand for both consumption and
investment output. But if Keynes' rejection of Say's law is
valid, the wage-cut theory cannot be valid. While it is true
that the extra workers and others who share in the newly-
created income will bring extra buying power into the market for consumption output, they will not bring enough extra
demand to absorb all the output. Some of the extra income
earned will be saved because consumption demand will not
increase as much as income. If investment does not increase,
employment cannot increase. There is nothing automatic
about increases in investment. This is the simple and essential point of Keynes' rejection of the wage-cut argument.

Whether or not the above analysis gives an accurate picture of the classical reasoning is not the main issue. The ultimate difference between Keynes and the classical school on
the effects of wage cuts on employment resolves itself into a
practical matter. Keynes denies and the classical school asserts that wage cuts can be a significant factor in restoring

full employment when there is widespread unemployment. Although Keynes assumes for the purpose of analysis that prices fall in proportion to the fall in money wages, leaving real wage rates unchanged, his argument does not hinge on the validity of this assumption. He never denies the possibility of some decline in real wages as a consequence of money-wage cuts. He does not even say that wage cuts can never result in some increase in employment. What he does deny most emphatically is that wage cuts are of practical significance in restoring higher levels of employment. The chief weakness which he finds in the theories of those who differ on this important practical matter is their lack of a theory of effective demand.

Let us examine the classical argument for wage cuts in terms most favorable for its success. Suppose employers *believe* they can make higher profits by an all-around wage cut. If they believe they can make larger profits, they will be willing to expand their output and increase employment. Only if the expectations of higher profits prove illusory will they reduce output and employment to the former level. Business men might expect to make larger profits and be able to employ more workers after a general all-around wage cut because they are accustomed to looking at the economic process from the viewpoint of their own individual businesses. It is obvious to the business man that a wage cut will lower his costs. It is not so obvious that the wage cut, even though economy-wide in scope, will reduce the demand for his product. He may expect to sell a larger output at a greater net profit just because his own costs are lower.

Let us assume that entrepreneurs, in view of their expectations of larger profits, hire more workers and expand their output after cutting the wage rates paid to their workers. Will they realize the larger profits which they expect? As we have seen from the principle of effective demand, profits can increase only if:

(1) The marginal propensity to consume is equal to unity so that the increased income will go entirely into consump-

tion demand, thereby clearing the market of the increased supply of goods produced as a result of increased employment. Say's law that supply creates its own demand comes into its own when there is no gap between the increment of income and the increment of consumption. Hence, no investment is necessary to keep the process of production going at its existing level. However, this cannot happen because employment will not fall, except possibly temporarily, below the point where the marginal propensity to consume is unity. This assumption is contrary to the fundamental principle that as income increases, consumption increases by less than income. Some of the increased output of goods could be sold to consumers but there would remain an unsold quantity of goods equivalent to the gap between the increase in income and the increase in consumption.

(2) There is an increase in investment demand equal to the gap between the increased income and the increased consumption. Such an increase in investment demand will occur only if there is an increase in the marginal efficiency of capital relative to the rate of interest since these two factors are the determinants of the inducement to invest. There is nothing in the nature of a wage cut that will lead *directly* either to a rise in the marginal efficiency of capital or to a fall in the rate of interest. Therefore, the producers who have added to their output will be unable to sell what they have produced except at losses. The losses may be concentrated in a few firms producing investment goods or they may be scattered among all types of firms. In any event, the business losses will result in a contraction of output. As workers are laid off, their incomes fall and the initial increase in demand for consumers goods begins to contract. This process continues until output and employment are lowered to the former level at which profits are maximized (or losses minimized). The practical refutation of the classical logic reveals itself in the form of business losses. The proceeds from the added output have fallen short of the cost of producing that added output. There is no sustaining basis for the employment of a greater number of

workers as a consequence of the economy-wide cut in money wages.

Classical economic theory is primarily the theory of a particular industry and as such is not designed to answer the important question of the effects of wage cuts on employment because it lacks a theory of effective demand. Keynes' *general* theory, on the other hand, is specifically designed to come to grips with this problem. The answer arrived at thus far is that there is clearly no *direct* tendency for a cut in money-wage rates to increase employment. Employment can increase only if there is an increase in the propensity to consume, or an increase in the marginal efficiency of capital, or a fall in the rate of interest. Any validity in the classical position must come about through indirect effects of wage cuts upon one or more of these three independent variables. There are many repercussions of a general cut in money wages upon these three variables, but we shall confine our discussion to the most obvious and important ones.

(1) *Propensity to Consume:* The effect of wage cuts on the propensity to consume is more likely to be unfavorable than favorable. In so far as the distribution of income is affected, there will be a redistribution from wage earners to other income recipients, especially entrepreneurs and rentiers. This represents a shift from a high-consuming to a high-savings group and will tend to lower rather than raise the consumption function. A stimulating influence, however, will be the price reductions that accompany wage cuts. The fall in prices will increase the real purchasing power of people's fixed money *wealth* and thereby tend to increase the consumption function.

(2) *The Marginal Efficiency of Capital:* The repercussion of wage cuts upon the marginal efficiency of capital which offers the best chance of increasing employment will be the reaction on the expectations of entrepreneurs. If the reduction in wages is a once-and-for-all wage cut, that is, a reduction not expected to be followed by further reductions, the marginal efficiency of capital will be favorably affected.

Entrepreneurs will be stimulated to make alterations and additions to plant and equipment and to build new plant while wage rates are at a minimum level. If a reduction in wages is expected to be followed by further wage cuts at a later date, the marginal efficiency of capital will be lowered because entrepreneurs, in anticipation of further cuts, will tend to postpone investment until wage rates have fallen to still lower levels.

The conditions which would give practical importance to this repercussion in its favorable aspect are extremely difficult to attain, except in an authoritarian economy. Under any system of relatively free labor and management, there can be no guarantee that once wage cuts have begun they will not be followed by further wage cuts. Labor as a whole and management as a whole seldom if ever act together in such a policy, and if labor were organized in strong unions, strikes would undoubtedly mar attempts to increase employment by lowering wage rates. In the probable event that labor would not act on a common front in permitting wage reductions, the weakest unions would probably be cut first, and having revealed their weakness would be vulnerable to further cuts. A slowly sagging wage level will have a highly unfavorable effect on the marginal efficiency of capital. This is acknowledged even by those economists whose theoretical models are designed to demonstrate that employment can be increased by lowering money wages.[1] A rigid money-wage policy would probably have a more favorable influence upon the marginal efficiency of capital than a policy in which wages sag slowly to lower and lower levels. If it is true that, as a matter of practical policy, a once-and-for-all wage cut is difficult to attain, especially under non-authoritarian conditions, it follows that the effect of lower money wages on the marginal efficiency of capital does not appear to offer much hope as a means for decreasing unemployment in a depression in democratic economies.

---

1. See A. C. Pigou, "Real and Money Wage Rates in Relation to Unemployment," *The Economic Journal*, September, 1937, Vol. XLVII, No. 187, page 405.

(3) *The Rate of Interest:* The most favorable repercussion of a general wage cut upon employment arises in connection with its possible influence in lowering the rate of interest. A fall in wages will normally be accompanied by a fall in prices. Lower wages and lower prices reduce the amount of money needed to carry on transactions (M_1). Assuming the total supply of money (M) remains constant, a lessening of the demand for transactions (M_1) will increase the amount of money available to satisfy the speculative motive (M_2), and this, as the preceding analysis of interest and money indicates, will tend to lower the rate of interest. The greater the fall in wages and prices, the greater the quantity of money released from active balances to inactive balances and, therefore, the greater the fall in the interest rate. The extent of the fall in the interest rate will depend not only upon the increase in money available to satisfy the liquidity preference for the speculative motive but also upon the shape of the liquidity function. If the liquidity function is elastic, the fall in interest rates will be less than if it is inelastic. Analytically, the process whereby lower wage rates lead to lower interest rates is no different from that whereby the total quantity of money (M) is increased in order to increase the amount of money available for inactive balances (M_2).

Although a flexible wage policy is *analytically* an alternative to a flexible money policy, there are important practical difficulties with the former which do not apply to monetary policy. To be successful as a check to unemployment, the reduction in wages in time of depression must be general, all-around, and simultaneous, and since labor as a whole does not bargain with employers as a whole, it is virtually impossible to execute such a policy in a democratic society with strong, independent, labor unions. Consequently, even though workers knew that wage cuts would mean more jobs for labor in general, in the absence of over-all collective bargaining, self-interest would lead any one sector of the labor supply to resist reductions in money wages. Those who accepted wage cuts first and in the greatest amount would suffer relative to other groups who resisted longer and finally acceded to lesser cuts.

Even if all wage earners could be persuaded to accept a policy of equal, all-around, money-wage reductions, they would be acting contrary to their own best interest unless all non-labor incomes were also reduced in the same proportion. Rentiers receiving income from bonds and other forms of contractual securities containing promises to pay fixed in terms of money would gain a real advantage at the expense of the working class if the latter accepted wage reductions while contractual incomes remained inviolable. Since sanctity of contract is one of the foundations of a business civilization, it is highly improbable that this condition essential to justice and to voluntary acceptance on the part of wage earners would be realized. Thus even the working class as a whole— at least the employed part of it—would be acting contrary to its best interests if it agreed to accept money-wage reductions of the type suggested by the classical theory. Keynes pointed to all these difficulties at the time of Britain's return to the gold standard under Chancellor of the Exchequer Winston Churchill in 1925.

Another strong objection to money-wage cuts arises because a lower price level increases the real burden of debt, both private and public. Entrepreneurs who are heavily in debt will find themselves saddled with still heavier real charges when prices fall and the money size of their obligations does not fall. A lower price level will increase the real burden of taxation required to service and repay the public debt. If the public debt is large, this becomes a major objection to any deflationary policy like wage and price reductions. The adverse effect of the increase in the real burden of debt will be somewhat offset by the favorable influence on the propensity to consume arising from the tendency for a fall in prices to stimulate spending out of fixed money wealth.

Should wages be increased in depression?

So far we have examined the effects of wage cuts on employment in depression. At the opposite pole is what may be called the "trade unionist argument" that the way out of depression is to raise money wages. Higher wages, it is argued, will increase purchasing power and employment. So far as the *direct* effects upon employment are concerned, this argument suffers from the same faults as the one for wage cuts. Higher wages will increase costs and prices by an amount that will offset the nominal increase in purchasing power. Real wages will remain at the same level. There will be an increase in nominal effective demand but no increase in real effective demand and therefore no increase in employment on a continuing basis. There is nothing in the nature of a wage increase to stimulate more demand for investment, and, as Keynes' theory of effective demand tells us, there can be no increase in employment unless there is an increase in the demand for investment sufficient to fill the gap between increased income and increased consumption.

The *indirect* repercussions of a rise in wage rates will probably be even less favorable to employment than wage cuts. While the effect may be to increase the propensity to consume through a favorable influence upon the distribution of income, both the marginal efficiency of capital and the rate of interest will tend to be influenced in a manner unfavorable to employment. An increase in wages in the depths of a depression when business is suffering losses from costs in excess of revenues is hardly likely to restore the confidence of the business community in the prospects for profitable operations. Of course, the announcement that higher wage rates are to go into effect at a specific future date may temporarily stimulate entrepreneurs to complete their investments before the higher wage rates become effective. After the higher rates go into effect, however, investment will fall back to less than its previous level to the extent that improvements that might have been spread evenly over time have been bunched in order to beat the higher cost period.

With regard to the rate of interest, the effect of higher wage rates will be unfavorable. Higher wages and higher prices will increase the requirements for money for transactions and, in the absence of an expansion in the total quantity of money, will drain the quantity available as a store of value. The interest rate will tend to rise with the consequent unfavorable reaction upon investment, income, and employment.

Conclusions on a flexible wage policy in relation to a flexible money policy

The foregoing examination of a flexible wage policy leads to the conclusion that neither wage cuts nor wage boosts are effective measures for increasing employment in depression. At best, a flexible wage policy is no better than a flexible monetary policy. In the most likely circumstances under which a flexible wage policy would have to be carried out in a non-authoritarian society, a flexible wage policy would be much less satisfactory than a flexible monetary policy.

It is important to view Keynes' conclusions on wage policy in the broad perspective of his position as a theorist and as an advocate of monetary policy. What his analysis amounts to, after all is said and done, is simply that a flexible monetary policy is an alternative to and on both economic and political grounds is preferable to a flexible wage policy. He acknowledges that money-wage cuts may increase employment slightly, but his main contention is that anything which might be accomplished by cutting wages can, as a matter of practical policy, be accomplished better by monetary policy.

Although Keynes' theory opposes the idea that labor is to blame for unemployment, his views do not constitute a defense of organized labor in any positive or partisan sense. This is evidenced by his rejection of money-wage increases as well as money-wage decreases. It is further evidenced by his acceptance in the *General Theory* of the classical view that an increase in employment will be accompanied by a fall in *real* wage rates, a conclusion which follows from his assumption of the principle of diminishing returns in the short run. When statistical investigations indicated that real wages did not in fact fall as employment rose, Keynes acknowledged he had accepted too readily the classical assumption in regard to falling real wages. However, if in fact real wages did not decline, he said his practical conclusions would be strengthened and his theory simplified.[2]

Although real wages may not rise in the short run, they will rise in the long run as a consequence of the increase in output per man hour which results from the greater amount of equipment per worker. Higher real wages may take the form either of rising money wages with stable prices, or of stable money wages with gradually falling prices. Keynes prefers the former of these two alternatives because a policy of rising money wages combined with a stable price level will (a) have a favorable influence upon the expectations of investors and hence upon the inducement to invest, (b) diminish the real burden of debt without inequities to the lending classes, who will receive in payment of their loans money of the same value as that which they gave up on advancing the loans, (c) give greater psychological encouragement to the active, producing, working class than will real wages in the form of constant money wages and falling prices, and (d) facilitate the transfer of resources out of declining industries into growing industries by raising money wages in the latter without having to lower them in the former (p. 271).

Nature of the issue between Keynes' theory and the classical theory

The foregoing discussion has referred to some points of disagreement between Keynes and the classical economists. In addition to the technical points already discussed, these issues raise the important question of the nature of controversies in economic theory. The reader should be warned that economic theory is a subtle discipline full of pitfalls for the unwary. When economists disagree in a fundamental way,

---

2. See "Relative Movements of Real Wages and Output," *The Economic Journal*, March, 1939, Vol. XLIX, No. 193, pages 40-41. In this article, Keynes states that Chapter 2 of the *General Theory* "is the portion of my book which most needs to be revised." *Ibid.*, page 40 n.

they seldom are able to settle their differences in a mutually satisfactory manner. Between the classical theory and Keynes' theory there are fundamental differences in the explanation of unemployment. The classical theory attributes unemployment to wages being too high (i.e., higher than they would be under thorough-going competition among wage earners), and Keynes attributes unemployment to an insufficiency of effective demand. What these two different positions mean in objective, operational terms is that the classical school sees the cure for unemployment in reductions in wage rates whereas Keynes sees the cure in an expansionary monetary and fiscal program designed to increase the volume of effective demand. This controversy concerning the theory of unemployment between Keynes and Professor Pigou, the chief representative of the classical school on this issue, has never been settled in any satisfactory manner despite long and drawn-out discussion.[3] However, when Professor Pigou finally conceded that he favors attacking the problem of unemployment by manipulating demand rather than by manipulating wages, the controversy for all practical purposes was settled in favor of Keynes.[4] The real issue between Keynes and Professor Pigou has always been one of intuition about the relative importance of things in the actual world. Keynes has triumphed because he possessed a superior insight into practical affairs combined with a remarkable ability to develop his insights into a systematic body of economic theory.

The way in which intuition or insight into practical affairs

---

3. In addition to the several books by Professor Pigou already referred to and Keynes' *General Theory*, especially chapters 2 and 19, see Pigou, "Real and Money Wage Rates in Relation to Unemployment," *The Economic Journal*, September, 1937, Vol. XLVII, No. 187, pages 405-422; Keynes, "Professor Pigou on Money Wages in Relation to Unemployment," *Ibid.*, pages 743-745; N. Kaldor, "Professor Pigou on Money Wages in Relation to Unemployment," *Ibid.*, pages 745-753; Pigou, "Money Wages in Relation to Unemployment," *The Economic Journal*, March, 1938, Vol. XLVIII, No. 189, pages 134-138; and Keynes, "Relative Movements of Real Wages and Output," *The Economic Journal*, March, 1939, Vol. XLIX, No. 193, pages 34-51.

4. See Pigou, *Lapses from Full Employment*, page v.

influences the formulation of economic theory may be further illustrated. A theory is an attempt to give a simplified explanation of some relatively complex area of experience. The process of simplification involves the selection of those aspects of experience which are regarded as most important in relation to the problem at hand, in this case unemployment. The theories which emerge are not and cannot be complete pictures of the actual world. They are simplified pictures, or models, of the economist's idea of what are the most important and relevant considerations. As Professor Pigou himself points out, the question whether the elements in the model are those which are most important in the actual world is a matter of intuition.[5] Quite naturally, each economist builds a model of the elements which his intuition evaluates as most important, although in model building some individuals are more heavily influenced by traditional approaches than others. The relative merits of the two theoretical explanations, or models, will depend to a large extent upon the relative acuteness of the intuition of the two economists in question. The logic of both models may be impeccable but their relevance may be worlds apart. Here the all-important point is that Keynes was endowed with a remarkably keen intuition or insight into problems of actual experience. This fact more than anything else appears to explain the great acclaim that his *General Theory* has received. Keynes' theory is not necessarily more logical nor otherwise more nearly perfect in terms of internal consistency than Professor Pigou's theory. It is just more relevant. Professor Pigou, on the other hand, feels, or at least used to feel, that his model contains those elements which are most important in the actual world. Professional and popular opinion does not appear to agree with him in this belief. Keynes' theory is considered of revolutionary significance because it stands for a course of action which is practicable in the modern world. It accepts collective bar-

---

5. "Real and Money Wage Rates in Relation to Unemployment," *The Economic Journal*, September, 1937, Vol. XLVII. No. 187, page 422.

gaining, minimum-wage legislation, and unemployment insurance, and points to a way of escape from unemployment
through increasing effective demand.

The Theory of Prices

Integration of monetary theory with the theory of value and output

The theory of prices, as this phrase is used in economic
analysis, is a study of the way in which changes in the quantity of money react upon the price level. Individual prices
are individual values expressed in terms of money, and the
level of prices in general is related in some systematic manner to the total quantity of money in the economic system. In
general, this relationship is such that an increase in the quantity of money is associated with a rise in the level of prices,
and a reduction in the quantity of money with a fall in the
level of prices. The details of this relationship between the
quantity of money and the level of prices are studied in connection with what economists call the quantity theory of
money.

Keynes' theory of prices, like the rest of his theory, is of a
more general nature than is the traditional doctrine.[6] He
accepts the traditional conclusion that increases in the quantity of money will be associated with increases in the level of
prices, but differs fundamentally from the traditional analysis of the causal process by which changes in the quantity of
money react upon the level of prices. From the foregoing
chapters, it is clear that the initial impact of an increase in
the quantity of money is to lower the rate of interest by in-

---

6. Keynes' purpose in referring to the traditional theory of prices is to contrast his own position with the generally accepted theory laid down in treatises
on the principles of economics. He does not attempt to assess the theory of
money and prices contained in the work of specialists in monetary and business cycle theory. Typical of the type of theory against which Keynes directs
his criticism is the work of Professor Taussig, who says, "We may brush aside
not only the notion that interest arises from the use of money but that the
rate of interest depends on the quantity of money. More money makes higher
prices, not lower interest." *Principles of Economics*, Fourth Edition. Vol. II,
page 8. New York: The Macmillan Company, 1939.

creasing the amount of money available to satisfy liquidity preference for the speculative motive. A lowering of the rate of interest tends to increase effective demand for investment, which in turn is associated with rising income, employment, and output. As income, employment, and output begin to rise, prices also begin to rise because of increasing labor costs resulting from the enhanced bargaining position of labor, diminishing returns in the short run, bottlenecks, and other reasons to be examined in this chapter. Employment and prices both rise, with the emphasis at first almost exclusively on increases in employment but shifting more and more to prices as the point of full employment is approached. Once full employment has been attained, no further increases in employment are possible, by definition, and further increases in effective demand become truly inflationary in the sense that they spend themselves entirely in rising prices.

Prices of individual commodities as well as the general price level of output as a whole correspond closely to costs of production, which change with variations in the volume of output. The general level of prices multiplied by output at any time determines the quantity of money absorbed in the active balances or active circulation (M_1). The rest of the total supply of money spills over into inactive balances (M_2), where, in conjunction with the state of liquidity preference, it determines the rate of interest. M_2 is a residual quantity which, with given prices and output, absorbs the increases and decreases in the total supply of money. Changes in the quantity of money do not affect prices directly, because prices are determined primarily by costs of production. The initial impact of changes in the total quantity of money falls on the rate of interest rather than on prices. The level of prices is affected indirectly through the effect of changes in the quantity of money upon the rate of interest acting as one of the three main determinants of the volume of output and employment (the other two main determinants being the marginal efficiency of capital and the propensity to consume). As output changes, costs of production change, and prices

adjust to changing costs of production. The demand for money
for transactions increases *because* prices and output rise.
Prices do not rise directly in response to increases in the
quantity of money, although they are indirectly influenced by
such increases. Keynes' analysis is sometimes spoken of as the
"contra-quantity theory of causation" because it treats rises
in prices as a cause of the increase in the quantity of money
for transactions instead of treating the increases in the quantity of money (for transactions) as a cause of the rise in
prices. Of course, the distinction between money for transactions and money as a store of value is absolutely essential to
this contra-quantity causation.

The great merit of Keynes' theory of prices is that it integrates monetary theory with the theory of value, which means
that it integrates monetary theory with what has been regarded as the main body of the principles of economics. The
theory of value teaches us that price, which is value expressed
in terms of money, is governed by the conditions of supply
and demand. In connection with supply and demand, the most
important concepts are marginal cost and marginal revenue
(which determine the extent to which output will be carried
since their equality designates the point of maximum profit),
and elasticity of short-period supply and elasticity of demand
(which determine the relative changes in output which correspond to relative changes in price of the commodity in
question). When Keynes comes to the theory of prices in general (price levels), he still emphasizes cost of production,
elasticity of supply, demand, and the other concepts which are
important in the theory of value or individual price. Prices
rise as costs of production rise; costs of production rise partly
because of the inelasticity of short-period supply of output
and employment; and the theory of demand is all-important
in calling forth the increased output and employment.

In addition to integrating the theory of value with the
theory of money, Keynes also integrates the theory of output
with the theory of money. In fact, it is through the theory of
output that value theory and monetary theory are brought

into juxtaposition with each other. For changes in the quantity of money are capable of changing the level of output. As the level of output varies, costs change, and as costs vary, values (prices) are affected. Since the theory of money is part and parcel of the theory of interest, and interest is intimately related to expectations concerning the future, it follows that discussions of the effects of changing expectations about the future must be stated in monetary terms. The emphasis shifts to money as a store of value, as a link between the present and the future. This emphasis is lacking in the traditional presentations of the general economic theory of value and output and monetary theory, and accounts to no small degree for the lack of integration of monetary theory with general economic theory in classical economics. The traditional statement of the theory of prices overlooks the influence of the quantity of money in the determination of the rate of interest, and thereby upon output, and goes directly from increases in the quantity of money to increases in the level of prices. This important omission in traditional economic theory arises from its assumption of full employment of resources. If full employment is assumed from the beginning, there is no possibility that an increase in the quantity of money, or anything else for that matter, can increase employment and output (in the short run). In ruling out by assumption changes in output, there is no need in the theory of price levels for the concepts that figure so prominently in the theory of value, such as marginal cost, elasticity of supply, and the theory of demand. In a sense, there is no occasion for integrating the theory of value with the theory of money. Since money cannot affect employment, it can influence only prices. This leads to the conclusion that *all* increases in the quantity of money tend to be inflationary, a conclusion quite valid under the assumption that resources are fully employed, but a nonsense conclusion when this special assumption is dropped. The theory of prices becomes nothing more than a theory of price levels, that is, of the value of money. Money is essentially a lubricant which is useful because it is more efficient than barter. The extremely important relations between changes in the quantity of money and changes in employment are ignored. The theory of the value of individual commodities is divorced from the theory of prices of commodities in general. Monetary theory remains outside the main body of economic theory, which is concerned with value and output.

It is to be recognized that there were some economists before Keynes who were not guilty of separating the theory of money from the theory of value and output, but this characterization holds true of the presentations found in treatises on the principles of economics. Perhaps it is best to make as few representations as possible as to just what the traditional position regarding the theory of prices and money has been because any positive assertion may be challenged on some plausible grounds. Whatever the traditional presentation may have been, it is clear that a theory based upon the assumption that unemployment is the normal circumstance and full employment the exception offers an opportunity for bringing together the theory of money and prices with the theory of value and output.

The reformulated quantity theory of money

It is possible by introducing a sufficient number of qualifications to formulate a simplified version of what may be called the reformed quantity theory of money. If there is perfectly elastic supply of productive factors when there is unemployment and perfectly inelastic supply when there is full employment, and if the increase in effective demand is proportional to the increase in the quantity of money, then the reformed quantity theory which takes into account the condition of unemployment as well as the special case of full employment may be stated as follows: "So long as there is unemployment, *employment* will change in the same proportion as the quantity of money; and when there is full employment, *prices* will change in the same proportion as the quantity of

money." (p. 296)[7] Before introducing the necessary qualifications to this reformulation of the quantity theory, let us
state the practical implication of this proposition in its barest,
unqualified form. It tells us when to fear and when not to
fear inflation. It tells us that, subject to the qualifying assumptions, inflation is not to be feared when there is large-
scale unemployment; and it tells us that once full employment has been attained, inflation does become a threat. Thus
it relieves us of the dread of inflation when we are plagued
with mass unemployment, and it warns us that once we have
conquered unemployment we must be on guard against inflation. Those who cry "inflation" in criticizing policies of
monetary expansion during the depths of depression like that
of the 1930's are either guilty of political propaganda or
lack understanding of the most elementary truths of monetary
theory and policy. For what is needed in depression is expansion of output, and the way to expand output is to increase
effective demand. Hence, monetary expansion by means of
public investment, low interest rates, and the encouragement
of spending rather than not-spending are all part of economic
policy designed to increase output and employment in a
period of depression.

The proposition that changes in the quantity of money will
affect employment when there is unemployment and will affect prices when there is full employment is no more than a
rough approximation to the truth. It is a generalized statement subject to so many qualifications that there is reasonable
doubt as to its usefulness as a leading proposition of monetary theory. Prices may rise substantially before full employment is reached, especially in the later stages of expansion.
These are not mere chance increases arising from fortuitous
circumstances. The increases in prices that occur as output
expands are more or less inevitably associated with expanding output and can be explained in terms of well-established
principles of economic analysis. The most important reasons

7. Keynes, *The General Theory of Employment, Interest and Money.* New
York: Harcourt, Brace and Co., Inc., 1936.

why costs and prices rise as employment increases are (1) the enhanced bargaining position of workers, (2) diminishing returns in the short run, and (3) bottlenecks in production.

(1) *Enhanced Bargaining Position of Workers as Unemployment Declines:* An increase in the demand for labor will tend to increase the money wages of workers. Both organized and unorganized workers, and especially the former, find themselves in a better bargaining position when employment is rising. The extent to which money-wage rates will rise depends, of course, upon the relative bargaining strengths of employers and wage earners, but regardless of their relative positions, a growing scarcity of labor will tend to enhance the position of wage earners and to weaken that of the employer, just as growing unemployment tends to have the opposite effect in periods of contraction. Entrepreneurs will be more willing to meet the demands of workers when business is improving because it is feasible to pass on increased costs by raising prices. This is true not only of competitive but also of various forms of monopolistic pricing. Monopolists and oligopolists may even welcome wage increases because they can use them as an excuse for price gouging which would otherwise be inexpedient because public opinion, which will tolerate higher prices when wages rise, will not tolerate unprovoked price increases. It is always easy to confuse the public on the question of how much a given wage boost will increase unit costs of production. The steel industry seems to have used the wage increase granted coal miners in 1947 to increase steel prices several times more than was justified on a basis of increases in the cost of coal.

Even though money-wage rates will rise, real-wage rates for workers in general will not rise because the increase in prices will be more than sufficient to offset higher money-wage rates. However, any particular group of workers which can push up its money-wage rates more rapidly than workers in general will gain at the expense of other workers and may be able to increase their money-wage rates more rapidly than the cost-of-living and thereby increase their real-wage rates. Because of this possibility, there is pressure on trade-union leaders to gain increases larger than the average granted to labor in general. To a considerable extent, the success of labor leaders will be measured in terms of their ability to gain larger concessions than other labor leaders. As full employment is approached, the inflationary dangers from competing labor groups increase. As a result there is a strong case for a unified labor movement rather than many different labor organizations, each of which competes with the other to secure better bargains. Sir William Beveridge has proposed a single national labor organization as a prerequisite for a guaranteed full employment program which is to avoid the danger of inflation.

Organized workers as a whole will probably gain larger concessions than unorganized workers as a whole. In the United States, where scarcely one third of the total number of wage and salary earners are members of organized labor groups, the opportunity for organized labor to get more than a proportionate share of the total increases in money wages is especially good. Of course, unorganized workers are also in a better bargaining position in an expanding labor market, but in relation to union labor they will probably find themselves falling behind. The distinction between wage rates and amounts of wages is also to be noted. Even though real-wage rates go down, workers who are employed more hours per week or more weeks per year may receive a larger annual real income. Workers who were previously unemployed will benefit from new-found employment, and previously employed workers whose real wage per hour may be going down because prices are rising more rapidly than money-wage rates, may work enough additional hours to gain a larger real wage per week or per year.

Increases in wage rates which occur during a period of expanding output will not be continuous but periodic, depending on the duration of trade-union contracts, and on the political strategy of trade-union leaders and employers. Increases in wages and prices will tend to be greatest in the sectors of the economy where expansion is most rapid. For example, if expansion begins in the construction industry, building trades-men and those working for firms which supply construction materials will be in a more strategic bargaining position than workers in other industries.

(2) *Diminishing Returns in the Short Run:* Prices will rise before full employment is attained also because of the tendency toward diminishing returns in the short run. Dimin-ishing return means that cost per unit of output rises as the volume of output increases. The short run is a period in which the amount of equipment is assumed to be given. When more men are employed to operate the existing equipment, there will tend to be a less than proportionate increase in output. If to start with, there is a large amount of idle equipment of the best quality as well as large numbers of idle workers, the tendency toward diminishing return will develop slowly. This will be especially characteristic of large-scale industries which operate on a mass-production basis. There may be a range, in fact, over which unit variable costs will decline. But neither men nor machines are of equal efficiency, and if it is assumed that the more efficient men and equipment are the first to be employed, then those subsequently employed will add a less than proportionate return. If the newly employed workers are less efficient than those previously employed and if the less efficient are paid the same time-wage as the more effi-cient, then the prime cost per unit of output must rise even though the equipment is of equal efficiency. If workers are re-warded in strict proportion to their efficiency, there will be con-stant unit cost rather than increasing unit cost. If the additional machinery put into use is less efficient than that already in service, increasing costs per unit of output will result even if the workers are rewarded in strict proportion to their effi-ciency. A machine with a greater spoilage of raw material fed into it is a typical illustration of an increasing cost situation caused by the employment of less efficient equipment; or a

machine which operates more slowly than other machines will not permit a worker to produce as much output as an equally efficient worker using more efficient machines. What is called "stand-by equipment" is less efficient, as a rule, and is placed in use only in emergencies when no other equipment is at hand and there is no time to procure more efficient machinery or when the demand for the particular output is not expected to continue long enough to justify the procurement of new equipment. Thus the lack of uniformity or homogeneity of resources is one important reason why the cost of production and the price based upon cost of production will rise as employment increases.

(3) *"Bottlenecks" in Production:* Even if all resources were perfectly homogeneous, increasing costs from diminishing returns would set in prior to full employment because all types of resources would not reach a point of full employment simultaneously. Skilled laborers may be fully employed when there still remain many unskilled workers in the ranks of the unemployed. Steelworkers may be out of work because of a temporary shortage of coal arising perhaps from the reluctance of workers to become coal miners; building may be held up because of a scarcity of plumbing materials; automobiles because of a shortage of rubber for tires, et cetera. Full employment of all resources requires that resources be available in certain proportions, which can be varied within limits, but beyond these limits real bottlenecks exist because the substitution of one resource for another is beyond the limits of technical feasibility. This disproportionality of available resources is especially serious in a recovery that follows a prolonged and severe depression like that of the 1930's. During that depression, there was a great decline in the number of skilled laborers because of death, retirement, loss of skill through idleness, and the small number of new apprentices coming into the skilled trades during the depressed years. In the upswing of the business cycle in the spring of 1937, an acute shortage of skilled workmen developed at a time when there were millions of unemployed

among the unskilled workers of the nation. Bottlenecks are accentuated by a rapid increase in output. In the great defense and war expansion from 1940 to 1943, shortages developed in many types of labor, materials, and equipment. Serious bottlenecks were experienced in aluminum, magnesium, steel, rubber, and in many other commodities. When a bottleneck is reached in one line of production, the price of the item in question tends to rise sharply, in the absence of price control, even though other prices are rising only gently. In the short run, supply is inelastic in the sense that output does not respond immediately to increases in prices. The increase in demand is diverted into a rise in price until the output has time to expand to meet the demand. Increases in prices of this sort are referred to as "bottleneck inflation."

"Bottleneck inflation" differs in a fundamental way from the general inflation that accompanies full employment of all other resources. For given sufficient time, bottlenecks can be broken by an increase in the output of the item in question. If there are no more workers available of a certain skill, more can be trained given sufficient time. If there is insufficient aluminum capacity, more can be built. If there is not enough rubber, more can be produced. The length of time that must elapse before the bottleneck is broken will, of course, depend upon technical considerations. Wartime shortages of skilled labor were met rather quickly in the United States because they were attacked with vigor and intelligence. The rubber shortage dragged on for years while various interest groups fought over who should supply the synthetic raw materials to replace the unavailable supplies of natural rubber. The increases in prices which result from particular shortages as compared with general shortages occur because resources are not perfectly interchangeable.

These are the chief factors which account for rising costs and rising prices in the phase of expansion short of full employment. Generally speaking, in contemporary industrial economies the rise in money wages resulting from the enhanced demand for labor is probably a more important factor contributing to higher prices than the tendency toward diminishing return.[8] The quantitative importance of the two factors will vary, however, with the scale of production, and the relation between costs and prices will vary with the degree of competition and monopoly, which in turn is likely to be related to the scale of production. Throughout the *General Theory*, Keynes takes as "given" the degree of monopoly and competition (p. 245). For the purposes of his analysis, competition and monopoly are not strategic factors. His theory of unemployment and of prices does not depend in any way on the presence or absence of either monopoly or competition. If the theory of effective demand is valid, unemployment would exist even though there were pure competition or absolute monopoly. Keynes' assumption that prices will rise when costs of production rise does not require the further premise that prices are equal to costs of production. Under competitive conditions prices will tend to equal total unit cost, and under monopolistic conditions prices will tend to exceed total unit cost. A monopolist will increase his prices when costs rise almost as readily as a competitive firm. The quantitative relation of costs to prices does depend, however, on the scale of production and the degree of monopoly. Under large-scale enterprise, the economies of full utilization which accompany expanding output may offset the increases in wage rates over a wide range of output. The tendency for prices not to rise because the two component parts of price tend to offset each other is reinforced if industrial producers are content with a smaller profit per unit of output as output increases. Where there is imperfection of competition, producers tend to maintain prices when output is falling and to increase prices by less than the full amount of the increases in unit cost when output is rising.[9] Hence, under monopolistic

8. See Keynes' post-*General Theory* article, "Relative Movements of Real Wages and Output," *The Economic Journal*, March, 1939, Vol. XLIX, No. 193, page 46.

9. *Loc. cit.*

conditions prices will tend to move with costs, but they tend to move by lesser amounts, and if total costs do not vary because higher wage costs are offset by lower non-wage costs, there may be a considerable stability of unit costs and a still greater stability of prices over a wide range of output. Exceptions occur in boom periods when producers are overwhelmed with orders they cannot fill. In these exceptional periods, wage boosts may be used as an excuse for price gouging, that is, for increasing prices much more than costs have increased. Wage increases become the occasion rather than the cause of unreasonable price increases.

In small-scale enterprise, diminishing return tends to act more strongly and competition is more effective. Costs move up and down with increases and decreases in output, and prices tend to be even more flexible than costs. Only in the long run does the equality of prices to total unit cost tend to prevail.

The two preceding paragraphs are in the nature of elaborations of the general thesis that in the early stages of expansion when there are abundant supplies of efficient resources, the general level of prices will probably not rise very much. As full employment is approached, the pressure for costs and prices to rise increases progressively because the bargaining strength of labor is greatly enhanced and the remaining unemployed resources become less and less efficient as the "bottom of the barrel" is scraped. The number of bottlenecks multiplies rapidly. Shortages are more and more difficult to overcome as substitutes are more difficult to find because the most satisfactory substitutes have already been fully employed, or nearly so. But as long as there is unemployment, increases in effective demand will increase employment. When full employment is at last attained, further increases in effective demand no longer increase employment. They spend themselves entirely on increases in prices. A condition of true inflation sets in as soon as full employment is reached. One of Keynes' definitions of full employment is the point beyond which output proves inelastic in response to further increases in effective demand.

As Keynes points out, there is a lack of symmetry on the two sides of the level at which true inflation sets in. A reduction in effective demand below this critical level reduces both prices and output, but above this point only prices (not output) increase. This lack of symmetry is explained by the resistance which workers and other factors of production offer to reductions in their money rewards. Money wages do not fall without limit as soon as unemployment appears. The resistance of wage earners to reductions in wages in conditions of unemployment gives a degree of stability to wages and prices which would not otherwise exist (p. 304). This does not mean, however, that unemployment could be cured if wages were flexible in a downward direction. Unemployment arises from a deficiency of effective demand which does not depend on the flexibility of wages and prices.

Long-term price movements

Even if full employment without inflation can be achieved, there remains the important question whether, with rising productivity per man hour and falling unit costs of production, prices in the long run should fall as costs fall or remain constant as money (and real) wages rise. Keynes recommends as the desirable policy a stabilization of prices, within limits, and rising money wages. The reasons for this preference have already been indicated in connection with the discussion of money wages.

References for Further Reading

Keynes, J. M., *The General Theory of Employment, Interest and Money*, Chapters 2, 19, and 21. New York: Harcourt, Brace and Company, 1936.

———, "Relative Movements of Real Wages and Output," *The Economic Journal*, March, 1939, Vol. XLIX, pages 34-51.

———, "Professor Pigou on Money Wages in Relation to Unemployment," *The Economic Journal*, December, 1937, Vol. XLVII, pages 743-745.

Bangs, R. B., "Wage Reductions and Employment," *The Jou nal of Political Economy*, April, 1942, Vol. L, pages 251-271.

Dunlop, J. T., "The Movement of Real and Money Wage Rates," *The Economic Journal*, September, 1938, Vol. XLVIII, pages 413-434.

———, "The Supply and Demand Functions for Labor," *The American Economic Review, Papers and Proceedings*, May, 1948, Vol. XXXVIII, pages 340-350.

Ellis, Howard S., "Some Fundamentals in the Theory of Velocity," *The Quarterly Journal of Economics*, May, 1938, Vol. LII, pages 431-472.

Hansen, A. H., "Cost Functions and Full Employment," *The Amer- can Economic Review*, September, 1947, Vol. XXXVII, pages 552-565.

Lerner, A. P., "The Relation of Wage Policies and Price Policies," *The American Economic Review, Papers and Proceedings*, March, 1939, Vol. XXIX, pages 158-169.

Marget, Arthur W., *The Theory of Prices*, 2 volumes. New York: Prentice-Hall, Inc., 1938 and 1942.

Pigou, A. C., "Real and Money Wages in Relation to Unemploy- ment," *The Economic Journal*, September, 1937, Vol. XLVII, pages 405-422.

———, "Money Wages in Relation to Unemployment," *The Eco- nomic Journal*, March, 1938, Vol. XLVIII, pages 134-138.

———, *The Theory of Unemployment*, especially Part V, Chapter III, "Wage Policy as a Determinant of Unemployment." Lon- don: Macmillan and Co., Ltd., 1933.

———, *Employment and Equilibrium*. London: Macmillan and Co., Ltd., 1941.

———, *Lapses from Full Employment*. London: Macmillan and Co., Ltd., 1945.

Rosenstein-Rodan, P. N., "The Coordination of the General Theories of Money and Price," *Economica*, August, 1936, Vol. III (new series), pages 257-280.

Tobin, James, "Money Wage Rates and Employment," in *The New Economics*, edited by S. E. Harris, Chapter XL, pages 572-587. New York: Alfred A. Knopf, 1947.

Sweezy, Alan R., "Wages and Investment," *The Journal of Political Economy*, February, 1942, Vol. L, pages 117-129.

CHAPTER 10

War and Postwar Inflation

An individual cannot by saving more protect himself from the consequences of inflation if others do not follow his example; just as he cannot protect himself from accidents by obeying the rule of the road if others disregard it. We have here the perfect opportunity for social action, where everyone can be protected by making a certain rule of behaviour universal.

J. M. Keynes, *How to Pay for the War,* page 70.

THUS FAR the theory of prices has been discussed only in relation to circumstances of less than full employment. In this connection, Keynes makes his most important contribution to the theory of prices by integrating the theory of value (individual prices) with the theory of money (price levels) and output. Prices are assumed to correspond closely to costs of production. Prior to full employment, prices rise because of increasing costs which are associated with higher money wages and with diminishing returns as the scale of output increases in the short run. After full employment is attained, further increases in effective demand spend themselves entirely in raising prices. Thus full employment is the point at which true inflation sets in and inflation is in this sense a phenomenon of full employment. True inflation occurs when prices rise without being accompanied by a rise in employment and output. Inflation is caused by further increases in effective demand after full employment is attained.

Although Keynes' most important contribution to the theory of prices is in relation to circumstances of less than full employment, he also has made important contributions to the theory of prices under full employment, that is, to the theory of inflation. Monetary changes which do not increase total production are significant in themselves in so far as they affect different people and classes in different ways and to different degrees. If inflation were to affect everyone in exactly the same way and in the same degree, it would have no importance whatsoever. Its tremendous social significance arises from the fact that it always does affect people and classes differently. Inflation takes wealth away from some people and hands it over to others in a manner which disregards the maxims of social equity. Yet this subtle thievery is perfectly legal. The inequity of inflation is an economic problem hardly less important than the vast waste associated with mass unemployment. One of Keynes' foremost preoccupations as an economist has been the process of inflation and means of minimizing its evil consequences. He has sometimes been called an "inflationist," but such a label is misleading. If he has shown a preference for inflation over deflation, it is purely a matter of the lesser of two evils. For deflation is a double evil—it redistributes wealth in an arbitrary manner and also impedes the creation of new wealth by causing unemployment. Inflation, except when it approaches breakdown proportions, errs only in the arbitrary redistribution of wealth. It does not, except indirectly, cause unemployment. Stability of the value of money has always been one of the goals of Keynes' analytical and programmatic skill. The brilliant suggestions put forth near the end of his life for financing the second world war with a minimum of inflation marks a worthy conclusion to this lifelong preoccupation.

Keynes applies the same concepts to the special case of full employment that he uses where unemployment prevails. No new techniques are required to explain the mechanism of inflation. Inflation merely represents the special case in which output ceases to be responsive to further increases in effective demand and as a result prices only, and not output, rise. Increases in the quantity of money still work their way into the economic system through liquidity preference, the rate of interest, the inducement to invest, the multiplier, and income. An increase in the total quantity of money goes first into idle balances (M_2), where it lowers the rate of interest. The lower rate of interest increases the inducement to invest, which is already adequate for full employment. The increase in investment causes income in money units to increase by more than the increase in investment, according to the principle of the investment multiplier. The increase in money income must be sufficient to cause an amount of saving out of that income to equal the increase in investment. Since income cannot increase in real terms (wage units), it increases in money terms by means of a rise in prices (a rise in the wage unit). This is a state of true inflation because prices are rising when employment and output are constant.

The gap between income and consumption, which holds the clue to the explanation of unemployment when there is an inadequacy of effective demand, is also the clue to inflation when there is an excess of effective demand. Unemployment exists when the amount of investment is insufficient to fill the gap between income and consumption corresponding to full employment. Inflation arises because investment is more than adequate to fill the gap between income and consumption at the level corresponding to full employment *at existing prices*. The sum of the effective demand for consumption and the effective demand for investment exceeds the aggregate income expressed in current prices. The adjustment which makes $Y = C + I$ and $I = S$ comes about through an increase in prices, money income, and money savings, until money savings are equal to the total amount of investment, also expressed in terms of a new level of prices. The equality between investment and saving is brought about by changes in the level of income when there is full employment as well as when there is less than full employment. The inflationary potential or inflationary gap is measured by the excess of consumption demand (D_1) plus investment demand (D_2) over income (Y) at full employment expressed in current prices. Potential inflation becomes actual inflation unless measures are taken to suppress it.

Measures to suppress an inflationary potential involve a reduction of total effective demand below its potential level. Suppression may take the form of a decrease in the propensity to consume or in the inducement to invest. The propensity to consume may be reduced by higher taxation or by an increase in the desire to save, which may be induced by appeals to buy bonds and other saving media, or, to some extent, by an increase in the rate of interest. Taxation intended to reduce aggregate consumption will be effective to the extent that it falls upon income which would otherwise be spent for consumption. A regressive tax will be a more effective curb to inflation than a progressive tax since the propensity to consume is proportionately higher for lower-income groups than for higher-income groups. The inducement to invest can be lowered by a rise in the rate of interest or by a fall in the marginal efficiency of capital. Since the private marginal efficiency of capital is largely beyond the reach of government control, restraints upon the volume of private investment must work mainly through the rate of interest by means of a restriction in the quantity of money. Reductions in government spending will also tend to suppress the inflationary pressures. To sum up, inflation arises because too much money is spent by individuals, businesses, and governments. The obvious way to prevent inflation is to reduce the total volume of spending. In so far as individuals and businesses tend to spend too much money, the government may take the excess away from them in the form of increased taxation or by inducing a higher ratio of saving to income. If full employment exists and government feels the need to spend more, as in time of war, inflation can only be avoided by withdrawing some of the potential private expenditures.

Wartime Inflation

Inflation is by no means unknown as a peacetime phenomenon, but it is an almost universal and inevitable accompaniment of war and postwar economic conditions. Perhaps it is not an exaggeration to say that inflation and full employment are the normal conditions of a wartime economy and that deflation and unemployment are the normal conditions of a peacetime economy in the present stage of capitalist development. After the primary postwar depression of 1920-21, the commodity price levels in the United States and other capitalistic countries of the western world showed a remarkable stability until the collapse of 1929. Even in the boom years of 1928 and 1929, commodity price inflation was not typical. The most important forms of inflation in the United States between 1922 and 1929 were in the prices of securities sold on the stock exchanges and in the amounts of profits earned by industrial enterprises.[1] On the other hand, commodity price inflation was an outstanding characteristic of the first and second world wars and their aftermaths. Hence any discussion of inflation in commodity prices which is to be close to actual experience must be concerned primarily with war and postwar conditions.

The social framework of Keynes' general theory of employment, interest, and money is that of a peacetime capitalist economy rather than of a wartime economy. Although Keynes envisages a large amount of governmental control in peacetime, the extent of regulation is small in comparison with that required by the exigencies of modern warfare. Consequently, Keynes' general theory is most useful as an instrument of analysis within the premises of peacetime capitalism. Yet the war experience is significant in relation to Keynes' theory in at least two important respects. First, war experience indicates clearly that a sufficient rate of governmental

---

1. "Profit inflation" is a special term coined by Keynes in his *Treatise on Money* to describe the condition when prices increase more than business costs or prices fall less than costs. See *Treatise on Money*, Vol. 1, page 155.

expenditure can soon bring even the wealthiest of the moderɪ industrial economies to full employment, at which point the drag of unemployment is replaced by the threat of inflation. Second, Keynes' suggestion of how to pay for the war, a plan offered in Great Britain in 1939, shows the flexibility and the fruitfulness for practical action of the kind of thinking that went into the general theory of employment, interest, and money.[2] There is nothing in Keynes' plan for preventing inflation in war that contradicts his explanation of unemployment in peace. The plan for war finance suggests the need for compulsory saving whereas the emphasis in the *General Theory* is upon the social disadvantages of thrift. The reversal of circumstances from peace to war calls for a reversal of emphasis. The plan for compulsory saving is an extension of Keynes' basic theory to wartime conditions. The change from peace to war calls for a shift in emphasis but involves no change in the framework of the analysis.

Wartime inflation is not basically different from peacetime inflation except in the greater pressures that exist in war and the more drastic remedies required to cope with these pressures. The fundamental principle is, to repeat, that the total effective demand for consumers goods (D_1) plus the effective demand for investment goods (D_2) exceeds the total value of output at full employment in terms of existing prices. In the absence of measures to suppress excessive demand, prices must rise until income is sufficient to permit saving to equal investment. Investment in a war economy is best thought of as all goods and services which are not for private consumption. Investment then includes all government outlays plus private capital accumulation.

In terms of the three independent variables which determine the volume of effective demand—the propensity to consume, the rate of interest, and the marginal efficiency of capital—it is the last which provides the stimulus to effective demand which in turn gives rise to inflation or the threat of

2. *How to Pay for the War.* New York: Harcourt, Brace and Co., Inc., 1940.

inflation in war. Wartime "investment" is not influenced to any important extent by changes in the rate of interest. War expenditures are largely a function of military requirements, taken in conjunction with estimates of the quantity of consumers goods, with a tendency to maximize war production and to minimize consumption output. War may be viewed as a great new industry whose colossal demands stimulate economic activity in every nook and cranny of the economic system. The expected yields which raise the marginal efficiency of government investment are mainly in terms of social and military advantages rather than pecuniary profits. In so far as wartime plant and equipment is furnished by private capital, the investments are made in the expectation that high yields will bring returns at least equal to the supply price within a fairly short period. Thus it is a sharp rise in the marginal efficiency of capital that increases effective demand and sets up the inflationary potential in a war economy.

Since the exigencies of war do not permit consumers goods to increase in response to effective demand from consumer spending, plans for preventing wartime inflation must focus upon suppressing current consumer demand. The fundamental problem is how to prevent consumption expenditure from increasing when income is increasing. "The fiscal problem," said Keynes with reference to British conditions in 1939, "is how to permit an increase of incomes by 15 to 20 per cent. without any of this increase being spent on increased real consumption."[3] Modern warfare requires more guns and less butter without regard for the fundamental psychological principle that as income rises consumption also rises. Belts must be tightened in war. And even if a nation is so fortunate as to be able to afford as much consumption as before the war, it certainly cannot permit consumption to rise according to the peacetime schedule of the propensity to consume. To hold the *amount* of consumption constant when income rises means to lower the schedule of the propensity to consume.

---

3. "The Income and Fiscal Potential of Great Britain," *The Economic Journal*, December, 1939, Vol. XLIX, No. 196, page 629.

Since the production of consumers goods cannot be adjusted upwards to correspond to normal consumer demand, the amount of consumer demand must be adjusted downward to correspond to the output of consumers goods. In other words, the schedule of the *propensity* to consume must be lowered so that the *amount* of consumption will not rise as income rises. If the propensity to consume is not lowered, a sharp rise in the prices of consumers goods is unavoidable. In war it is hardly possible by normal means to adjust the division of consumer output and non-consumer output to the proportions which income recipients will voluntarily choose to spend and not to spend. In the absence of unusual measures, the increasing money expenditure coming into the consumer market for a fixed or declining volume of consumers goods and services will cause a sharp increase in the prices of consumers goods. Price fixing and rationing are subsidiary measures for depressing the propensity to consume special commodities. They are incapable of suppressing effectively and efficiently the general flow of consumer demand.

Alternatives in war finance

Bearing in mind that the primary problem of war finance is to restrict consumption expenditure when income is rising, the alternative policies for attaining this objective are relatively few in number. The problem is less that of lowering the absolute level of consumption than of preventing consumption from rising when income is rising rapidly. The alternative means of lowering the general propensity to private consumption are: (1) to increase taxation on consumption expenditure, (2) to rely upon voluntary saving plus increases in normal taxation, (3) to institute a system of compulsory saving aimed primarily at consumption expenditure.

(1) *Increase Taxation:* Since it is the potential expenditures of the lower income groups which must be suppressed, increases in taxes which would provide any solution to the inflation problem must fall most heavily upon these groups. Heavy taxation upon the rich will do little to lessen aggregate

expenditure for consumption because a very large part of the incomes of the wealthy is either taxed or saved. While the rich consume more than the poor in proportion to their number, the rich do not consume enough in the aggregate, especially in time of war when extravagances are unpatriotic and many types of luxury goods and services are not produced at all, to make any practicable reduction in their consumption of consequence. Keynes found in 1939 in Great Britain, that the income group with five pounds (about $20) per week constituted about 88 per cent of the population, received 60 per cent of the total personal income, and accounted for two-thirds of the total consumption of the country. In this low-income group, incomes had risen on an average of 15 per cent in the first year of the war and there were not enough consumer goods available to permit them to consume anything like 15 per cent more than before the war. At best the absolute level of consumption of those whose incomes remained below five pounds might have been maintained at the prewar level.

About the only taxes which would drain off a sufficient amount of the increase in consumer demand of the low-income classes to serve as an effective check to the inflation of prices of consumers goods would be a stiff wage tax or a retail sales tax. Such taxes are highly regressive and therefore violate a cardinal principle of justice in taxation. Special taxes on wages meet very strong political opposition from the ranks of labor, especially if they are severe enough to be effective. Keynes estimated the necessary rate to be 20 per cent on wages, in addition to the income tax with lowered exemptions. He estimated that a retail sales tax which would be adequate would be too high to be borne by the very lowest income groups and therefore would need to be levied on non-essentials at a rate of about 50 per cent. Only the financial purists, he said, would insist that it is possible for a country with the income structure of the United Kingdom to finance a war effort of the size needed in 1940 out of current taxation. Such taxation was, Keynes contended, both socially unjust and politically impracticable. No modern government of a capitalistic nation has ever financed war expenditures out of taxation to a sufficient degree to avoid inflation.[4]

(2) *Voluntary Saving:* Governments usually rely upon voluntary saving to fill the gap between total war expenditure and receipts from taxation. The only fault of voluntary saving as a preventive of war inflation is its inadequacy. The inadequacy arises because the income groups which account for the bulk of increased consumer spending in wartime are not the groups which are likely to save voluntarily enough of their incomes to reduce consumer demand to equality with the amount of consumer goods available in terms of prewar prices. No amount of saving by the rich nor any amount of taxes levied upon the rich will suffice to reduce the spending of the poor out of their enhanced incomes. It is not reasonable that the lower income groups will suddenly develop habits of saving which will render reliance on voluntary saving a satisfactory anti-inflation policy. Peacetime quiescence in the injustices of economic inequality cannot be perpetuated in wartime by mere appeals to the patriotism of the poor. A family which has not been able to afford roast beef before the war because of inadequate income is not likely to refrain voluntarily from indulging a little during the war when its income has risen sufficiently to bring roast beef within its economic grasp. Patriotic appeals to forestall inflation which rest upon the assumption that those who ate roast beef before the war may do so during the war, while those who were unable to afford roast beef before the war shall refrain from eating it during the war must surely fall upon deaf ears as well as outrage our sense of social justice. This is the essential nature of the problem. Although roast beef and some other commodities may be rationed, consumption

---

4. Professor William J. Fellner has contended that a proportionate income tax of 10 per cent applied to all income without exception and superimposed upon the income tax structure that actually prevailed would have prevented inflation in the United States during the second world war. See "Postscript on War Inflation: A Lesson from World War II," *American Economic Review.* March, 1947, Vol. XXXVII, No. 1, page 47.

demand in general can be restrained efficiently only by some stronger means than an appeal to voluntary saving on the part of the lower income groups. There is no evidence from experience to indicate that voluntary saving has ever been adequate to prevent inflation in time of war, no matter how intense and how widespread the appeals to save.

There is an element of subtle deception in the belief that war finance can be adequately taken care of by "normal" methods, that is, by increasing the rates of existing taxes and by voluntary saving stimulated by propaganda. When voluntary saving is inadequate without inflation, it increases with inflation. For a sufficient degree of inflation will always occur to raise the yield of taxes and voluntary saving to the necessary level. This method whereby so-called voluntary saving is increased through inflation is typically followed by governments in wartime. Governments do not employ it willingly. It is not usually a conscious policy but what Keynes calls "Nature's remedy," the consequence which follows by default, in the absence of an adequate, positive program against inflation. It is all the more dangerous because governments slip into it unconsciously and perhaps under the delusion that it "works." It does "work" in the sense that a government which follows it will always find the cash to pay for its purchases of home-produced goods, but it does not work in the sense that it can prevent inflation. It works only because of inflation. Keynes seems to have been the first to articulate explicitly the essential nature of this inflationary process. In his *Treatise on Money* (II, pp. 173-176) he characterized British financing of the first world war as one of increasing voluntary saving and taxation through inflation. A similar description could be applied to war finance in the United States in the first and second world wars and to Britain in the second world war, although in the latter case the process was modified by a belated adoption of Keynes' plan for compulsory saving. In fact voluntary saving through inflation involves a mechanism which characterizes all inflations and has a significance which transcends the wartime cases. The essence of the process is that price inflation raises the level of money income until saving out of income is equal to investment, or in the case of a wartime governmental budget, price inflation raises national income to the point where taxes and voluntary saving are adequate to finance government expenditures. "Nature's remedy . . . is a rise of prices sufficient to divert real resources out of the pockets of the main body of consumers into the pockets of the entrepreneurs and thence to the Treasury, partly in the shape of a higher yield from existing taxes, particularly Excess Profits Tax, and partly in contributions to loans out of the increased savings and reserves of the entrepreneurs."[5]

The process is perhaps best explained with reference to an arithmetical example reduced to the simplest possible assumptions. Suppose the national income and the national output are $160 billion at the beginning of a war before any inflation has taken place; that the war effort requires an expenditure of $85 billion on the part of the government; that private investment is zero; that taxes amount to $45 billion and voluntary saving to $25 billion out of the $160 billion income. A total of $70 billion comes into the government coffers from taxes and loans and leaves the receipts short of expenditures by $15 billion. Now this sum of $15 billion needed to balance the government's expenditures is exactly equal to what remains in the hands of the public in the form of voluntary savings. This is inevitable by the rules of arithmetic. For the government has taken $85 billion out of the total national output of $160 billion (in prewar prices) and there are no goods left over for which the extra income in the hands of the public can be spent. If prices do not rise, people will find themselves with $15 billion left after buying all the goods available in the market. If prices rise, as they undoubtedly will when $90 billion are available for $75 billion worth of goods (in prewar prices), the higher prices will swell the national income by $15 billion so there is just as

5. Keynes, "The Income and Fiscal Potential of Great Britain," *The Economic Journal*, December, 1939, Vol. XLIX. No. 196, pages 630-631.

much left over as before. Prices will rise by 20 per cent to bring the supply of goods into equality with the money demand. Those who sell goods worth $75 billion for $90 billion will have extra income of $15 billion.[6]

If this extra income is not captured in loans and taxes, there will be a further rise in prices when the additional $15 billion comes into the market in the second round of the inflationary process. If this happens, the volume of money income coming into the market for a constant supply of consumer goods will increase cumulatively. The prices paid by the government for war goods will also increase as other prices and costs rise. The net outcome, if this happens, is a progressive inflation without limit.

Fortunately, this is not what actually happens. The initial rise in prices transfers real income from the main body of consumers to entrepreneurs because prices rise faster than wage and salary rates. Real-wage rates are diminished and real profits are inflated. This represents a shift in real income from the lower to the higher income classes of society. The increase in aggregate national income is concentrated in the hands of a limited number of business entrepreneurs, a group which Keynes refers to as the "profiteers." The personal incomes of the profiteers are subject to very high marginal rates of taxation under the personal income tax, and their extra business profits are subject to almost confiscatory rates under the wartime excess-profits tax. As a result, the extra income which arises from the initial rise in prices, of 20 per

6. We may express the quantitative relations as follows: Consumption expenditure (C) + Saving (S) + Taxes (T) = Consumption output (C') + Private Investment (I) + Government Expenditure (E).

$$C + S + T = C' + I + E$$
$$90 + 25 + 45 = 75 + 0 + 85$$

But C' must equal C, and S + T must equal I + E,
$$90 + 30 + 55 = 90 + 0 + 85$$

Thus saving plus taxes are brought to equality with private investment plus government expenditure as a result of a rise in money income of $15 billion, of which $10 billion are taxed and $5 billion are voluntarily saved. The rise in income is a purely monetary one which results from an expenditure of $90 billion for consumers goods previously worth $75 billion. An inflation of 20 per cent has taken place in the prices of consumers goods.

cent in our example, is almost entirely taxed away. Most of what is not taxed may be voluntarily saved because it is in the hands of one of the saving classes of society. Most of the excess demand will be mopped up. Instead of a 20 per cent increase in the money demand for consumers goods at the second round, there may be, for example, only a 2 or 3 percent increase. Voluntary saving will have increased as a result of the rise in prices and income to the extent necessary to fill the gap between the government's total expenditure and what it collects in taxes.

This is an expedient way for a government which quails at bolder programs to meet its war expenditures. It permits real resources to be taken away from the mass of consumers by letting prices increase faster than wages. The resources taken from consumers are handed over to profiteers. Then most of the extra profits of the profiteers are taken away in the form of taxes or of loans to which they voluntarily subscribe. The profiteers are in effect tax collectors for the government. The process is not intolerable as long as the profiteers remain merely the agents and do not become the principals in taking resources away from the mass of consumers. It works with more social justice if the excess "booty" which has accrued to the profiteers is taxed away and not merely borrowed by the government. If it is merely borrowed, the profiteers retain a claim on the future although they have done nothing to deserve such claims. In order to assure more equity and avoid unjustified gains remaining in the hands of the profiteers, a capital levy should be assessed on war-won wealth quickly at the conclusion of hostilities.

Even though the excess purchasing power arising from the initial increase in prices is entirely mopped up by taxes and voluntary saving, the inflationary process is not permanently stopped. Workers whose cost of living has risen by 20 per cent will demand higher wages to compensate for the higher cost of living. In the absence of controls over wage bargaining, the increased demands of workers may be met by employers with relatively little resistance, both because they wish to retain their workers and because there is not much incentive to keep down business costs when tax rates are at confiscatory levels. Fortunately, some costs are fixed and do not increase even if wages rise. Wage increases take time to negotiate and wars do not last forever. England got through four years of the first world war with something less than a doubling of prices. Voluntary saving was always adequate to meet the necessary expenditures above taxation with the help of a sufficient amount of inflation. The limited meaning of the term "voluntary" should be borne in mind. Keynes points out that this so-called voluntary saving method "is a method of *compulsorily* converting the appropriate part of the earnings of the worker which *he* does not save voluntarily into the voluntary savings (and taxation) of the entrepreneur."[7] So the method of voluntary saving merely limits the amount of inflation. It does not prevent inflation. The effect of inflation is similar to a regressive tax. It leaves the working class with no claim against the future and with no more consumption goods than they would have enjoyed in the aggregate if there had been no inflation. In the second world war, Keynes suggested a plan whereby inflation could be avoided and the working class would have a share in the claims on the future.

(3) *Compulsory Saving:* The Keynes plan to pay for the second world war is known as the "deferred-pay" or "compulsory-saving" plan. Its provisions, which were for the purpose of preventing inflation, were: (a) A deduction from current wages and salaries to be credited to a savings account which would remain blocked for the duration of the war. This savings deduction is in addition to the income tax withholding. The very lowest incomes would be exempt from both tax and savings deductions, and those just above the lowest level would be subject to a savings but not a tax deduction. The proportion of the total deduction which represented taxes would increase as income increased. Interest would be paid

7. *How to Pay for the War,* page 69. Italics in the original.

on savings at 2½ per cent per annum. (b) At the appropriate time after the war, the savings accounts would be unblocked and become available for spending. The propitious time for unblocking this purchasing power would be when a deficiency of effective demand threatened to lead the economy into a postwar depression. (c) Other provisions included the payment of cash allowances to all families with children, an iron ration at fixed prices supported by governmental subsidies, permission to unblock some savings for exceptional and unavoidable emergencies such as illness and hospitalization, credits for prewar commitments to mortgage payments and life insurance premiums, and a capital levy for raising funds with which to make payment of the deferred incomes.

In wartime, the budget problem of how to pay for the war and the inflation problem of how to keep prices down should be approached from the consumption end. The borrowing problem then becomes "child's play."[8] The aggregate amount of wartime consumption for all classes in Britain was assumed to be fixed, regardless of the method used to finance the war. The problem of consumption was therefore one of equitable distribution of a fixed amount of goods and services. This amount was less than the aggregate prewar consumption. Keynes offered his plan of deferred pay as the only means whereby war sacrifices could be in proportion to ability to bear them. Taxation alone was not a practicable means, and voluntary saving could be made adequate only if assisted by inflation. The Keynes plan was intended to permit some increase above the prewar level in the consumption of those with incomes below 75 shillings ($15) per week, no change in the aggregate consumption of all those with incomes below 5 pounds ($20) per week, and a reduction on the average of about one-third in the consumption of those with incomes above 5 pounds ($20) per week. The progressive incidence of the plan accorded with the well-established principles of

---

8. Keynes, "The Income and Fiscal Potential of Great Britain," *The Economic Journal*, December, 1939, Vol. XLIX, No. 196, page 633.

social justice which a democracy should extend rather than abandon in time of war.

The low-income groups (below $20 per week) would be able in the aggregate to buy just as much as they enjoyed before the war and just as much, if not more, than they would be able to enjoy during the war under any alternate plan, and at the same time they would have savings left over with which to buy things after the war. The extra rewards for some of the extra effort expended during the war would be merely deferred and not taken away for good. Under Keynes' plan, the working class as well as the capitalist class would share in the ownership of the national debt, a privilege usually enjoyed by the capitalist class alone. Under the probable alternative of price inflation, the working class would spend all its money during the war, get no more for it, and sacrifice the privilege of spending after the war some of the money earned during the war. "Inflation . . . allows them to spend and deprives them of the fruit of spending."[9]

The deferred-pay plan is consistent with a maximum freedom of choice on the part of consumers in deciding what to consume. In contrast, a system of universal rationing presupposes that all consumers have approximately the same tastes, an assumption obviously far from valid. A few commodities like sugar, bread, and salt may be rationed in equal allotments without interfering with consumer preference, but for most items entering into consumption, tastes of individuals differ so widely that it is far better to limit the total amount of spending and let the individuals decide for themselves what they will buy. This does not mean that rationing and price control can be dispensed with altogether. It does mean that direct controls over consumption are not the most suitable method for controlling the over-all distribution of consumers goods. If, in addition to rationing, all prices are fixed and there is an excess of purchasing power, people find themselves with money in their pockets when there is nothing to

---

9. *How to Pay for the War*, page 49.

buy. If the prices of essentials only are controlled, the excess buying power is diverted to the uncontrolled items whose prices tend to skyrocket. There then develops great pressure to divert materials into those activities where prices and profits are high. Hence, it becomes necessary to control the flow of materials into channels where they are most essential rather than where they are most profitable. Such controls necessarily involve extensive interference with personal and business affairs and unavoidably degenerate into widespread "black market" operations.

Since the problem of avoiding inflation is to be attacked from the consumption end, it is misleading to suppose that the issue is primarily one of borrowing directly from the public rather than from the banking system. The amount of money that can be borrowed from the banks without setting up inflationary pressures depends on the liquidity preference of the business community and of investors for the transactions, precautionary, and speculative motives. In wartime, when investment is strictly controlled, the rate of interest is not of direct consequence in relation to the volume of investment. However, the limits to the ability of the economic system to absorb new money will be indicated by a sharp rise in the prices of securities (an undue fall in the rate of interest). In the expansion of economic activity in the early phases of war, the volume of money needed for transactions will increase because of larger output, higher prices (caused by increasing costs and profits), and higher wages. There is also need for more money to satisfy the precautionary holdings arising from large tax liabilities and other contingencies. Keynes estimated that war activity in Britain required an increase in cash holdings of from 20 to 25 per cent over prewar needs. Therefore, in the early stages of war it is desirable for the Treasury to sell bonds to the banking system. Borrowing from the banking system should not, however, be continued beyond the expansion stage. It is a once-and-for-all source of financing the governmental budget. After the supply of money has been adjusted to maximum activity, the total quantity of money should be kept approximately constant for the duration. Borrowing thereafter should come directly from the public rather than from the banking system.[10]

Financing the war and preventing inflation in Britain in the early 'forties offered a perfect opportunity for social action of the type represented in the deferred-pay plan because it was one of those situations in which each benefits by a rule that applies to all. Compulsory saving was a social guarantee that each would be protected in doing for his own good what was also good for others providing all behaved in the same way. A single individual cannot protect himself against inflation by saving when others are not saving. Therefore, in the absence of assurance that others will save, the individual has less incentive to do so, even though he would prefer to save if he knew that everybody else would do likewise. Under war conditions, if all save, all will be benefitted by lower prices now and by having something left over to spend in the future. But if some save while others do not, all will pay higher prices for a fixed amount of goods; the spenders will have nothing left over and the value of the savers' money will diminish in value as a result of the spending of the non-savers. Authorities who appeal to individuals to save under these circumstances but do not take steps to protect the value of the savings are guilty of half-way measures. The desirable policy is to make the rules for saving the same for all. That is what Keynes' plan of deferred pay was intended to do.

Postwar Inflation

The foregoing analysis which has related the principle of effective demand to the problem of wartime inflation may be applied with only minor modifications to postwar or peacetime inflation. Inflation is always caused by an excess of effective demand above the level needed for full employment, just as unemployment is always caused by a deficiency of ef-

---

10. Keynes, "The Income and Fiscal Potential of Great Britain," *The Economic Journal*, December, 1939, Vol. XLIX, No. 196, page 635.

fective demand below the level required for full employment. Inflation and unemployment are the twin evils of the failure to harmonize the volume of effective demand with the basic aims of full employment and stable prices. If the volume of investment exceeds the size of the gap between income and consumption at full employment, prices rise until the size of the gap is accommodated to the amount of investment. In war, when government expenditures are fixed by military necessity, steps to avoid price inflation are confined to lowering the current private propensity to consume, that is, to reducing private consumption until the gap between income and consumption is large enough to accommodate government expenditure plus private capital formation. In wartime the latter is of minor significance. In peacetime, price inflation may be attacked either by widening the size of the full employment gap between income and consumption until it is accommodated to the volume of investment, or by reducing the amount of investment to fit the size of the gap between income and consumption in terms of existing prices. This is merely to say the exigencies of peace are less than those of war. The effective demand for either consumption or investment, or both, may be adjusted to make the aggregate demand equal the level required for full employment without inflation.

Consumption

The means whereby the propensity to consume may be lowered are the same in peace as in war, that is, taxation, voluntary saving and compulsory saving, supplemented by price control and rationing. However, the political and social atmosphere for executing these measures is much less favorable in peace than in war. Much of the voluntary abstinence exercised by consumers during war is purely a temporary phenomenon induced by the psychological satisfaction of submitting to patriotic sacrifices. Government bonds are more readily purchased in war than in peace by the great mass of consumers. With the cessation of war there is a strong psychological release from the self-imposed sacrifices of war in favor of a propensity to spend the savings which have accumulated during the war. This psychological impatience reflects itself in free spending and in political pressure for a quick end to price controls, rationing, high taxes, and bond purchases. A compulsory-savings plan which might be politically acceptable in war, as it was to some extent in England but not in the United States during the second world war, is not likely to be tolerated in peace, although an increase in social security deductions might be used for this end to the mutual benefit of workers and non-workers alike. There may be irony but there is no paradox in the circumstance that the more successfully inflation is staved off during war, the less likely it is to be staved off after war. The bigger the dam, the bigger the deluge when the dam gives way, and analogously, the greater the success attained in restraining consumer spending in war, the greater will be the difficulty of holding back the flood of potential effective demand which the public is impatient to release as soon as the war is over. If political and personal impatience gains the upper hand before the conversion from military to civilian production is completed, the increase in prices is likely to be very great indeed. Hence, it is not so strange that inflation is often more severe in a postwar than in a war period.

Postwar inflation is not inevitable. The controls which work in war will work in peace if they are given a chance. There is no necessary reason why the purchasing power that has been dammed up in war need be permitted to break loose when the war is over. Reductions in military demands that follow the end of war ease the pressures that tend to raise prices. The inflation that struck the United States after the second world war was a consequence of the political immaturity of the general public in relation to the purpose and functions of such controls. A public steeped in the tradition that "free" competition is the cure-all for economic ills, fell easy prey to those who, whether out of self-delusion or self-interest, proclaimed that the end of price control and a return to competition would bring down prices. Urged on by a flood of propaganda, there was a headlong rush to end all controls. Without public support to continue controls, the fight against inflation was lost because no system of controls can work effectively unless it has the co-operation of the general public. Administrative rationing, which is never justified except for its greater equity as compared with the "natural" rationing of higher prices, was scrapped. This undermined price control which was quickly beaten down to a skeleton and finally placed on the ash pile in the middle of 1946. In the first six months following the end of price control in June of 1946, wholesale prices rose 25 per cent as compared with a rise of only 10 per cent in the four years from mid-1942 to mid-1946. Retail prices and the cost of living were held down quite successfully during the war but surged wildly upward following the removal of OPA controls. In some instances people with low incomes were forced to eat less because their pocketbooks were exhausted by high prices. After a Congressional investigation of prices, Senator Flanders reported in September of 1947 that many white collar workers in New York were undernourished because they were unable to afford the food required for a balanced diet. This is the manner in which the "law of supply and demand" redistributes real income in periods of inflation. It takes away from some and gives to others in ways which bear no necessary relation to what social consensus would regard as equitable. An advantage of positive social action is, of course, that equity may be consciously taken into account.

The three elements of effective demand in war are government expenditure, private consumption, and private capital formation. At the conclusion of a great war, the first element falls precipitously while the second and third rise sharply. Postwar inflation is partly a question of whether the decrease in the first element exceeds or falls short of the increase in the other two. In the United States from 1945 to 1946, government purchases fell by $52 billion, while private consumption expenditure rose $22 billion and total investment (gross domestic plus net foreign) rose by $21 billion. Meanwhile, with price controls still in effect, the cost of living index rose only 4 points, from 129 in June, 1945, to 133 in June, 1946 (1935-1939 = 100). From 1946 to 1947 government purchases fell by only $2 billion, private consumption expenditure rose by $21 billion, and total investment (gross domestic plus net foreign) rose by $7 billion. With government purchases leveling off, and consumption and investment expenditure continuing to rise, and in the absence of price controls, the cost-of-living index soared from 133 in June, 1946, to 157 in June, 1947, and reached 172 in June, 1948.[11]

Although the magnitudes of government expenditure, private consumption, and investment are the most important considerations in relation to price movements, there are other important factors bearing on price movements in immediate postwar periods. On the output side there is the major problem of converting from military to civilian production. Contemporary industrial society is characterized by an extremely complicated technology which is not easily converted from one line of production to another. There must elapse at the end of any major war a critical period during which final output falls below the potential maximum because of the change in the direction of production. Industrial disputes between labor and management also tend to delay the return to a full level of peacetime production. If during this critical conversion period, pent up demands from the war are permitted to surge into the market for whatever is available, the inevitable consequence is a sharp rise in prices. Price inflation occurs when a surplus of effective demand comes into the market to purchase the available supply of goods. Inflation can be attacked either by reducing the quantity of effective demand or by increasing the quantity of goods. In the short run, it may be necessary to suppress the effective demand. In the long run, the prodigious productive capacity of modern technology is the surest guarantee against inflation.

---

11. The cost-of-living data are those of the U.S. Bureau of Labor Statistics, and the national income and product data those of the U.S. Department of Commerce.

At the close of the second world war there existed an immense backlog of unsatisfied demand for consumers goods of all types. By the end of 1946 the supply of many non-durable goods had caught up with demand, and there was concern over the growing size of inventories. A longer period is required to meet the backlog of demand for durable consumers goods than for non-durables. However, by the fourth quarter of 1947 nearly all consumer durables were being produced in sufficient volume to meet an unprecedented current demand and, in addition, to cut into the backlog from the war. Radios, vacuum cleaners, washing machines, refrigerators, and automobiles were being turned out more rapidly than in the previous peak year of 1941. Only in the case of automobiles was current output failing to gain rapidly on demand. It was predicted in the spring of 1948 that any serious weakening in aggregate demand was likely to originate in the consumers durable goods sector of the economy.[12]

Investment

Private Capital Formation: In the short run, under conditions of full employment, investment is always carried on at the expense of consumption. Postwar conditions usually favor a strong inducement to invest as well as a strong propensity to consume, to cause a two-fold pressure toward an inflationary rise in prices. The inducement to invest is determined by the rate of interest and the marginal efficiency of capital. The fiscal and monetary policy followed in the United States during the second world war tended to accentuate the downward trend of interest rates. During recent years the long-term rate of interest has been reduced to about three per cent on gilt-edged corporate bonds and to less than three per cent on long-term government bonds. Short-term interest rates are even lower than long-term rates. These low interest rates, taken along with the high marginal efficiency of capital which follows the destruction of capital assets in war areas and the

---

12. See L. J. Atkinson, "Backlog Demand for Consumers' Durable Goods," *Survey of Current Business,* April, 1948, Vol. XXVIII, No. 4, pages 15-21.

war-enforced cessation of investment in many types of capital assets even in non-war areas, leads to a high level of private investment in the years following a major war. In addition to the task of restocking inventories to normal levels, there exists a heavy demand for durable producers goods. Plant and equipment which has worn out or become obsolete during the war will require replacement, and the business community will be eager to get on with its war-deferred programs for plant expansion. During 1946 gross private domestic investment (including housing) in the United States rose to $25 billion, and in 1947 to $28 billion, as compared with only $9 billion in the prewar year 1939. That part of domestic investment consisting of plant and equipment expenditures, especially in manufacturing, showed signs of leveling off in 1948, but nevertheless it continued to exert a major inflationary pressure. The great postwar housing boom is an inflationary factor, and many years will be required to fill the postwar demand. Inflationary pressures on rents and building materials promise to continue for an extended period. The longer period of time which must elapse before the demand for housing can be met is the justification for retaining rent controls after other forms of price control have been eliminated.

Exports: From the point of view of any national economy, net exports—that is, exports in excess of imports—represent a form of investment. Net exports are production in excess of current consumption, which is the fundamental meaning of investment. The huge demand from Europe and other foreign areas for American goods for rehabilitation and reconstruction is one of the great and continuing sources of inflationary pressure which has followed the second world war. Millions of tons of food, locomotives, coal, steel, clothing, and almost every conceivable type of item are being shipped abroad in response to desperate needs of these areas for the goods that will enable the people to survive and to rebuild on the rubble heaps left by the most destructive conflagration in the history of the world. At one point during 1947, the net exports from the United States rose to a rate of nearly one billion dollars per month. This means that from this source alone incomes were being earned by workers and owners in the United States to the extent of nearly a billion dollars a month in excess of the value of the goods available for purchase. The removal of goods from the domestic economy naturally leaves less to buy and creates relative shortages which, taken in conjunction with other conditions of the postwar period, tends to drive up prices. These pressures are temporary because they are peculiar to the aftermath of a great war. They will not continue indefinitely both because of the inability of foreigners to pay dollars and because the foreigners will not wish to continue to buy American goods on so vast a scale when their own domestic productive capacity is restored. But as long as these demands for exports continue and as long as dollars are available in the hands of foreigners to pay for them, net exports will contribute to higher prices for goods sold within the United States.

The rate of net exports fell off rather sharply toward the end of 1947 and in the early months of 1948, but passage of the Foreign Assistance Act in the spring of 1948 gave assurance that they would continue at a high level until 1952 or 1953. During 1948 the foreign aid program contributed to aggregate demand and thus to domestic inflation. In later years it may provide some protection against large-scale domestic unemployment. In the long run, repayment of foreign loans will depend on the willingness of the United States to accept large imports of goods. During the 1920's the United States played the comic role of insisting that debts from the first world war be paid while making repayment virtually impossible by raising tariff walls to an all-time high. If the American economy continues to operate as it did during the 1920's and 1930's, it may be better off if the postwar loans of the second world war are never repaid because a net import of goods, representing negative investment, working through the multiplier principle, might be a major factor contributing to unemployment and depression. One of the ironies of our economic system is that foreign demand, which in later years would provide a bulwark against unemployment in the United States, is concentrated in a period in which it contributes to inflation.

Large Government Expenditures: Government expenditures constitute part of aggregate effective demand. At the conclusion of the second world war the total outlays of the federal government declined sharply from the wartime levels, but remained very high in comparsion with about $8.5 billion in the late 'thirties and less than $4 billion in the 'twenties. In the first three years after the war, annual outlays had not fallen below $35 billion and appeared destined to increase rather than decrease. In combination with a high private propensity to consume and a strong private inducement to invest, large government expenditures are a major force contributing to rising prices.

Fiscal policy is the best weapon against inflation in peace as well as in war. Since inflation is caused by too much spending, its cure lies in curtailing spending. Reductions in government expenditure is one method and higher taxes is another method for lessening demand. Strangely, it is sometimes argued that the best way to combat inflation is to reduce taxes because they discourage investment, which will increase the supply of goods. This is a dangerous contention from the point of view of an effective anti-inflationary program. Where there is already full employment, additional investment reduces the flow of current consumer output and increases the flow of current consumer demand. Consumers goods which will come onto the market in the future after new factories have been built will not help to avoid inflation now. Timing fiscal policy in order to regularize the flow of effective demand is the core of the problem. Too much demand at one time, followed by too little demand at another time, has been responsible for the boom-and-bust pattern which has characterized the free enterprise economies since the Napoleonic Wars. If an economy is already in the throes of inflation, it will only intensify its malady by lowering taxes. Reduction of the federal income tax in the spring of 1948 illustrates how economic wisdom is often sacrificed to political expediency. With full employment and with prices already rising, the public was given more money to spend at the very time Congress was voting to spend billions for the Foreign Assistance Act and was preparing to increase by more billions the outlay for armaments. Under such circumstances, more money left in the pay check means more money taken out at the grocery store. In peace as in war, when the public spends more money for a fixed quantity of goods it is rewarded only with higher prices. Unfortunately, the money illusion is strong enough to protect the political profiteers. Higher rather than lower taxes are appropriate to a period of inflation.[13]

While government is not a net contributor to inflation as long as it takes more money away from people than it pays out to them, it can always suppress inflationary tendencies by increasing the amount of money it takes away or by reducing the amount it pays out. A budget surplus is in the nature of a negative investment, just as a government deficit is in the nature of a positive investment. By increasing the size of the surplus in its cash budget, the government may provide an offset to the large positive investment for private capital formation and for net exports, and help to reduce the gap between income and current consumption to a size consistent with full employment without inflation.

References for Further Reading

Keynes, J. M., *The General Theory of Employment, Interest and Money,* Chapter 21. See Index for other references. New York: Harcourt, Brace and Company, 1936.

———, *How to Pay for the War,* especially Chapter 9. New York: Harcourt, Brace and Company, 1940.

---

13. An alternative to higher taxation is greater saving. It is interesting that one of the foremost American economists, Professor Sumner Slichter, recommended in early 1948 a plan for compulsory saving similar to that recommended by Keynes during the second world war. See Sumner Slichter, "The Problem of Inflation," *The Review of Economic Statistics,* February, 1948, Vol. XXX, No. 1, page 5.

————, *Monetary Reform.* New York: Harcourt, Brace and Company, 1924.

————, *A Treatise on Money.* 2 volumes. New York: Harcourt, Brace and Company, 1930.

Fellner, William, *A Treatise on War Inflation.* Berkeley: University of California Press, 1942.

————, *Monetary Policies and Full Employment.* Berkeley: University of California Press, 1946.

Hansen, A. H., *Economic Policy and Full Employment,* Chapters I, XX, and Appendix D. New York: McGraw-Hill Book Company, Inc., 1947.

Harris, S. E., *Inflation and the American Economy.* New York: McGraw-Hill Book Company, Inc., 1945.

————, *Prices and Related Controls in the United States.* New York: McGraw-Hill Book Company, Inc., 1945.

Klein, L. R., *The Keynesian Revolution,* Chapter VI. New York: The Macmillan Co., 1947.

Salant, W. A., "The Inflationary Gap," *The American Economic Review,* June, 1942, Vol. XXXII, pages 308-314.

"Ten Economists on Inflation," *The Review of Economic Statistics,* February, 1948, Vol. XXX, pages 1-29.

(See also the items listed for Chapter 9.)

CHAPTER 11

Further Applications of Keynes' General Theory of Employment

With Keynes, practical advice was the goal and beacon-light of analysis . . .

Joseph A. Schumpeter, *The American Economic Review,* September, 1946, page 504.

THIS CHAPTER illustrates a few of the uses that have been made of Keynes' *The General Theory of Employment, Interest and Money* in some of the more important fields of economic policy. Previous chapters have indicated the relation of the *General Theory* to monetary policy, fiscal policy, public works, and inflation. In this chapter the fruitfulness of Keynes' work is further illustrated with reference to business cycles, international trade, and international finance.

Business Cycles

In offering an explanation of what determines at any time the prevailing level of employment and income, Keynes' *General Theory* provides also an explanation of the business cycle since the business cycle is nothing more than a rhythmic fluctuation in the over-all level of employment, income, and output. During the past decade, Keynes' general theory has become the focal point of discussion in the field of business-cycle analysis. It should be clear, however, that his work is not a theory of the business cycle as such. It is much more and also much less than that. It is more than a theory of the business cycle in the sense that it offers a general explanation for the level of employment, quite independently of the cyclical nature of changes in employment. It is less than a complete theory of the business cycle because it makes no attempt to give a detailed account of the various phases of the cycle, and does not examine closely the empirical data of cyclical fluctuations, something which any complete study of the business cycle would presumably attempt to do. Keynes' Chapter 22 entitled "Notes on the Trade Cycle" serves as a link between his general theory of employment and the conventional subject matter of business-cycle theory.

Keynes finds the essence of the business cycle in variations in the rate of investment caused by cyclical fluctuations in the marginal efficiency of capital. The rate of interest, which along with the marginal efficiency of capital determines the rate of investment, is relatively "sticky" or stable and is not a motivating force in cyclical fluctuations, although it does act as a reinforcing factor, especially in the financial crisis which often marks the early stage of depression. Likewise, the propensity to consume is relatively stable and is not an important factor accounting for cyclical fluctuations. Thus, of the three independent variables determining the volume of employment (the marginal efficiency of capital, the rate of interest, and the propensity to consume), it is the marginal efficiency of capital which plays the all-important role in business cycles. When it is recalled that the marginal efficiency of capital is nothing but another name for the expected rate of profit on new investment, we arrive at the very common-sense observation that business cycles in a profit economy result from variations in the rate of profit, or more specifically, from fluctuations in expectations as to what the rates of profit on varying types of investment will be in the future. In Chapter 7, it was noted that instability is the leading characteristic of the marginal efficiency of capital in the short run, as distinct from the secular tendency to decline in the long run under the impact of an increasing abundance of capital assets.

The "marginal efficiency of capital" differs from the more conventional "rate of profit" primarily in the emphasis in the former upon the *expected* as contrasted with the realized rate of return on capital assets. Our earlier discussion of expectations, including the place of the stock exchange in their determination, indicates the precarious nature of knowledge upon which expectations are based and explains why the marginal efficiency of capital is subject to sudden and violent changes. The multiplier, resting upon the fundamental principle that as income increases (decreases), consumption also increases (decreases), but by less than income, explains the cumulative nature of expansion and contraction. Once started in a given direction, activity in the whole economic system continues in that direction until checked by the exhaustion of the forces which push it upward and downward. These upswings and downswings move erratically rather than smoothly. Although there is great instability in economic life, there are limits to the degree of instability. The range within which cyclical fluctuations occur is explained by the principle that when income changes, consumption changes, but by lesser amounts.

The concept of the business cycle implies, in addition to the cumulative nature of economic forces that gradually exhaust themselves, some degree of regularity in the timing and duration of these alternate expansions and contractions. Therefore, a theory of the business cycle must explain the *cyclical* nature of economic fluctuations. Some types of economic fluctuations are not of a cyclical nature, but there are economic movements which are sufficiently regular in their recurrence to justify the concept of the business "cycle." Keynes suggests that these movements were more characteristic of the nineteenth century than they are of the twentieth. In the nineteenth century, the tremendous forces of economic growth and expansion maintained the marginal efficiency of capital at a level which, taken in relation to the rate of interest, was high enough to permit variations between full employment and less than full employment, i.e., between good times and bad times. In the twentieth century, the slowing down of factors like population growth and geographical expansion and the great increase in the accumulation of capital assets have, except in time of war and for a few years thereafter, rendered full employment virtually unattainable in an economy following the traditional policies of laissez-faire capitalism. The threat of secular stagnation has replaced the business cycle as the major problem of economic policy. But even within the framework of secular stagnation, cyclical movements persist. There are still business cycles even though they are fluctuations between bad and worse times rather than between good and bad times.

Course and phases of the business cycle

If we begin our sketch of the business cycle with the period of expansion that leads into the boom, we find investment going on at a rapid pace. The outlook is optimistic, confidence in the future is firm, the marginal efficiency of capital is high, and employment is rising. The prevailing opinion is that business activity will continue to improve for an indefinite period. Through the multiplier effect, each increment of new investment stimulates consumption to cause a multiple increase in income. As expansion enters the boom stage, the economic forces which tend to lower the marginal efficiency of capital begin to assert themselves. The high marginal efficiency of capital is subjected to pressure from two directions —from increasing costs of production of new capital assets as shortages and bottlenecks of materials and labor develop, and from the increasing abundance of output from recently completed capital assets which tends to lower some yields below expectations. The marginal efficiency of capital remains high only as long as optimism prevails and confidence in the future remains. Ultimately, the belief that high rates of return from new capital assets can continue indefinitely will reveal itself as an illusion. Costs of production continue to rise and output from competing investments continues to flow into the market.

The realities of costs and competition finally triumph over psychological optimism. When this occurs, as it inevitably must, optimism gives way to skepticism and then to pessimism. At this point, the marginal efficiency of capital collapses with a suddenness that may be catastrophic. All of the psychological forces which are so important in the erratic behavior of the stock exchange play a leading role in explaining the fall in the marginal efficiency of capital. As Keynes says, "It is of the nature of organized investment markets . . . that, when disillusion falls upon an over-optimistic and over-bought market, it should fall with sudden and even catastrophic force." (p. 316)[1] Investments which were made in anticipation of six per cent may, as a result of rising costs and falling yields, fall to only two per cent in conditions of high employment. But when over-optimism is replaced by over-pessimism, unemployment spreads, and the investment which would yield two per cent under high employment conditions may yield nothing at all under conditions of widespread unemployment.

The turning point from expansion to contraction is thus explained by a collapse in the marginal efficiency of capital. The change from an upward to a downward tendency takes place suddenly, and in this respect differs from the turning point from contraction to expansion, which occurs more gradually and often imperceptibly. The contraction which follows the collapse of the marginal efficiency of capital is likely to proceed at a rapid pace both because of the multiplier effect and because of a rise in the rate of interest. When investment begins to fall, the multiplier works in reverse. Each dollar of decreased investment multiplies itself into several dollars of decreased income. Employment goes tumbling down as investment falls off. The rate of interest rises because liquidity preference rises. The desire to liquidate inventories as well as securities before prices fall far, the reluctance to buy while prices are falling, and the need for money to meet contractual obligations at a time when sales are falling, all tend to

---

1. *The General Theory of Employment, Interest and Money.* New York, Harcourt, Brace and Co., Inc., 1936.

increase the strength of liquidity preference. The rise in the rate of interest is reflected in a fall in the prices of securities, especially bonds, whose yields are fixed in money. When a long-term bond paying $40 a year, previously selling at $1000, falls in the market to $800, the market rate of interest on this type of security has risen from 4 to approximately 5 per cent. Once the rate of interest begins to rise, the expectations of further rises tend to increase still further liquidity preference for the speculative motive. With everyone wishing to sell and no one wishing to buy, and with the prices of securities and goods tending to fall precipitously in a beggar-thy-neighbor fashion, money becomes the safest form of asset in which to store wealth during the economic crisis.

The collapse of the marginal efficiency of capital is the predominant cause of the crisis. Although many of the same forces which precipitate the collapse of the marginal efficiency of capital also raise the rate of interest through their influence upon expectations affecting liquidity preference, the sharp rise in liquidity preference occurs *after* the marginal efficiency of capital has collapsed. The rise in liquidity preference leading to a sharp increase in the rate of interest contributes to a further decline in investment and renders the slump intractable. This increase in the interest rate which occurs after the onset of the crisis is to be distinguished from smaller increases which usually take place during the boom as a result of increases in the demand for money to facilitate a larger volume of transactions.

The drastic fall in security prices on the stock exchange which accompanies the collapse of the marginal efficiency of capital tends to lower the propensity to consume. Equity holders are less prone to spend on consumption when the value of their investments is going down than when the value of their investments is going up. Although the propensity to consume depends primarily on current income, it is also influenced by capital gains and capital losses, even though these may be purely "paper" gains and losses and do not affect realized income. A man is more likely to feel he can

afford a new automobile each year when his stocks are high
and going higher than when his stocks are low and going
lower. Keynes suggests that a rising stock market may be
essential to a satisfactory propensity to consume in a "stock-
minded" country like the United States (p. 319).

Just as the collapse of the marginal efficiency of capital is
the predominant cause of contraction in business activity, so
its revival is the chief requisite of recovery. Restoration of
business confidence is the most important yet the most difficult factor to achieve. After contraction has been under way
for a time, it may be possible through proper monetary management to lower the rate of interest, but in the absence of a
return of confidence, the marginal efficiency of capital may
remain so low that no practicable reduction in the rate of
interest can stimulate substantial investment. Even if the rate
of interest were to be lowered to zero, business men would
not borrow if they had no expectation of making profits.[2]

The interval which must elapse before recovery will set in
is conditioned by (1) the time necessary for the wearing out
and obsolescence of durable capital, and (2) the time that
elapses before excess stocks, which accumulate toward the
end of the boom, can be absorbed. Just as the marginal efficiency of capital, or rate of profit, is pushed down during
expansion by a growing abundance of capital goods, so it will
be pushed up during contraction by a growing scarcity of
capital goods as a consequence of depreciation and obsolescence. Although the length of time is not rigidly determined,
it will be related to the average durability of capital assets at
the particular stage of economic development of the business
cycle in question. Average durability of capital assets will

---

2. It is often argued that a zero rate of interest would lead to an infinite
amount of borrowing and by this route to inflation. This conclusion does not
follow. If loans are for a finite period and if there is no guarantee that they
will be renewed, as is the case in the banking world, there is no reason to
assume that a zero rate of interest would have any great stimulating effect in
the depths of a severe depression. Investment would not increase as long as
the marginal efficiency of capital were less than zero, as it may well be for
some time after its collapse. See William J. Fellner, *Monetary Policies and
Full Employment*, page 169. Berkeley: University of California Press, 1946.

change over time, and as it changes the length of the period of contraction will tend to change in a corresponding direction.

The length of the contraction period is also conditioned by the time required to absorb excess stocks of goods left over from the boom. When the slump sets in and demand falls, entrepreneurs must choose between selling currently at losses or storing their goods until prices rise again to profitable levels. The latter alternative is conditioned by the carrying costs of stocks of goods. The costs of storage set a limit to the number of months or years over which stocks can profitably be carried. This time interval differs for different types of goods and with the storage facilities of different firms. For the economy as a whole, however, there will be a fairly definite period beyond which the carrying costs of stocks become prohibitive.

During the time that stocks are being depleted, total production may be less than total consumption. The absorption of excess stocks *per se* represents disinvestment or negative investment, which has a depressing effect on employment, just as positive investment has a stimulating effect on employment. If disinvestment through stock absorption is sufficiently widespread and sufficiently rapid, total income may temporarily fall below consumption. Such a situation can be only temporary because effective demand is self-perpetuating at a level where income is equal to consumption, that is, where there is no gap between income and consumption so that no investment is required to fill the gap. When consumption exceeds income, the average propensity to consume is greater than unity. According to the principle of effective demand, income will tend to rise at least to the level at which the average propensity to consume is unity. At any rate, when the absorption process is complete and disinvestment ceases, some improvement in employment will be experienced even though there is no increase in consumption and no positive investment.

The pattern of the cycle is also influenced by changes in the volume of working capital, or goods in process, as distinct from stocks of finished goods. Disinvestment in working capital begins earlier, and reinvestment also begins earlier, than in the case of stocks of finished goods. So far as stocks and their carrying costs are causal influences, Keynes estimates the period of contraction should not as a rule exceed three to five years in a modern industrial economy. Thus, the time required for durable assets to wear out and the time required to absorb surplus stocks together explain the approximate length of time before the marginal efficiency of capital will recover from the collapse it suffers at the end of the boom.

The rate of interest plays a part in the transition from contraction to expansion, although, as in the transition from expansion to contraction, it is secondary in importance to the marginal efficiency of capital. During the period of contraction which prepares the way for the recovery of investment, the rate of interest has a "natural" tendency to fall as a result of the decrease in the quantity of money required for business and income transactions. Even in the absence of a deliberate monetary policy aimed at lowering the rate of interest, the decline in prices and in the number of transactions will make additional funds available to satisfy the demand for money as a store of value. Although liquidity preference for the speculative motive may remain high, the increased quantity of money available to satisfy this motive may be sufficient to lower the rate of interest to a significant extent. The lower rate of interest, combined with a gradual recovery of the marginal efficiency of capital, will in time increase the inducement to invest and cause the expansion phase of the business cycle to set in once again. The length of the boom will be determined, roughly, by the time necessary to produce a sufficient increase in capital assets to cause a break in the marginal efficiency of capital, which leads once again into depression.

The investment multiplier and the trade cycle

A factor in Keynes' theory of the business cycle which is of significance, even though he does not develop it in his chapter on "Notes on the Trade Cycle," is the investment multiplier. As a rule, the investment multiplier falls in the expansion phase of the cycle and rises in the contraction phase. This cyclical change, or perhaps it might more appropriately be called an anti-cyclical change since it moves against the cycle, means that the multiplying power of equal amounts of investment becomes less and less with each further increase in employment and income. Each addition to income and employment becomes more costly in terms of investment. Each higher level of economic activity becomes more difficult to attain than the preceding level in terms of investment. As a multiplier of income, investment gradually weakens until at the peak of the boom it is at its lowest point of efficiency. In contraction, the decline in income and employment is accompanied by a rising multiplier. At each lower level a fall of one dollar in investment will result in a relatively greater fall in income, so that contraction is speeded up in depression by a rising multiplier just as expansion is slowed down in the boom by a falling multiplier. Of course, the multiplier principle works in both directions with equal force at any point in the cycle. In the boom, when the multiplier has a low value, say, of 2, an additional dollar of investment will increase income by only $2, but by the same token, a decrease of $1 in investment will lower income by only $2. In deep depression when the multiplier has a high value, say of 5, a further fall in investment of $1 results in a fall in income of $5; but by the same token, an increase in investment of $1 will lift income by $5. The violence of contraction after the collapse of the marginal efficiency of capital is to be explained by the large absolute amount of fall in investment rather than by a high multiplier value. As business activity dwindles to lower levels, the absolute amount of the fall in investment declines but this tends to be offset by a rising multiplier.

The fall of the multiplier in expansion and its rise in contraction is explained by changes in the propensity to consume. The principle that short-run or cyclical changes in income are accompanied by smaller changes in consumption in the same direction means that as income rises, the absolute size of the gap between income and consumption increases, and as income falls, the absolute size of the gap between income and consumption diminishes. A rise in community income will result in a smaller *proportion* of income being spent for consumption, and a fall in community income will result in a larger *proportion* of income being spent for consumption. As a rule to which there may be exceptions, when community income is high a smaller proportion of *additions* to income will be spent for consumption than when community income is low. When income is high, the community will spend a lesser proportion of its total income and also a lesser proportion of additions to its income than when income is at a low level. This indicates a declining average and a declining marginal propensity to consume. In terms of saving, in contrast to consumption, the rule is that the community will save a larger proportion of its income and a larger proportion of additions to income in a boom than in a depression. The multiplier, being equal to the reciprocal of the marginal propensity to save, will therefore tend to be lower in a boom when income is high, than in a depression when income is low. If, for example, the marginal propensity to save is ½ in the boom, the multiplier will be only 2, whereas if in the bottom of a depression the marginal propensity to save is only ⅕, the multiplier will be 5. Therefore, in the boom an additional dollar of investment will increase income by only $2, whereas in the depths of depression a dollar of investment will increase income by $5. In the boom, the amount of investment necessary to maintain a high level of employment will be large both in the absolute sense and also in the relative sense that an additional dollar of investment will support only $2 of increased income. In depression, a relatively small amount of investment may be capable of keeping income at a level considerably above consumption, because each dollar of additional investment will stimulate a $5 increase in income.

Although in depression a relatively small investment is capable of keeping income at a level considerably above consumption, it is also true that a small fall in investment leads to a relatively large fall in income—in the above example a fall of $1 in investment leads to a $5 fall in income. Once contraction begins and investment continues to fall, perhaps until it reaches zero or even less, and the multiplier increases in size, what is there to prevent employment from falling until no one is employed? The answer, of course, is the principle of effective demand. Although the multiplier grows in size, the total or absolute dependence of employment upon investment becomes less and less as income falls. Since income falls faster than consumption, the absolute size of the gap between them becomes smaller and smaller until at some point considerably below full employment but also considerably above zero employment, the gap disappears entirely. Income falls to equality with consumption, and may temporarily fall below consumption. At or below the point where income equals consumption, no investment is required to stabilize the level of income. This is the level of basic national income at which supply does create its own demand and which is self-sustaining without investment. Here employment is stabilized and will rest indefinitely until investment revives and begins to lift it upward once again. Hence Keynes' theory of effective demand and the multiplier principle derived from it explain both the instability which characterizes the business cycle and also the limits of the instability.

Keynes' theory vs. overinvestment and underconsumption theories of the cycle

In a strict sense Keynes' theory of the business cycle is neither an overinvestment nor an underconsumption theory, although it has much more in common with the latter than with the former. Most underconsumption theories of the cycle explain underconsumption in terms of previous overinvestment which releases a flood of goods so great than consumer demand is incapable of absorbing them. As long as the point of reference is full employment, overinvestment and underconsumption amount to the same thing. Strange as it may seem, the starting point of many explanations of the business cycle is full employment so that many underconsumption theories are also overinvestment theories. If overinvestment were the true cause of the business cycle, the remedy for a slump would be to raise the rate of interest in order to check excessive investment during the boom. Keynes, however, is opposed to raising the rate of interest for the purpose of checking investment during expansion. He suggests a depression can best be avoided if the boom is perpetuated by creating conditions which will maintain a high rate of investment. During booms there develop maladjustments which should not be perpetuated, but, broadly speaking, the fault of the economic system is not too much investment but too little. Investment can be increased by lowering and not by raising the rate of interest. Investment of the right type should continue without interruption until capital assets cease to be scarce and their rate of return is reduced to zero. Keynes calls this the point of "full investment." Only beyond the point of full investment would "overinvestment" have any definite meaning. It would mean that additional investment would lower the marginal efficiency of capital to a negative rate. Since there would be no incentive to invest at losses, net investment would cease at the point of "full investment."

Keynes agrees with the underconsumptionists that an unequal distribution of income contributes to an inadequate demand for consumption goods and services, but he disagrees with their view that depression is caused by an oversupply of consumer goods flowing from previous overinvestment. The fault of most underconsumption theories lies in placing the blame for depression and unemployment on savings which are invested, whereas stress should be placed on potential savings which are not realized because of lack of investment. The fault is more one of underinvestment than of overinvestment. Keynes recommends attacking unemployment along two fronts—by increasing consumption and investment simultaneously.

Keynes' stress on underinvestment rather than underconsumption is associated with his conservative attitude toward economic reform He recognizes that the need for more investment grows out of the limited ability to consume which, in part at least, grows out of the concentration of income in capitalistic society. Socialistically inclined underconsumption theorists like John A. Hobson believe the remedy for unemployment lies in increasing the propensity to consume through a reconstruction of the economic system, whereas Keynes accepts the existing social structure and the accompanying distribution of income and advocates making up for the deficiency in consumer demand by increasing investment demand. Keynes apparently feels that when the point of "full investment" in his sense is reached, the redistribution of income will have automatically been taken care of because the reward for owning as such will have disappeared in a process he calls the "euthanasia of the rentier." Keynes recognizes there is a strong case for redistributing income in a manner which will increase the propensity to consume before the point of "full investment" is reached, but this suggestion is incidental rather than central and is not implemented in his theoretical apparatus.

International Economic Relations

Long before Keynes wrote *The General Theory of Employment, Interest and Money,* he was one of the leading critics of conventional views on monetary problems in the international as well as in the domestic field. Nearly all of Keynes' writings are filled with direct and indirect applications of his theories to international economic relations. The *General Theory* is more concerned with domestic than with international economics, but even this work has significant applications to international economic theory and policy. A few of these applications are developed in Chapter 23 of the *General*

Theory and others are elaborated elsewhere in his writings, especially in connection with his participation in the formation of the International Monetary Fund and the International Bank for Reconstruction and Development. Keynes was the chief author of the British plan for an International Clearing Union, which was later integrated with the American plan at Bretton Woods to form the Fund and the Bank.

The favorable balance of trade as investment

Since the time of Adam Smith, nearly all academic economists have been severe critics of what they regard as the "fallacies" of mercantilism. Keynes' criticisms of the classical theory lead quite naturally to a sympathetic attitude toward many mercantilistic ideas which economists have regarded as long since dead and buried. Although it would be misleading to call Keynes a "mercantilist," his position on some important issues is much nearer the mercantilist than the classical position.

A cardinal principle of mercantilism was high esteem for a "favorable balance of trade," by which was meant an excess of exports of goods and services over imports of goods and services. To the mercantilists, a favorable balance of trade was a technique whereby an individual nation sold more than it purchased abroad in order that it might collect the difference, or "balance," in gold and silver. Precious metals were regarded as a particularly desirable form of wealth. For nations which did not mine gold and silver within their borders, the businesslike method of acquiring them was to sell more goods than were bought in order that the balance could be collected in money, that is, in gold and silver. Classical economics teaches that the idea of a favorable balance of trade and the desire for large stores of precious metals are irrational and illusory. According to classical doctrine, gold and silver are not true wealth and it is irrational to attempt to accumulate large supplies of them. It is also irrational to want to send more goods out of the country than are brought into the country, since this leaves the nation poorer in real wealth. The so-called favorable balance of trade is an illusory technique for obtaining gold and silver except for a brief period, because the importation of precious metals increases the quantity of money within the domestic economy and, by causing prices to rise, renders the domestic economy a less favorable market in which to buy. With prices at a higher level as a result of the increase in the quantity of money, foreigners will buy less and some domestic buyers who previously purchased at home will be driven to purchase abroad because of higher domestic prices and lower foreign prices. The lower foreign prices result from the unfavorable balance of trade of countries sending gold and silver to the home country. The precious metals, which for a time flow into the domestic economy, will set in motion price movements that will cause them to flow out of the country again.

Keynes finds considerable merit in the mercantilist theory of the favorable balance of trade and points out important fallacies in the classical argument. The favorable balance of trade is desirable from the view of maintaining employment because to the domestic economy it represents a form of investment. As the *General Theory* shows, domestic employment can be maintained by a high rate of investment, which may be either domestic or foreign. The current rate of foreign investment is determined by the excess of exports over imports, that is, by the size of the favorable balance of trade. An increase in the favorable balance, either in the form of increased exports or of decreased imports, increases employment in the same way domestic investment increases employment. The multiplier effect and all the rest work in the same manner for foreign as for domestic investment. The total investment of a nation is the excess of its production over current domestic consumption. So far as the employment-creating effects are concerned, it does not matter what form the exports take. They may all be goods for current consumption by foreigners, or they may be capital goods which will be used for building up the productive capacity of the foreign

nation. The excess of exports over imports, which is investment from the domestic point of view regardless of their
form, may represent from the world point of view either consumption or investment. The foregoing chapters have emphasized repeatedly that, given the propensity to consume, the
maintenance of employment depends upon the volume of investment. Employment can increase only if there is an increase in investment. If there is unemployment at home, an
increase in the size of the favorable balance of trade represents new investment to the nation in question and will, like
domestic investment, increase income not only by the amount
of investment but by some multiple of it, depending upon
the size of the multiplier. A high rate of investment has always been a necessary condition for the successful functioning of capitalist economies. Hence, any policy which tends
to promote investment is desirable in capitalistic economies.
The mercantilists, who wrote during the period of early capitalism, were therefore fundamentally correct in their insight
which led them to advocate a favorable balance of trade.

A favorable balance of trade works in yet another way to
promote domestic employment. The importation of precious
metals resulting from the favorable balance increases the
domestic quantity of money, lowers the rate of interest at
home, and stimulates a larger volume of domestic investment.
During early capitalism when the money supply was more
closely tied to gold and silver, the importation of precious
metals had a greater influence upon the rate of interest than
would be true under the managed currencies of contemporary
capitalism. In so far as unemployment was a threat during
early capitalism—which it was to some extent—and in the
absence of positive measures to prevent it, there was merit in
the mercantilistic desire to attain a favorable balance of
trade.

Keynes' sympathetic treatment of mercantilist theories does
not mean he advocates a return to the policies historically
associated with these ideas. He does show, however, that the
practical statesmanship of the mercantilists did not rest on

fallacious reasoning but upon shrewd insights into the functioning of the economic system which they sought to guide. In order to promote the favorable balance of trade, they resorted to export restrictions and, more important, to import restrictions like protective tariffs. In the mercantilist period these trade restrictions may have been the most effective means for realizing a favorable balance, but Keynes points out that export and import controls are not necessarily the best means for achieving a large favorable balance of trade and a high level of domestic employment. During the nineteenth century, for example, he suggests that complete freedom of trade was the policy best designed to promote a maximum balance of trade for England. Thus, the British advocates of free trade in the nineteenth century were not necessarily less nationalistic in their outlook than the mercantilists. Nevertheless, the mercantilist perspective was such as to overlook many of the advantages of an international division of labor. Protectionism may yield advantages to some nations, but it is much less likely to benefit the world as a whole than free trade.

Free trade vs. protectionism

New light is shed upon the controversy of free trade versus protectionism by Keynes' *General Theory*. The traditional case for free trade proves too much because it ignores unemployment. If it is true that employment depends on effective demand, as Keynes contends, and that effective demand may be inadequate to provide full employment, then it is quite possible for a single nation to increase its employment through a system of protective tariffs, and in this manner to increase the demand for domestic labor at the expense of foreign labor. Only if full employment is assumed, does the conclusion necessarily follow that a country will be better off if it buys abroad whatever it can purchase more cheaply than it can produce at home. Then real wages and other forms of income will be maximized because incomes are proportional to productivity and productivity is maximized when each country produces those items in which it enjoys the greatest comparative advantage, exchanging surpluses of these commodities to other countries for the things in which other countries have the greatest comparative advantage. Like all classical theory, this argument for free trade is based on the assumption of full employment. Where full and continuous employment prevails, there is little doubt concerning the validity of the free trade argument. Under full employment, real national income is maximized when unit costs of production are minimized, as they are under free trade. An industry requires protection only if it is less efficient than the same industry in some other country. Hence, protection interferes with the most economical use of national and world resources. Protection causes productivity to be less and real income to be less than they would be if each nation produced those things for which its resources are best suited under conditions of free world trade. Under protectionism, the national income may be greater than under free trade because of a higher level of employment resulting from a higher level of effective demand. The wastes of unemployment may outweigh the wastes of a poor allocation of resources. The alternative to employing workmen less efficiently under protectionism may be no employment at all. Of course, the higher unit costs of production are in themselves a national disadvantage to be weighed against the advantages of greater employment. From the viewpoint of a single country, the question of tariffs is simply which of these two counteracting tendencies will yield the larger real national income. Protection is more likely to increase real national income in periods of large-scale unemployment than in periods of small-scale unemployment. As in all cases where Keynes' theory challenges the conclusions of classical theory, the key to the whole matter is his assumption of less than full employment. There is no inconsistency, except in the different assumptions, between the theory which justifies free trade under conditions of full employment, on the one hand, and on the other hand the theory which justifies, under conditions of less than full employment, protective tariffs as a means to increasing national welfare by raising employment and real national income.

The strongest case against protective tariffs in a world of unemployment is that they, like mercantilistic policies in general, are nationalistic. Benefits to one nation are gained at the expense of ,other nations. If protective tariffs increase employment in one country, they do so at the price of increased unemployment in other countries. Although a favorable balance of trade is equivalent to investment for the nation which exports more than it imports, for the world as a whole, it does not represent investment. World exports must equal world imports, which means that the excess of exports from some nations is offset by an excess of imports to the rest of the nations of the world. All nations cannot export more than they import and' thus all cannot enjoy the benefits of a favorable balance of trade. Increases in employment which result from the favorable balance in one nation may be matched by decreases in employment in other nations of the world.

Foreign Exchange Stabilization

The international gold standard, which was closely associated with classical economic theory and its general laissez-faire attitude toward economic policy, was one of the earliest objects of criticism by Keynes. In his first book, *Indian Currency and Finance* (1913), he compared the conventional gold standard unfavorably with the gold exchange standard. In the *Tract on Monetary Reform* (1923), Keynes advocated a managed currency which he thought would permit a greater stability of the domestic price level than could be achieved under the gold standard, combined with short-term stability and long-run flexibility of foreign exchange rates. Keynes remained a relentless critic of orthodoxy in foreign exchange policy, and finally toward the end of his career, when his views on gold became generally accepted, he saw the objective outlined in his *Tract* realized in the International Monetary Fund set up at Bretton Woods.

Criticism of the international gold standard

The great fault of the international gold standard, as it operated after the first world war, was that it tended to cause deflation and unemployment in countries with an excess of imports over exports. During the 1920's England returned to the gold standard at a subsequent cost that was to prove more than she could bear, and in 1931 gold was abandoned after doing great harm to the world and to the British economy. A gold standard requires that a nation, usually through its monetary authority, stand ready to buy and to sell gold at a price fixed in terms of its domestic currency. When a nation is importing more goods than it is exporting, gold tends to go abroad to offset the unfavorable balance of trade. If the deficit in exports continues for a time, a wholesale loss of gold can be prevented only if the monetary authority takes positive steps to protect the national stock of gold. The theory of the gold standard is that the drain on gold will cause prices to fall in the deficit nation, and the influx of gold will cause prices to rise in the country with a surplus of exports. By virtue of flexible domestic prices, the country exporting gold becomes a better place in which to buy and the country importing gold a less favorable place in which to buy. The result, according to theory, is a reversal of the flow of goods and the flow of gold.

In the 1920's, when gold was flowing into the United States and out of Britain at an unprecedented rate, American prices did not rise as they should have for the automatic gold standard adjustments to take place. The failure of American prices to rise was partly because the American monetary authority, the Federal Reserve System, was fearful of the effects of rising prices and so did not allow imported gold to be used as a basis for credit expansion, and partly because there was a lesser connection between gold stocks and domestic prices than the gold standard theory takes for granted. Probably the latter was much the more important reason. In Britain, domestic prices did not fall according to the postulates of the gold standard, partly because of inflexible wages and prices, and partly because of a decreasing connection between gold stocks and domestic prices. Hence, the "automatic" adjustments presupposed in the traditional theory of the gold standard were missing. Instead of lower prices, Britain got unemployment. In order to protect the nation's declining gold stocks, the British bank rate was raised to attract foreign lending to London and to discourage foreign lending by Englishmen. An increase in the bank rate meant an increase in the domestic rate of interest, which in turn led to a fall in domestic investment, income, and employment. As domestic incomes fell, the demand for imports fell because people at home had less money to spend abroad. As a result, the unfavorable balance of trade was reduced. In England, as imports fell in relation to exports, the foreign exchange rate rose because the demand for foreign currencies (dollars) in relation to the home currency (pounds) was reduced. Less foreign currency was needed to settle the fewer purchases being made abroad.

To rescue the gold standard in a deficit nation under modern conditions means to sacrifice control of the domestic rate of interest; it means a reduction in investment, employment, and income via high interest rates; it means deflation at home, which, among other things, involves an attempt to lower costs in home industries to the point where they will be able to compete on favorable terms in foreign markets; it means pressure to reduce wage rates as a means for getting lower costs of production, and lower wage rates are resisted by organized labor; it probably means industrial strife, strikes, and interrupted production. After all these painful adjustments, the gold standard may be saved but at a price which no nation can afford to pay. Keynes concluded early in the 'twenties that unemployment and deflation, the inevitable consequences of the gold standard in a nation in Britain's position at that time, were evils which far outweighed the advantages of the gold standard.

Proposal for exchange stability
without the gold standard

Nevertheless, an undeniable advantage of the gold standard is the stability of exchange rates among gold standard countries. Stable foreign exchange rates encourage international trade by enabling those who buy from foreigners and those who sell to foreigners to know how much they will have to pay and how much they will receive in terms of their own domestic currency. Imports must be paid for in money acceptable to foreign sellers, and exports are sold to foreigners whose foreign currency must be converted into currency acceptable to the domestic sellers. Unstable exchange rates add unnecessarily to the risks of international trading. The leading problem of international finance is how to preserve the stability of foreign exchange rates, which the international gold standard did provide, without subjecting domestic economies, especially those which are importing more than they are exporting, to the ravages of unemployment and deflation which result from the high interest rate required to make the gold standard work. During the inter-war years after the breakdown of the gold standard throughout the world, there developed a hodge-podge of exchange controls, quota systems, blocked currencies, and barter agreements. These stop-gap measures are clearly unsatisfactory in a well-ordered world economy. They sacrifice many of the economic gains from an international division of labor because nations which sell under bilateral agreements are unable to buy except from the country to which they sell, and often what they might want from these countries is not available to them. To escape from these evils as well as from the ill effects of the gold standard on domestic stability, yet to gain short-term stability and long-term flexibility of foreign exchange rates, was the purpose of Keynes' proposal for an International Clearing Union. This proposal was made by the British Government in 1943 while Keynes was serving as a special adviser to the British Treasury.

In describing to the House of Lords the official British

proposal for the International Clearing Union, a plan of which he was the chief but not the exclusive author, Keynes summarized the main purpose as follows: "The principal object can be explained in a single sentence: To provide that money earned by selling goods to one country can be spent on purchasing the products of any other country. In jargon, a system of multilateral clearing. In English, a universal currency valid for trade transactions in all the world. Everything else in the plan is ancillary to that."[3] When a British textile manufacturer pays for cotton purchased in the United States, the American seller does not necessarily wish to use the proceeds of his sale to buy things from England. Nor does any other American necessarily wish to buy British goods. In so far as Americans wish to buy abroad at all, they may wish to offset the sale of cotton to Britain by the purchase of coffee from Brazil or natural rubber from the Netherlands Indies or by some combination of such purchases of imports. It is prerequisite to the widest international division of labor that Americans be able to use their foreign exchange secured from cotton sales to Britain to purchase wherever and whatever they wish. Under the International Clearing Union, the pounds paid by British buyers of American cotton would be converted into an international form of money known as "bancor" and credited to the account of the United States, which could then spend it for goods and services anywhere in the world. Every nation would have an account in "bancor" which would be debited or credited whenever purchases or sales were made in international trade. Individual countries' accounts would be cancelled against each other and the remaining balances cleared through the International Clearing Union. The clearing technique which has so long been part of domestic banking facilities was to be carried over into the field of international financial relations.

The Keynes plan for an International Clearing Union was, like all of Keynes' peacetime programs, expansionist in na-

3. *Parliamentary Debates on an International Clearing Union*, House of Lords, page 76. May 18, 1943, British Information Service.

ture. It provided for the establishment of large initial credits of the new international money, "bancor," which credits were in the nature of overdraft facilities so familiar in British banking. The amount of the initial credit alloted to each nation was based on the volume of foreign trade before the war. In contrast with the American or White Plan, the plan actually adopted at Bretton Woods, the Keynes plan called for no contribution of gold to the International Fund. However, gold was not completely ignored in the Keynes plan because the new international money, "bancor," could be purchased with gold even though it could not be converted into gold. Thus, countries with large stocks of gold or countries which mine large quantities of gold would not suffer from its de-monitization.

One of the merits claimed by Keynes for the International Clearing Union was that it would get around the difficulty caused when some nations export without importing to an equal extent. Under the gold standard, gold flowed to the na-tions with a favorable balance of trade and thereafter the gold was removed from circulation so far as world trade was concerned. Between the two world wars, most of the world's monetary gold came into the possession of the United States, only to be buried under the ground at Fort Knox, Kentucky. This represented a form of international hoarding which did not decrease the total amount of money actually held but did reduce the amount in active circulation and re-duced the effective demand for goods and services.

The failure of a strong exporting nation, e.g., the United States, to make use of its balance represents a fall in effective demand in world trade. It represents sales which are not fol-lowed by purchases. Under the Clearing Union, a nation ex-porting more goods and services than it imports could use its balance only to purchase goods from some other countries. Its balance could not be converted into gold for hoarding. Keynes believed one of the novel features of his plan was its attempt to mitigate international hoarding, to free in the in-ternational field the effective demand which tended to get locked up in buried gold. However, his plan was only a beginning and the measures in this respect were relatively mild. Nations which sold and refused to buy would find themselves with growing idle balances of "bancor" which they could not withdraw or convert into gold. They would be exposed to the world and to themselves as guilty of anti-social behavior. Keynes felt that moral pressures as well as enlightened self-interest would lead the offending creditor nations to take corrective steps to increase their international purchases and thereby reduce their unused balances. He said to the House of Lords: "We have lately come to understand more clearly than before how employment and the creation of new incomes out of new production can only be maintained through the expenditure on goods and services of the income previously earned. This is equally true of home trade and of foreign trade."[4] Keynes was striving to carry over into international economics the principles of effective demand outlined in his *General Theory* for domestic economics.

The International Clearing Union was more than an attempt to extend the principles of the general theory of employment to the field of international economic relations. It represents a natural and necessary complement to the closed-economy economics of the *General Theory*. The International Clearing Union, as well as the International Monetary Fund which was actually established, was intended to integrate domestic economic systems into the international economy without sacrificing domestic stability. The traditional gold standard integrated domestic economic systems into the international economy at the price of domestic stability, caused by high interest rates, depressed investment, unstable prices, and unemployment. The International Clearing Union retained the one chief virtue of the gold standard—short-term stability of foreign exchange rates—in a manner consistent with the domestic stabilization of employment at a high level by means of low interest rates, stable domestic price levels, and such other measures as public investment, et cetera

4. *Ibid.*, page 77.

which may be required for the purpose. In the long run, the
Keynes plan allowed for flexibility in foreign exchange rates
to the degree necessary to adjust to long-term changes in the
relation of the domestic to the international economy. This
adjustment was to be one of changing the external value of
the domestic currency to coincide with its domestic value,
rather than making the adjustment the other way around, as
required under the international gold standard.

References for Further Reading

Keynes, J. M., *The General Theory of Employment, Interest and
Money*, Chapters 22 and 23. Also Chapters 11 and 12. New
York: Harcourt, Brace and Company, 1936.

——, *Monetary Reform*, especially Chapter III on "The Theory of
Money and of the Foreign Exchanges." New York: Harcourt,
Brace and Company, 1924.

——, *A Treatise on Money*, especially Books IV, VI, and VII.
New York: Harcourt, Brace and Company, 1930.

——, "The Balance of Payments of the United States," *The Economic Journal*, June, 1946, Vol. LVI, pages 172-187.

——, "The Objective of International Price Stability," *The Economic Journal*, June-September, 1943, Vol. LIII, pages 185-187.

——, "The International Clearing Union," A speech delivered by
Keynes before the House of Lords, May 23, 1944. Reprinted in
The New Economics, edited by S. E. Harris, pages 359-368.
New York: Alfred A. Knopf, 1947.

——, "The International Monetary Fund," A speech delivered by
Keynes before the House of Lords, May 23, 1944. Reprinted in
The New Economics, edited by S. E. Harris, pages 369-379.
New York: Alfred A. Knopf, 1947.

Angell, J. W., *Investment and Business Cycles*. New York: McGraw-
Hill Book Company, Inc., 1941.

Harrod, R. F., *The Trade Cycle*. London: Oxford Press, 1936.

Kaldor, Nicholas, "A Model of the Trade Cycle," *The Economic
Journal*, March, 1940, Vol. L, pages 78-92.

Kalecki, Michal, *Essays in the Theory of Economic Fluctuations*.
New York: Farrar and Rinehart, Inc., 1939.

Lerner, A. P., *The Economics of Control*, Chapter 23 on business
cycles and Chapters 26, 27, and 28 on foreign trade. New York:
The Macmillan Company, 1944.

Metzler, L. A., "Keynes and the Theory of Business Cycles," in *The New Economics*, edited by S. E. Harris, Chapter XXXIII, pages 436-449. New York: Alfred A. Knopf, 1947.

Robinson, Joan, "The International Currency Proposals," *The Economic Journal*, June-September, 1943, Vol. LIII, pages 161-175.

Williams, John H., *Postwar Monetary Plans and Other Essays*. Third Edition. New York: Alfred A. Knopf, 1947.

CHAPTER 12

The Development of Keynes' Thought and the Social Philosophy Toward Which It Leads

> Whilst, therefore, the enlargement of the functions of government, involved in the task of adjusting to one another the propensity to consume and the inducement to invest, would seem to a nineteenth-century publicist or to a contemporary American financier to be a terrific encroachment on individualism, I defend it, on the contrary, both as the only practicable means of avoiding the destruction of existing economic forms in their entirety and as the condition of the successful functioning of individual initiative.
>
> J. M. Keynes, *The General Theory of Employment, Interest and Money*, page 380.*

THE FOREGOING chapters have dealt almost exclusively with Keynes' *The General Theory of Employment, Interest and Money*. This work, which was published in 1936 when Keynes was fifty-two years of age, marks the breaking point with the classical school and the working out of a system of economic theory along anti-classical lines. Preceding this event, Keynes had been an adherent of the general classical tradition. While his break with the classical school may appear to have been

---

* Harcourt. Brace and Co., Inc., 1936.

quite sudden, his earlier writing and thinking contain many elements of his later position. In the present chapter an attempt is made to trace the gradual development of Keynes' thought during the period in which he accepted the classical theory and to show why, after so many years, he changed to the unorthodox position which is presented in the *General Theory* and outlined in the preceding chapters.

There was nothing capricious or fortuitous about Keynes' break with the classical tradition. It grew out of long experience from which there developed gradually the conviction that classical economics is inadequate to deal with the pressing problems of contemporary economic society. The practical implications of classical economics are essentially laissez-faire, and laissez-faire was dying during the first world war and the years which followed. Keynes wrote a tract called *The End of Laissez-Faire* in 1926. Since his theory was always geared to policy, the logical outcome of the conviction that laissez-faire was dead must have led rather surely in time to the further conviction that classical economics as an adequate system of thought was also dead. To develop a systematic body of theory to replace the classical principles required time. The formative period of the *General Theory* was the decade or more prior to its publication, when it became apparent that England would not make a full recovery from the primary postwar depression. The *Treatise on Money* (1930) is in this sense a transitional work, but the real break with the classical theory came after the *Treatise* and culminates in the *General Theory*. Yet, in a broader sense, Keynes' formative period begins with his very first writing, which contains criticisms of orthodox economics. The main question to be answered is why such a book as the *General Theory* came to be written. This involves the forces at work in the environment, and the reaction of Keynes to these forces. If the *General Theory* is a great work, as surely it is, the answer to this question of why it was written must enrich our appreciation of its meaning and influence. This task might have been performed before the general theory itself was explained, but it was felt that the story of its development would have greater significance if the reader first knew what the final outcome of this process of development was to be. While this procedure would not be desirable in mystery thrillers, it seems the best approach to a solid body of economic thought.

A word should be inserted concerning the nature of Keynes' challenge to traditional economics. He has not questioned the method or the scope of classical Anglo-Saxon economics. His challenge is rather to the content, that is, the assumptions, of the classical doctrine. As previously indicated, Keynes contends that his theory is a *general* theory of employment of resources, whereas the classical theory pertains only to a special case, the case of full employment. Critics of the classical conception of the appropriate method and scope of economics will not find Keynes' general theory satisfactory, even though they may feel it is an improvement over the classical position. However, if the matter is viewed pragmatically, in a manner which takes as fundamental the relation between theory and policy, Keynes' new departure has been quite as useful in challenging the old tenets of economic policy as a challenge directed at method and scope could have been. It seems clear that the greatness of Keynes' work lies in its impact on economic policy.

Development Prior to the Great Depression

The general thesis of the following discussion is that Keynes changed from a classical to an anti-classical economic theorist because of a change in his ideas about economic policy. His anti-classical economic theory is derived from his practical position, which may be characterized as an attack on financial capitalism and a defense of industrial capitalism.

The framework of interpretation for this thesis attributes to Keynes a dualism between the financial and the industrial aspects of modern capitalism. The terms "financial" and "industrial" capitalism are not used by Keynes, but they may be approximately identified with his distinction between "finance" and "industry" or between "financial circulation" and "industrial circulation," as he employs these categories in his *Treatise on Money*. Keynes defines "finance" as "the business of holding and exchanging existing titles to wealth, . . . including Stock Exchange and Money Market transactions, speculation and the process of conveying current savings and profits into the hands of entrepreneurs." He defines "industry" as "the business of maintaining the normal process of current output, distribution and exchange and paying the factors of production their incomes for the various duties which they perform from the first beginning of production to the final satisfaction of the consumer."[1] In the *General Theory*, the dichotomy between "industry" and "finance" reappears in the form of the distinction between M_1, or money held to satisfy the transactions and precautionary motives (industry), and M_2, or money held to satisfy the speculative motive (finance).

As long as Keynes remained an adherent of the general classical tradition and was preoccupied with short-run monetary problems, he had no occasion to develop a theory of capitalism. In his later thinking, however, he began to question aspects of the fundamental structure of capitalism, even to the point of foreseeing as a condition of its survival the disappearance of all rentier capitalism. In these later writings, especially the *General Theory*, the ever-present distinction between "finance" and "industry" became the framework for his fragmentary theory of capitalism. Even in these later stages of his thought, Keynes did not develop a theory of capitalism in the self-conscious sense in which Werner Sombart, or Karl Marx, or Thorstein Veblen developed theories of capitalism. The chief task of the present section is to trace the development of Keynes' early thinking in terms of the distinction between "finance" and "industry."

Keynes was not the cloistered scholar that many, if not most, of his fellow economists have been. In his preoccupa-

---

1. *Treatise on Money*, Vol. I, Chap. XV, "The Industrial Circulation and the Financial Circulation," page 243. New York: Harcourt, Brace and Company, Inc., 1930.

tion with the world of affairs as well as with the world of theory, he found it necessary to divorce himself from the orthodox tradition and, in the process of estrangement, was led to a position which has long and interesting antecedents. This is, as Keynes partly recognized, the tradition of the monetary heretics such as Silvio Gesell, Proudhon, the Ricardian socialists, the mercantilists, and even of the canonists, with their strictures against taking interest.[2]

Keynes' early opposition to orthodox *monetary* theory is evident in his first important publication, *Indian Currency and Finance* (1913).[3] This work was essentially an attack on the report of the British Fowler Committee of 1898, which had recommended the adoption of the gold standard for India.[4] Though *Indian Currency and Finance* is for the most part a technical treatment of a special problem, Keynes draws certain conclusions which have terms of reference much broader than the problem of Indian currency and finance. He was impressed by the uneconomic consequences to India of her propensity to hoard great stores of gold and silver. At the time (1913), the price levels of western Europe were being prevented from a rapid increase only because India—the "sink of precious metals"—was absorbing large amounts of gold which were flowing in great quantities from newly opened mines, especially those of South Africa, where production had just reached its zenith. Consequently, the gold standard was not working so badly in Europe. However, Keynes warned Europe not to continue to leave "the most intimate adjustments of our economic organism at the mercy of a lucky prospector, a new chemical process, or a change of ideas in Asia."[5] These ideas regarding Indian currency and finance foreshadow Keynes' later stress on hoarding as a

2. "A Self-Adjusting Economic System?" *The New Republic*, February 20, 1935, Vol. LXXXII, No. 1055, page 35.

3. London: Macmillan and Company, Ltd., 1913. See especially page 99.

4. See *Report of the Royal Commission on Indian Currency and Finance*, Vol. I. London: His Majesty's Stationery Office, 1926.

5. *Indian Currency and Finance*, page 101.

brake on economic progress and on his preference for a managed currency instead of the "automatic" gold standard.

In *The Economic Consequences of the Peace* (1920), Keynes' chapter on "Europe Before the War" has particular significance for any study of his subsequent economic writings because here he sketches his long-view perspective of the capitalist process. His emphasis is upon the underlying instability of the outwardly placid currents of European capitalism before the war, a war which "had so shaken this system as to endanger the life of Europe altogether."[6] In numerous passages, Keynes expresses a skepticism which suggests a starting point for the rather far-reaching changes in social relations called for by the program of the *General Theory*. The relations between the laboring and capitalist classes are portrayed as a game of deception and of double bluff, designed to attain the maximum accumulation of capital, but resting on a psychological base so unstable that it might crumble if either the laboring class or the capitalist class should cease to be satisfied with a rate of consumption very small in comparison with the creation of wealth:

It was not natural for a population, of whom so few enjoyed the comforts of life, to accumulate so hugely. The war has disclosed the possibility of consumption to all and the vanity of abstinence to many. Thus the bluff is discovered; the laboring classes may be no longer willing to forego so largely, and the capitalist classes, no longer confident of the future, may seek to enjoy more fully their liberties of consumption so long as they last, and thus precipitate the hour of their confiscation.[7]

The laboring class did not consume more because its members received rights to only a small share of the national dividend. The capitalist class preferred the enjoyment of the power of accumulated wealth to the enjoyment of consumption on a large scale. "It was precisely the *inequality* of the distribution of wealth," Keynes wrote, "which made possible those vast accumulations of fixed wealth and of capital im-

---

6. Page 25. New York: Harcourt, Brace and Howe, 1920.

7. *Economic Consequences of the Peace*, page 22.

provements which distinguished that age from all others. Herein lay, in fact, the main justification of the Capitalist System."[8] Whether the laboring class would be satisfied with its lot and whether, in the light of uncertainty, the capitalist class would continue to venture its capital were crucial issues. Keynes never embraced capitalism wholeheartedly. He favored it because "Capitalism, wisely managed, can probably be made more efficient than any alternative system." But capitalism "in itself is in many ways extremely objectionable."[9]

Whereas exercise of the duty of "saving" by the capitalist class, coupled with inequality of wealth and income, yielded maximum accumulation in pre-1914 Europe, such saving was, on the whole, irrational:

The duty of "saving" became nine-tenths of virtue and the growth of the cake the object of true religion . . . the cake increased; but to what end was not clearly contemplated. . . . Saving was for old age or for your children; but this was only in theory,—the virtue of the cake was that it was never to be consumed, neither by you nor by your children after you.[10]

This passage is interesting because, like the *General Theory*, it attacks thrift as an irrational type of behavior. It also stresses the importance of habit in influencing the propensity to save, and thus contrasts with the view that interest is the reward for saving. Keynes' subsequent refutation of the classical theory of interest rests on his repudiation of the idea that interest is a reward for saving, or for waiting, or for abstinence.

Following publication of *Economic Consequences of the Peace*, Keynes plunged into some of the most important postwar European controversies on economic policy. During the decade of the 'twenties he was concerned primarily with three problems: an appeal for reduction of war debts, reparations, and debt service; opposition to postwar deflationary tenden-

---

8. *Ibid.*, page 19.

9. *Laissez-faire and Communism*, pages 76-77. New York: New Republic, 1926.

10. *Economic Consequences of the Peace*, page 20.

cies in Britain; and opposition to the return to the gold standard. In the Preface to a collection of his more important miscellaneous writings of the 1920's, Keynes characterized his general attitude toward these, and all other similar issues, as "the profound conviction that the Economic Problem of want and poverty and the economic struggle between classes and nations is nothing but a frightful muddle, a transitory and an *unnecessary* muddle."[11] Here we see the liberal mind at work attempting to reconcile the grave issues of the day. Liberalism as a habit of mind tends to impute evil to wrong thinking rather than to irreconcilable conflicts embedded in the structure of society. This thesis that ideas are more powerful than vested interests and that by changing our minds we can change the world recurs frequently in Keynes' writings, for example, in the closing paragraph of the *General Theory*. So we find Keynes always ready with a plan, a compromise, or an amendment for resolving the problem at hand.

In the huge war debts, Keynes saw a menace to stability everywhere. As remedies, he suggested that the German cash reparations be reduced to a low figure ($10 billion) and that the interallied war debts and interest thereon be cancelled.[12] If carried out, his recommendations would have involved immediate recognition of a large national "sacrifice" by the United States and to a lesser extent by Great Britain. However, he believed the reparations and war debts among nations could not and would not be paid under any circumstances likely to exist, and therefore it was better to recognize this in advance than to suffer political and economic instability only to come out with the same result on debts in the end, default and *de facto* cancellation. The artificial financial transactions arising from war debts and reparations would, he predicted in 1920, react adversely upon the prosperity of industry.

By 1930, Keynes saw his 1920 predictions concerning war debts verified. The huge international transfers arising from

11. *Essays in Persuasion*, page vii. New York: Harcourt, Brace and Company, Inc., 1932.

12. *Economic Consequences of the Peace*, pages 256-282.

war debts, in conjunction with the international gold standard (after 1925), were responsible for the failure of interest rates in Britain to fall to a level compatible with full employment, according to Keynes. In 1930, Keynes maintained that the current long-term interest rates were 50 per cent above the prewar level. During the middle 'twenties, these rates started to decline and would have continued to decline, in Keynes' opinion, except for the gold standard and the war-debts-reparations muddle. The high market rate of interest led to an inadequate volume of investment, which in turn was the primary factor leading to depression in British industry at a time when most of the great capitalist countries were enjoying a considerable degree of prosperity. Keynes estimated that his country's deflationary postwar policy, associated with high interest rates, war debts, and the gold standard, decreased the production of wealth during the decade of the 'twenties by more than one billion pounds.[13]

In order to reduce the huge internal British debt arising from the war, Keynes advocated a capital levy in 1920.[14] As the next best alternative at that time, two years after the close of the war, he favored a reduction in the stipulated interest rate on the public debt. However, Keynes deemed this proposal as well as the capital levy impracticable, on equity grounds, except in the first few years after the close of the war. As a third choice immediately following the war and as first choice after the lapse of several years, he advocated a long-term rise in the internal price level as the best method for reducing the burden of the war debt. The significant point about these three proposals, however, lies in their similarities rather than in their differences. Each is a variation on the common theme that, in the interest of the economy as a whole, the "real" burden of rentier capitalist claims against the active, producing classes should be lightened. In France, Keynes said, the value of the franc would be determined in

---

13. *Treatise on Money*, Vol. II, page 181.

14. See Keynes' testimony on the capital levy before the Committee on National Debt and Taxation, *Minutes of Evidence* (1927), Vol. II, pages 534-540.

the long run by the proportion of earned income that the French taxpayer would permit to be taken from him to pay claims of the rentier.[15]

Keynes' bias against financial capital is indicated by the underlying theme of the *Tract on Monetary Reform* (1923). In the first paragraph of the Preface, he attributes all the major ills of capitalism to monetary instability.[16] Unemployment, insecurity, business losses, uncertainty, profiteering, and speculation "all proceed, in large measure, from the instability of the standard of value." Keynes argued for a managed currency, in place of the traditional gold standard to which most economists and statesmen were then assuming Britain would return at an early date. The managed currency should be directed toward stabilization of the internal price level, thus avoiding the speculative dangers of excessive inflation as well as the retarding forces of deflation.

Although he objected to both inflation and deflation, Keynes viewed moderate inflation as the lesser evil because "it is worse, in an impoverished world, to provoke unemployment than to disappoint the *rentier*."[17] In the past there had always been a tendency toward a secular rise in prices (inflation), and this had been to the good because "depreciated money assisted the new men and emancipated them from the dead hand; benefited new wealth at the expense of old, and armed enterprise against accumulation. . . . It has been a loosening influence against the rigid distribution of old-won wealth. . . . By this means each generation can disinherit in part its predecessors' heirs."[18] On the other hand, deflation permits the "dead hand of the past" to retard the wealth-producing entrepreneur. If Britain continued to foster a deflationary policy, said Keynes, an increasingly large share of the na-

---

15. "The French Franc," *The New Republic*, January 27, 1926, Vol. XLV, No. 582, page 266.

16. The American edition is called *Monetary Reform*. New York: Harcourt, Brace and Company, Inc., 1924. The following references are to the American edition.

17. *Ibid.*, pages 44-45.

18. *Ibid.*, pages 12-13.

tional income would accrue to the rentier class. An intolerable burden would fall on the productive classes, and the consequences would be inimical to the welfare of the community as a whole.

In his fight against deflation, Keynes collided head on with the policy of the conservative British government. In his budget message of 1924, Winston Churchill, then Chancellor of the Exchequer, announced that the United Kingdom would return to the international gold standard at the prewar parity by removing the embargo on gold exports. The gold standard was restored in April, 1925. Shortly after Mr. Churchill's message appeared, Keynes issued a pamphlet entitled *The Economic Consequences of Mr. Churchill,*[19] in which he predicted many dire results from the government's policy. At the time Churchill announced this policy, the pound was approximately 10 per cent below the prewar value in terms of gold. Prewar parity meant a pound worth $4.86, whereas the prevailing rate of exchange valued the pound in terms of dollars at $4.40. The return to gold at prewar parity amounted to a 10 per cent reduction in the prices of British export goods, without compensating decreases in costs of production at home. Keynes labeled the government's policy a "cold-blooded Income Deflation."[20] Automatically pressure was placed on industries producing for export—very important industries in the British economy—to reduce their costs, especially wages, in order to offset the reduction in prices.

Great Britain alone among the great powers had not recovered from the first postwar depression. Industry generally and export industries in particular were already (1925) in a distressed condition, and unemployment was at an all-time high.[21] Keynes said the Churchill policy would result in more

---

19. The American edition is entitled *The Economic Consequences of Sterling Parity.* New York: Harcourt, Brace and Company, Inc., 1925. The following quotations are from the American edition.

20. *Treatise on Money,* Vol. II, page 182.

21. See John H. Clapham, *An Economic History of Modern Britain,* Vol. III, pages 542-545. New York: The Macmillan Company, 1938.

distress to industry, more unemployment, and strikes against those firms and industries which attempted to cut wages.

In this pamphlet, *The Economic Consequences of Mr. Churchill,* Keynes devoted one chapter to an analysis of the coal industry, the leading export industry, pointing out that Churchill's policy would lead to a coal strike and perhaps to something much worse:

The working classes . . . attacked first are faced with a depression of their standard of life, because the cost of living will not fall until all the others have been successfully attacked too; and, therefore, they are justified in defending themselves. . . . They are bound to resist so long as they can; and it must be war, until those who are economically weakest are beaten to the ground. . . . The plight of the coal miners is the first, but not—unless we are very lucky—the last. of the Economic Consequences of Sterling Parity.[22]

The validity of Keynes' prophecy was verified in 1926 when resistance by the coal miners to lower wages precipitated the general strike, which in almost any other country might have developed into revolution. The general strike was surely the greatest single catastrophe in the interwar crisis of British capitalism.

How did Keynes' opponents in this controversy view the return to gold at prewar parity? How did they justify this policy and what did they expect to gain thereby? Chancellor Churchill maintained that the return to gold was "no more responsible for the condition of affairs in the coal industry than is the Gulf Stream."[23] Churchill reported in his budget message that the return to gold was dictated by the absence of any alternative if England was to bring her financial system into agreement "with reality."

The "compelling reality" which dictated England's return to the gold standard seems to have been the shift of international financial transactions from London to New York. International banking and associated services had been one of England's largest sources of income. If the return to gold was

22. *Economic Consequences of Sterling Parity,* pages 9, 23.

23. *Ibid.,* page 8; also pages 20, 21, 28.

to be made at all, there was "compulsion" that it be made at prewar parity because, in the words of the Macmillan Committee (1930), the international financial world would have been immensely shocked if the world's greatest prewar creditor nation were deliberately by a positive act to reduce the value of its currency below par.[24] Any other policy would have meant a further loss of confidence in the London money market and an accentuation of such trends as the tendency of the Dominions to base their financial transactions on the dollar rather than on the pound. The government's policy was designed to restore position and prosperity to bankers, rentiers, and other financial interests without much conscious regard for the effects of such a policy upon British industrial entrepreneurs. Keynes, the champion of industrial capital and the antagonist of financial capital whenever these two interests clashed, denounced the government's policy with all the logic and rhetoric at his command.

The unfortunate consequences of Mr. Churchill's policy were not confined to the coal, textile, machine, iron and steel, and other industries producing for export markets. All industries, and especially those requiring new investment for expansion or rationalization, suffered because, in order to attract and protect a gold balance adequate to maintain the gold standard, the Bank of England's discount rate and consequently all interest rates in Britain had to be maintained at an abnormally high level. Shortly after Churchill's announcement that England would return to the gold standard, the Bank of England advanced its discount rate to a high level in order to assure sufficient gold to prepare for removal of the embargo on the export of gold during 1925. This policy led to a restriction of credit to industry and was accompanied by an increase in unemployment.

The government's policy found support among those who gave first emphasis to London's monetary and financial power and those who were naïvely unaware how much the world

---

24. Great Britain, Committee on Finance and Industry, *Report*, page 109. London: His Majesty's Stationery Office, 1931.

economy had changed from the prewar era when the gold standard had not been incompatible with domestic prosperity in industry. *The Times* of London pointed out that the higher discount rate was necessary to attract funds which were then going to New York because the United States had remained on the gold standard. "Once back on the gold standard we should find that foreign balances which have been kept in New York should return to us and our financial and monetary power would be greatly increased."[25] In contrast with the optimistic tone of *The Times*, Keynes took the gloomy view that a return to the gold standard would compel the Bank of England to act in a manner inimical to industrial prosperity. The rules of the gold standard under the circumstances then existing in Great Britain necessitated a high bank rate and a consequent restriction of credit to business. The inevitable result, Keynes predicted, would be discouragement of industrial enterprise and intensification of unemployment.[26]

Keynes did not deny *The Times'* assertion that this policy might greatly increase his country's financial and monetary power. His statement does represent, however, a strenuous objection to a policy that attempted to gain a large share of international banking business at the expense of domestic industry and employment.

Another objection made by Keynes to the Churchill policy also represents a criticism of financial capital. This refers to the windfall gains accruing to rentiers or functionless investors as a result of the deflation policy: "When we raise the value of sterling by 10 per cent, we transfer about $5,000,-000,000 into the pockets of the *rentiers* out of the pockets of the rest of us, and we increase the real burden of the National Debt by some $3,750,000,000. This . . . is inevitable."[27]

The "dead hand of the past," which Keynes deprecated in his *Tract*, again stood as one of the chief barriers to a rational program. As a firm believer in the power of persuasion

---

25. *The Times*, London, March 5, 1925, page 15.
26. *Economic Consequences of Sterling Parity*, pages 18-19.
27. *Ibid.*, page 11.

to reconcile group conflict, Keynes thought it possible that the trade unionists might be willing to accept a reduction in money-wage rates were it not for the automatic transfer of wealth to the rentier class. But, in the light of this transfer, he thought it both unjust and inconceivable that the representatives of labor could be reconciled to reductions in money wages. Prime Minister Stanley Baldwin in an interview with the coal miners' representatives stated: "All the workers in this country have got to face a reduction of wages . . . to help put industry on its feet."[28] Keynes predicted that the laboring classes would resist the Churchill-Baldwin policy until they were "beaten to the ground." His prediction proved literally true.

In Britain's gold-standard controversy of the 1920's, industrial interests clearly stood opposed to the interests of English international finance and of the rentier. Here, as always, Keynes stood for and advocated a course of action that placed him in the position of a defender of industrial capital and a critic of financial capital. He was not acting as a champion of the working class. Here as elsewhere Keynes did not object in principle to reductions in money-wage and real-wage rates. His position was that, as a matter of practical policy, it was impossible to secure the necessary reductions in money-wage rates without causing strikes and increasing unemployment, which would interfere with the continuity of industrial production.

When the Macmillan Committee was seeking an explanation for Britain's depressed economic condition of the 1920's, Keynes, who was a member of the committee, maneuvered Bank of England officials like Montagu Norman and Sir Ernest Harvey into positions in which they were compelled to confess a disregard for the welfare of home industry. By implicitly placing the blame for Britain's industrial depression on the banking policy of the nation, Keynes expressed his ever present criticism of finance capital.

---

28. See Allen Hutt, *The Post-War History of the British Working Class*, page 89. New York: Coward-McCann, 1938.

Before the Great Depression, Keynes believed that monetary reforms were adequate for attaining whatever social reforms were necessary. He had said in 1925, "Mr. Churchill's Budget is the real source of our industrial troubles."[29] His optimism concerning the possibilities of monetary reform is indicated by the following statement:

The supporters of Monetary Reform, of which I, after further study and reflection, am a more convinced adherent than before, as the most important and significant measure Great Britain can take to increase economic welfare, must expound their arguments more fully, more clearly, and more simply, before they can overwhelm the forces of old custom and general ignorance . . . . [It is] my belief that fluctuations of trade and employment are . . . the greatest and the most remediable of the economic diseases of modern society, that they are mainly diseases of our credit and banking system . . . .[30]

The British election of 1929 was the occasion for a new development in Keynes' practical outlook. His position as a purely monetary reformer was qualified by the addition of public works and government loans to the agenda of social control. Unemployment was the leading issue in the campaign in which Lloyd George was the leader of the Liberal party and Stanley Baldwin and Ramsay MacDonald the leaders of the Conservative and Labour parties, respectively. Lloyd George offered a public works program as the remedy for unemployment. In support of the Liberal party program, Keynes, in collaboration with Mr. H. D. Henderson, issued a pamphlet entitled *Can Lloyd George Do it? An Examination of the Liberal Pledge.*[31] Keynes supported Lloyd George's promise that his proposed public works program would involve no rise in taxation, since the increased primary and secondary employment would augment the taxable national income while decreasing expenditures for unemployment relief in amounts sufficient to offset the additional outlays for public works. In attempting to establish the validity of these

---

29. *Economic Consequences of Sterling Parity*, page 25.

30. "The Return Towards Gold," *The New Republic*, March 18, 1925, Vol. XLII, No. 537, pages 92, 93.

31. London: The Nation and Athenaeum, 1929.

promises, Keynes and Henderson tried to make quantitative estimates of the relation between initial outlay in public works and the final increase in national income. This, so far as Keynes is concerned, marks the genesis of the so-called "theory of the multiplier," which is a refinement of the common-sense insight that, in an environment of unused resources, an expenditure for public works will increase the national income not only by the amount of the direct government outlay but by some multiple of it.[32]

Here we see public works emerging in a liberal democracy during the interwar period as a program designed to place new purchasing power in circulation after it was found virtually impossible to force funds into circulation in times of depression merely by manipulation of the banking mechanism.[33] The extension of government activity in the form of public works was in no sense intended to be an entering wedge for socialism. On the contrary, public works as well as monetary control were part of the liberal program for avoiding socialism.

The Break With the Classical Theory

Keynes changed from an orthodox to an unorthodox general economist in the period between his *Treatise on Money* (1930) and his *General Theory* (1936). His transition to a distinctly anti-classical position was precipitated at that time by the incompatibility between the policy Keynes advocated and the practical implication of classical principles of economics. In its theoretical aspect, the *Treatise* makes no attack on the main body of traditional economic principles but is confined to a pretentious monetary theory of the trade cycle.

---

32. Keynes and others have credited R. F. Kahn with the invention of the multiplier theory. This is true only in the sense that Kahn first gave it a refined technical formulation. The basic insight and a clear explanation of its practical significance is clearly expressed in the Keynes-Henderson pamphlet of 1929, whereas Kahn's article in *The Economic Journal* did not appear until 1931.

33. For a standard textbook view of the relation between monetary control and public works, see James Arthur Estey, *Business Cycles; Their Nature, Cause, and Control*, page 405. New York: Prentice-Hall, 1941.

The practical problem envisaged is control of the trade cycle. The general tone is optimistic. There is no hint in Keynes' writings and speeches during 1929 that he foresaw the stock market crash, nor, in 1930, that he realized its severity. Public works were viewed as a temporary expedient, as indicated by a statement made in May, 1929: "In three to five years we should be able to employ every one without the aid of special schemes. . . . We must lift ourselves out of the rut. Once we have succeeded in doing that, our business men will be able to run things for themselves."[34]

This optimistic tone is replaced in the *General Theory* by doubts concerning the survival powers of capitalism. Rather than mitigation or elimination of the trade cycle, the problem in the *General Theory* is one of implementing a declining capitalism against the loss of the self-recuperative powers that characterized it during the nineteenth century. The uniqueness and objectives of the *General Theory*, both as a proposal for practical action and as an attack on the old principles of economics, can be appreciated only by understanding Keynes' shift in viewpoint.

The most important event influencing Keynes during this transition period seems to have been the financial crisis of 1931. The economic depression that began in 1929 appeared to him as a recurrence of earlier trade cycles until it developed into a severe crisis two years later. Whereas in his *Treatise* Keynes refers to the "slump of 1930," in 1931 we find him asking, "Can we prevent an almost complete collapse of the financial structure of modern capitalism? One begins to wonder and to doubt."[35] On another occasion, in June, 1931, he said, "We are today in the middle of the greatest economic catastrophe . . . of the modern world."[36]

In this pessimistic frame of mind, Keynes collided head on

34. *The Times*, London, May 29, 1929, page 9.

35. *The World's Economic Crisis and the Way of Escape*, page 57. New York: Century Company, 1932.

36. Quincy Wright, ed., *Unemployment as a World-Problem*, page 3. Chicago: The University of Chicago Press, 1931.

with the classical view that personal thrift and reduced government spending are desirable because individual saving and a balanced budget facilitate recovery from depression. According to the traditional view, accumulating savings would lower interest rates and thus encourage investment. What the traditional view called "savings," Keynes saw as "hoarding," which resulted not in increased investment but in decreased employment. He protested against the competitive struggle for liquidity, and labeled acts of curtailed expenditure for useful things "anti-social acts."[37] His insight that a preference for liquidity may have far-reaching anti-social consequences is developed in the *General Theory* as the basis for the liquidity-preference theory of interest, which from an anti-classical point of view is the most important theoretical concept in the *General Theory*. Although the preference for owning money rather than other forms of wealth is a common type of social behavior, which becomes accentuated in crises, it became all-important in the Keynesian model as a result of a historical impression on the part of one who by training, experience, and traditional anti-rentier bias was sensitive to its consequences for industrial production.

Keynes' thought was crystallized into an anti-classical mold during the financial crisis of 1931 by the tenacity with which the British government stuck to principles of orthodox finance, and the strong opposition that most of his fellow economists offered to Keynes' policy suggestions. In the face of shrinking effective demand, Parliament passed the Budget and Economy Act in August, 1931. This measure supposedly followed the rules of "sound" finance, since it was directed toward a balanced budget. A policy of cutting wages, reducing relief payments, and retrenching on housing and road building followed the Economy Act. Keynes characterized this triumph of the "Treasury view" in its most extreme form as a curtailment of purchasing power, whereby "if the theory which underlies all this is to be accepted, the end will be that

---

37. *The World's Economic Crisis and the Way of Escape*, page 61.

no one can be employed except those happy few who grow their own potatoes."[38]

An aspect of the financial crisis of 1931 was England's effort to remain on the gold standard. Events at this time were a sequel to the return to gold in the middle 'twenties and, when England was forced to abandon the gold standard in September, 1931, represented a partial fulfillment of Keynes' prophetic statement of 1925: "The British Public will submit their necks once more to the Golden Yoke, as a prelude, perhaps, to throwing it off forever at a not distant date."[39] The return to gold had restored to some extent the international financial prestige of London, but it also reacted, as Keynes said it would, to the distress of industry in Britain. In 1931, the demand for a balanced budget was in part motivated by a desire to bolster confidence in the pound in order to prevent a drain of English gold reserves. It appeared that events had justified Keynes' prognostications of 1925. He predicted strikes and strikes had resulted; he said the gold standard was unworkable and so it had proved to be; he said industry would suffer under the gold standard and suffered it had. In 1931 we find Keynes mournfully picturing himself as a Cassandra whose predictions were prophetic but whose prophecies were never heeded. This whole unhappy episode of the return to gold seems destined to live in British opinion as the "straitjacket of 1925-1931."

A considerable portion of the *General Theory* is devoted to a polemic against the so-called classical political economy. In offering advice on matters of policy, Keynes found his efforts frustrated because of the conflicting practical advice given by his fellow economists. We may refer briefly to controversies with Professors Pigou and Robbins and Sir William Beveridge during the years preceding publication of the *General Theory*.

---

38. "The Budget," *The New Statesman and Nation,* September 19, 1931, New Series, Vol. II. No. 30, page 329.

39. "Is the Pound Overvalued?" *The New Republic,* May 6, 1925, Vol. LXII, No. 544, page 287.

Professor Pigou, in testimony before the Macmillan Committee, attributed unemployment to interferences with the "free working of economic forces," and to wage rates "out of adjustment with the general conditions of demand."[40] Pigou insisted that his analysis was on the "real" and not the "money" level. Keynes, as a member of the questioning committee, tried to get Pigou to shift from the "real" to a "money" analysis, but without success.

In *The Theory of Unemployment* (1933) and in *Economics in Practice* (1935), Pigou continued to emphasize the "real" as against the "monetary" analysis. From his theoretical analysis he concluded that unemployment is caused primarily by wage rates which are too high, and that money and interest are unimportant both in explaining unemployment and in finding ways of eliminating it. Speaking of a policy of lower wage rates, Pigou says, "This policy, if it could be practically carried out, would in my view, be a true antidote, within its limits, to slump conditions. It would not abolish, but it would effectively lessen the waste of unemployment."[41] Pigou's theoretical position, combined with the advice that he gave on practical affairs, is of special interest in explaining the sharp anti-classical position taken by Keynes in the *General Theory*.

In 1931, Sir William Beveridge denounced Keynes' proposal to levy a general protective tariff, with rebates on all imported materials entering into exports. Beveridge criticized the proposal in typical classical fashion when he asserted a protective tariff could do only harm, because the reduction in imports that would follow would result in a reduction of exports. Keynes replied that, contrary to the classical assumption implied in Beveridge's argument, "There is . . . no simple and direct relationship between the volume of exports and the volume of imports."[42]

---

40. Committee on Finance and Industry, *Minutes of Evidence*, Vol. II, page 78.

41. A. C. Pigou, *Economics in Practice*, page 51. See also page 70. London: Macmillan and Company, Ltd., 1935.

42. *The Times*, London, April 2, 1931, page 6.

Lionel Robbins, like Beveridge, invoked traditional free-trade arguments to ridicule Keynes' suggestions for protective tariffs and referred to his proposals as "petty devices of economic nationalism." True to the classical tradition, Robbins attributed the current economic distress to economic frictions, and in particular to wage rates that were too high to permit full employment. Robbins accused Keynes of being so muddled over the wage question that he was blinded to the obvious need for a downward readjustment in wage rates. "If he had not been so anxious to discredit his late associates and to destroy that which he once adored," said Robbins, "he might have chosen terms less glaringly inconsistent with his own earlier pronouncements."[43]

Undoubtedly Keynes' new position on the relation of protectionism to unemployment was, to orthodox economists, one of the most distressing changes in his thinking because free trade was one of the cornerstones of classical economics, and repudiation of free trade was in direct contradiction to the position Keynes had previously taken. For example, in 1923 he had written, "The claim to cure unemployment involves the Protectionist fallacy in its grossest and also in its crudest form."[44] In the *General Theory*, Keynes explicitly repudiates this earlier position and maintains that protectionism may be an aid to national employment. As previously indicated, the free-trade argument, which is valid under conditions of full employment, requires qualification for all types of duties and bounties when the assumption of full employment is dropped and maximum national income rather than minimum unit cost of production is taken as the criterion for judging desirable policy. Keynes never became a true advocate of protectionism, but on occasions such as the crisis of 1931, when international economic co-operation seemed hopeless, he viewed tariffs as a lesser evil than unemployment. His critical

43. Lionel Robbins, "A Reply to Mr. Keynes," *The New Statesman and Nation*, March 14, 1931, New Series, Vol. I, No. 3, page 100.

44. "Free Trade for England," *The New Republic*, December 19, 1923, Vol. XXXVII, No. 472, page 87.

attitude toward free trade was but one specific illustration of the change that had taken place in his thinking. The correspondence between controversy in theory and controversy in policy suggests that Keynes' transition to a distinctly anti-classical position was greatly influenced by his conviction that classical theory is vicious in its practical implications.

Thus Keynes' break with his past in economic theory was more abrupt than the accompanying change in his practical point of view. There had been important and fundamental changes in his views on policy, but they were in nearly all cases nascent in his earlier writings. His strong predisposition to be critical of certain social classes and institutions crystallized in the *General Theory* into a theory of the capitalist process and found expression in a program more sweeping than anything he had previously proposed. For example, while Keynes was always antipathetic toward rentiers, it was not until the *General Theory* that his program envisaged complete disappearance of the rentier class. To take another example, the significance of inequality of income distribution for the instability of capitalism was clearly stated in the *Economic Consequences of the Peace,* but Keynes had never, prior to the *General Theory,* advocated a program that took the broader implications of this inequality and instability into account. During the years that intervened between *Economic Consequences* and the *General Theory,* inequality of income and wealth was viewed by Keynes as a condition favorable to economic progress, albeit a capricious one, but in the *General Theory* inequality is in a very fundamental sense the root cause of unemployment and the greatest barrier to economic progress, "progress" being defined in the classical sense of capital accumulation.

By 1935, Keynes had become a self-acknowledged heretic from the general body of classical doctrine. In an article provoked by a discussion among English economists on the problem of poverty and potential plenty, Keynes maintains, contrary to the classical theory, that the capitalist economic system is not self-adjusting. Chiefly responsible for the lack of automatic adjustment to an equilibrium at full employment was the special nature of the rate of interest.[45] He refers to the traditional theory of interest as the "fatal flaw" in the whole of orthodox thinking of the past century. By repudiating the classical theory of interest and substituting a monetary theory of interest, Keynes believed he was on the way (in 1935) to a general theory of what determines the level of effective demand and the volume of aggregate employment, and therefore to a theoretical explanation of poverty in the midst of potential plenty.

The foregoing discussion has shown that Keynes was predisposed to be critical of orthodox economic policy and theory from the beginning of his career. The evolution of his position as a practical reformer went on more or less continuously from the time of his first important publication on *Indian Currency and Finance*. Although Keynes was critical of monetary and trade cycle theory early in his career, the change in his position as a general economic theorist came rather abruptly in the period between his *Treatise on Money* in 1930 and his *General Theory* in 1936. After accepting, or at least tolerating, the orthodox principles of economics for fully twenty of his mature years, Keynes found himself during the financial crisis of 1931 in a position where the breach between the policies he was advocating and the principles upon which he had been nurtured became too great to tolerate longer. The old principles, particularly as they related to the theories of interest, money and employment, were cast aside for a new set of doctrines in his *General Theory*.

---

45. "Now I range myself with the heretics. I believe their flair and their instinct move them towards the right conclusion . . . . There is, I am convinced, a fatal flaw in that part of the orthodox reasoning . . . due to the failure of the classical doctrine to develop a satisfactory and realistic theory of the rate of interest." "A Self-Adjusting Economic System?" *The New Republic*, February 20, 1935, Vol. LXXXII, No. 1055, page 36.

Political Liberalism, Class Loyalties, and Anti-Marxism

Keynes' major purpose may be characterized as an attempt to buttress political liberalism with a new economic program and to fortify this economic program with a new political economy. In this sense, Keynes follows in the tradition of the great British economists since Adam Smith, all of whom were liberals, with the possible exception of Malthus, and none of whom questioned the fundamental efficacy of private property. Smith and Ricardo were the champions of a new liberalism, which in their time was founded on laissez-faire. Beginning with John Stuart Mill, the advice given by classical economists on matters of practical policy became increasingly interventionist.[46] Keynes differs from his liberal predecessors in the extent of intervention which his program entails and in his willingness to lop off the dead wood of rentierism, of which all the classical economists, again with the exception of Malthus, were critical. Keynes is the first great British economist in this tradition explicitly to repudiate laissez-faire. The spirit of individualism still pervades his thinking quite as intensely as it did that of nineteenth-century British economists. Of government participation in economic life, Keynes says: "I defend it . . . both as the only practicable means of avoiding the destruction of existing economic forms in their entirety and as the condition of the successful functioning of individual initiative." (p. 380)[47]

In politics, Keynes was always a self-avowed, self-styled liberal. As a member of the British Liberal party, he consistently rejected the political philosophies of both the Conservative and Labour parties. The Conservatives were to him the "Die Hards," the representatives of the "Do-Nothing Party," led by men "incapable of distinguishing novel mea-

---

46. Jacob Viner, "Marshall's Economics, The Man and His Times," *The American Economic Review*, June, 1941, Vol. XXXI, No. 2, page 225.

47. *The General Theory of Employment, Interest and Money*. New York: Harcourt, Brace and Company, Inc., 1936.

sures for safeguarding Capitalism from what they call Bolshevism."[48] Keynes rejected the notion of class struggle, as seen both from the conservative and from the labor side. When Winston Churchill quit the Liberal party to join the Conservatives, Keynes said it would be fortunate for the Liberal party if all those who believed like Churchill "that the coming political struggle is best described as Capitalism *versus* Socialism, and, thinking in these terms, mean to die in the last ditch for Capitalism," were to do the same.[49]

Keynes rejected membership in the Labour party primarily because it is a class party, and if there is to be a class struggle in politics Keynes wished to be associated with the bourgeoisie and not the "boorish proletariat." In listing his objections to joining the Labour party, Keynes wrote in 1925:

To begin with, it is a *class* party, and the class is not my class. If I am going to pursue sectional interests at all, I shall pursue my own. When it comes to the class struggle as such, my local and personal patriotisms, . . . are attached to my own surroundings. I can be influenced by what seems to me to be Justice and good sense; but the *Class* war will find me on the side of the educated *bourgeoisie*.[50]

Keynes' criticisms of the Labour party referred to the inherent difficulties of securing leadership capable of acting in the interests of the community as a whole. The class character of the party requires its leaders to depend upon an appeal to "widespread passions and jealousies" against those who have wealth and power, rather than upon an appeal to reason and to justice. There is danger that an autocratic inner ring will seize control of labor and make decisions in the interest of that element within the Labour party which "hates and despises existing institutions and believes that great good will result merely from overthrowing them—or at least that to

---

48. *Essays in Persuasion,* page 327.

49. *Ibid.,* page 343.

50. *Ibid.,* page 324. The British election of 1945 seems to indicate that many of the "educated bourgeoisie" disagree with Keynes regarding membership in the Labour party. Approximately one-half of the Labour Members of Parliament elected in the overwhelming Labour victory are from middle-class professions and trades.

overthrow them is the necessary preliminary to any great good." The progressive Liberal has the advantage over the most admirable Labour representative because "He can work out his policies without having to do lip-service to Trade-Unionist tyrannies, to the beauties of the class war, or to doctrinaire State Socialism."[51] Although Keynes acknowledges elements of potential good in the Labour party, the class character of the party itself imposes limitations on its capacity for dealing appropriately with social and economic issues.

The economic counterpart of Keynes' political bias against the Labour party is reflected in his preference for social services instead of higher money wages as the best means of bettering the standard of life of the wage-earning class. Speaking with reference to England, Keynes maintained in 1930 in the midst of depression that a rise in wage rates would increase costs to an internationally uneconomic level. These higher costs, he said, would tend to drive British capital abroad, whereas the benefits of higher wages could be secured through social services paid for out of taxes which would not have the disadvantages of higher wages.[52] During 1939 and 1940, when Britain was threatened by dangerous inflation, Keynes appealed to the working class to accept his liberal plan of "forced savings" as the only method by which the long-run interests of wage earners could be safeguarded.

Keynes always dealt with the wage problem indirectly and never developed anything that could properly be called a theory of wages. He strenuously objected to reductions in money-wage rates during depression periods, but on the other hand he did not advocate higher wage rates. The direct problem to him was one of interest rates, profit expectations, distribution of income, effective demand, money supply, money standards, and stock market speculation, but never wages as such. In *How to Pay for the War* is a typical statement: "I

51. *Ibid.*, page 342.

52. "The Question of High Wages," *The Political Quarterly*, January, 1930, Vol. I, No. 1, pages 110-124.

have not attempted to deal directly with the problem of wages. It is wiser, I expect, to deal with it indirectly."[53]

Although Keynes frequently addressed his proposals to the working class, the latter never received them with much enthusiasm. Keynes' plan in *How to Pay for the War* provoked from a British labor group a critical reply in the form of a pamphlet entitled, *The Keynes Plan—Its Dangers to Workers*.[54] Keynes was accused of fighting the battle of the capitalists, however well meaning he may have been, and his plan was characterized as a subtle argument for reducing real wages. The idea of postwar payment of wages earned during the war was scornfully labeled "pie in the sky." Among the important reasons why Keynes' plan was not acceptable to these labor critics were: (1) The funds for payment of deferred wages were to be raised by a levy on capital after the war at a time when there was danger of a depression. That funds could be raised in this manner at such a time was considered highly doubtful. (2) There was a long tradition of broken promises of the government to labor, the most prominent case cited being the Sankey Commission case of 1919. (3) Inflation of prices might reduce to practically nothing the real value of wages to be paid in the future. The pamphlet denied Keynes' basic premise that the total quantity of consumers goods going to labor during the war was fixed, and therefore denied also that labor had nothing to lose under the plan. As an alternative to Keynes' plan, it was proposed that labor should increase its real wages now at the expense of profits. If necessary this should be done by government operation of vital industries on a non-profit-making basis, without compensation being paid to the owners for "being deprived of the opportunity for profiteering." The tone of the argument shows clearly that Keynes' plan struck an unsympathetic chord with these socialistically inclined Labourites.

Keynes' repudiation of the classical position with respect to the self-adjusting nature of the modern economy and his

---

53. *How to Pay for the War*, page 55.
54. London: Farleigh Press, 1940.

proposals for government control of investment did not lead him to advocate collectivism. In fact, he is much further from the socialist position than that archclassicist, Professor Pigou, who in his *Socialism versus Capitalism* (1937)[55] becomes virtually a socialist. For the most part, Keynes ignores the socialist argument that social ownership of the means of production is essential, but his occasional references indicate a strong opposition to collectivism. This is illustrated in a negative way by the foregoing discussion of Keynes' political and class biases. It is illustrated in a positive fashion by his lack of regard for the work of Marx, his opposition to socialization of the instruments of production, and his attitude toward Soviet Russia.

Apart from a bare recognition that Marx had something to say about effective demand, Keynes was always scornful of the work of Marx. "Marxian Socialism," he wrote in 1925, "must always remain a portent to the historians of Opinion —how a doctrine so illogical and so dull can have exercised so powerful and enduring an influence over the minds of men, and, through them, the events of history."[56] Discussing the Soviet Union after his visit there in 1925, Keynes wrote, "How can I accept a doctrine which sets up as its bible, above and beyond criticism, an obsolete economic textbook which I know to be not only scientifically erroneous but without interest or application for the modern world?"[57] Keynes' praise of what he calls the "anti-Marxian socialism" of Silvio Gesell, the stamped-money reformer, illustrates his own anti-Marxian bias. Gesell was just such a critic of financial capital and staunch defender of private industrial capitalism as we have indicated Keynes to be. Keynes' judgment of the relative merits of Marx and Gesell, so apparently false in the light of history, would seem to reveal much more about Keynes

55. London: Macmillan and Company, Ltd., 1937.

56. *Laissez-faire and Communism*, pages 47-48.

57. *Ibid.*, page 99.

than it does about either Marx or Gesell.[58]

In a manner characteristic of the outlook of a financial reformer, Keynes has viewed social ownership of the means of production as an unimportant issue. He wrote in 1926 that large-scale enterprise tends to socialize itself because the shareholders become dissociated from the management. The direct personal interest of management under these conditions is in the general stability and reputation of the enterprise, and the making of large profits becomes secondary to management. This optimistic acceptance by Keynes of the separation of ownership from control in modern corporate enterprise stands in sharp contrast to the alarm expressed by many economists.[59] Keynes' attitude toward nationalization of railroads also minimizes the importance of socialization of the means of production. "There is . . . no so-called important political question so really unimportant, so irrelevant to the re-organization of the economic life of Great Britain, as the Nationalisation of the Railways."[60] On another occasion Keynes speaks of "the falsity of the supposed historic antithesis between socialism and individualism."[61] These and similar views, expressed before he departed from the classical position, are reasserted in the General Theory, where he states, "It is not the ownership of the instruments of production which it is important for the State to assume," (p. 378) and also in his references to the "anti-Marxian socialism" of Gesell. In spite of the high degree of government intervention involved in Keynes' program, it is clear that he remained

58. "I am no Marxian. Yet I sufficiently recognize the greatness of Marx to be offended at seeing him classed with Silvio Gesell and Major Douglas."— J. A. Schumpeter, in his reveiw of Keynes' General Theory in the Journal of the American Statistical Association, December, 1936, New Series, Vol. XXXI, No. 196, page 793n.

59. For example, by Thorstein Veblen in Absentee Ownership and Business Enterprise in Recent Times; the Case of America. New York: B. W. Huebsch, 1923; and by Adolf A. Berle and G. C. Means in The Modern Corporation and Private Property. New York and Chicago: Commerce Clearing House, 1932.

60. Laissez-faire and Communism, page 64.

61. The Times, London, August 1, 1927, page 7.

fundamentally an individualist in his economic and social philosophy.

Keynes' perspective on social and economic issues is also revealed by his attitude toward Soviet Russia. Following his visit there in the 'twenties, Keynes concluded that, if communism had a future, it was as a new religion and not as a more efficient form of economic organization. He appears to have been tremendously impressed with Soviet economic inefficiency:

On the economic side I cannot perceive that Russian Communism has made any contribution to our economic problems of intellectual interest or scientific value. I do not think that it contains, or is likely to contain, any piece of useful economic technique which we could not apply, if we chose, with equal or greater success in a society which retained all the marks . . . of British bourgeois ideals.[62]

Nevertheless, Keynes thought that what was happening in Soviet Russia was important, much more important, for example, than anything happening in the United States during the 1920's. Communism, he thought, would survive in spite of its economic inefficiency because, unlike capitalism, it does not place economics and religion in separate compartments. Capitalism, wrote Keynes, "is absolutely irreligious, without internal union, without much public spirit, often, though not always, a mere congeries of possessors and pursuers. Such a system has to be immensely, not merely moderately, successful to survive."[63] While expressing the belief that capitalism, rightly organized, is probably more efficient than any other form of economic organization, capitalism is in itself highly objectionable on moral grounds. The business man motivated by the "love of money" is tolerable as a means but not as an end. This feeling that contemporary capitalism is

---

62. *Laissez-faire and Communism*, page 130. There is no evidence from Keynes' published writings that his fundamental skepticism of and dislike for the economic structure of Soviet Russia ever changed in any important respect. On the contrary, such positive evidence as exists in occasional references in his later writings indicates a continuation of his earlier bias. See *General Theory*, pages 380, 381; *How to Pay for the War*, pages 7, 53, 55.

63. *Laissez-faire and Communism*, page 131.

spiritually and morally bankrupt probably explains, at least in part, the psychological basis for Keynes' consistent attacks upon the financial abuses and speculative orgies of this system.

Here one finds in Keynes something of the medieval schoolman, to whom avarice was a deadly sin. But as the later canonists found, there is a dilemma where private prop' erty renders indistinguishable the motives of speculation (finance) and enterprise (industry). The solution is a com' promise which in the ideal society reduces all income to the reward for labor, including profit as a special type of wage, but eliminates "usury," that is, income from lending money.[64] Neither with the canonists nor with Keynes does the criticism extend to the institution of private property in the means of production.

The historic significance of Keynes' new political economy is that it furnishes the theoretical basis for a new liberalism, which, unlike classical liberalism, rejects laissez-faire. The concept of a pre-established harmony of economic forces, which Eli Heckscher has described as the fundamental pre-conception of laissez-faire, is absent from Keynes' thinking. In this sense Keynes fits into the mercantilist tradition, which likewise uniformly lacked the postulate of pre-established harmony.[65]

Because a private property economy lacks pre-established harmony, social controls are needed to prevent it from plung-ing to its own destruction. The greatest disharmony of laissez-faire capitalism is that full employment becomes increasingly difficult to attain with the progressive accumulation of wealth. The dilemma of poverty in the midst of potential plenty arises because the increase of wealth necessitates a

---

64. See R. H. Tawney, *Religion and the Rise of Capitalism*, pages 48-49. Hammondsworth, Middlesex, England: Pelican Books, 1938. For Keynes' stric-tures on usury, see his *General Theory*, pages 241, 340, 351, 353. For Keynes' acceptance of the labor theory of value, see the *General Theory*, pages 213, 214.

65. Eli F. Heckscher, *Mercantilism*, Vol. II, especially pages 316-324. Lon-don: G. Allen and Unwin. 1935.

greater quantity of investment, while at the same time accumulation weakens the inducement to invest. The dilemma is heightened because the power to consume is limited by the unequal distribution of wealth which is characteristic of laissez-faire capitalism. The general perspective from which Keynes projected both his earlier and his later theory and practice was that of liberalism. The essence of his liberalism is a criticism of financial capitalism, combined with a strong desire to establish an environment in which industrial capitalism, the system of private enterprise, can function. His work in this sense is essentially conservative and oriented toward a preservation of the status quo.

The General Theory as a Program of Action

Thus far the present chapter has traced the development of Keynes' thought and has indicated the general point of view within which this development took place. The ultimate significance of the theory which emerged from this process of development resides in the program of action with which it is associated. Being critical of the status quo, Keynes calls for a program of social reform, but, not being revolutionary, he envisions the execution of his program within the framework of the existing social order. There is no plea in Keynes' work for a total reconstruction of economic society along socialistic lines. At the same time, however, the explicit and inferential changes called for are hardly of a mild variety. They are severely liberal. Above all, they are dedicated to a preservation of civil rights and liberties and to the creation of an economic environment which will allow the individual to realize his full potentialities. Any society which tolerates mass unemployment not only fails to produce the goods and services of which it is capable, but denies to millions of individuals the dignity of creative labor and the possibility of self-realization of personality. Therefore, the first prerequisite of a better society is the abolition of unemployment. The second prerequisite is a more equitable and less arbitrary distribution of wealth and income (p. 372).

The immediate steps

The immediate proposals suggested by Keynes for promoting a high level of employment have been indicated in connection with the discussion of various parts of his theory and need only be summarized here before passing to his long-range view of social change. Fortunately, the steps which will promote a higher level of employment will also result in a more equal distribution of income and wealth. The most important proposals in Keynes' program for increasing employment are the following: (1) Progressive taxation to raise the community propensity to consume; (2) Public investment and public control of private investment to compensate for and to reduce the magnitude of fluctuations in the marginal efficiency of private investment; (3) Strong monetary authority to control the supply of money and lower the rate of interest.

(1) Since unemployment develops because our society as organized must produce much more than we have the economic ability to consume at full employment, the two approaches to full or nearly full employment are to increase the ability to consume and to raise the volume of investment to a level at which it will fill the gap between total income and consumption at full employment. Increasing the ability to consume means increasing the propensity to consume so more will be consumed at given levels of a national income. Keynes' main suggestion in this connection is to use progressive taxation to redistribute the social income from individuals with a low propensity to consume (the rich) to those with a high propensity to consume (the poor) and thus raise the community's average propensity to consume.

(2) Investment may be increased either by raising the marginal efficiency of capital or by lowering the rate of interest. The marginal efficiency of capital has its operational or practical meaning in what Keynes calls the "socialisation

of investment." As indicated in Chapter 7, Keynes does not say precisely what he means by the socialization of investment, but the proposal seems to suggest control of private investment of a rather far-reaching nature as well as public investment on an expanded scale. Private investment should be encouraged in every possible manner. However, private investors are very sensitive to government controls and there is danger that attempts to foster private investment may react unfavorably on the marginal efficiency of capital. This means there is not a great deal that can be done in a positive way to increase private investment through the marginal efficiency of capital. Some good may be achieved by a heavy transfer tax on all stock-market transactions. Such a tax would discourage buying and selling of stocks merely for the capital appreciation and might mitigate the dominance of speculation over enterprise in the securities market. Legislation like the American Securities and Exchange Act is in line with Keynes' desire to eliminate the worst faults of financial capital. Generally speaking, however, not much can be done to stabilize private investment at a high level. Therefore, a public investment authority like the Board of Public Investment suggested by Keynes in 1938 (see Chapter 7) should stand prepared to compensate for the fluctuations and inadequacies of private investment with public investment projects. The Council of Economic Advisers established under the Employment Act of 1946 is the type of government agency which might perform a similar function in the United States. Although the Employment Act of 1946 hardly goes beyond the advisory stage, its preamble represents a step in the direction of Keynes' philosophy of the role of government in maintaining high levels of employment. In the preamble Congress declares, "It is the continuing policy and responsibility of the Federal Government to use all practicable means consistent with its needs and obligations and other essential considerations of national policy, and with the assistance and cooperation of industry, agriculture, labor and state and local governments, to coordinate and utilize all its plans, functions and resources for the purpose of creating and maintaining, in a manner calculated to foster and promote free competitive enterprise and the general welfare, conditions under which there will be afforded useful employment opportunities, including self-employment, for those able, willing, and seeking to work, and to promote maximum employment, production, and purchasing power."

(3) The third of the fundamental determinants of employment, the rate of interest, finds its operational meaning in the proposal for a strong monetary authority with rigorous control over the total quantity of money as a means of lowering the rate of interest in order to stimulate private investment. In this suggestion for a strong central banking authority Keynes gives practical expression to the liquidity-preference theory of the rate of interest. In a series of articles on "How to Avoid a Slump," appearing in *The Times* of London in January, 1937, Keynes affirmed his faith in the ability of the central monetary authority to push down and keep down the long-term rate of interest to a level compatible with a flow of investment that would insure against an economic slump. He was aware that once a boom collapsed into a slump, the profit expectations of potential investors would probably fall so low that no reduction in interest rates could stimulate recovery from depression. As noted in the chapter on interest, it is important not only to push down the interest rate, but to give assurance that it will stay down in the future, since one of the great obstacles to a low long-term rate is the anticipation that the rate may rise in the future.

The long view

Even if these immediate proposals were put into effect and worked successfully, they would prove inadequate in the long run because the marginal efficiency of capital would continue to decline whereas the rate of interest could not be lowered by ordinary means below a level of, say, two per cent. Investment would therefore cease, and widespread unemployment would return to plague the economic system. Consequently, some means other than conventional bank control over the quantity of money must be found to lower the long-term interest rate from two per cent down to zero. Keynes makes no specific proposal for accomplishing this necessary step. He praises the principle behind the stamped-money plan of Silvio Gesell, who suggested that money, like other commodities, should be made to incur carrying costs in order to discourage storing wealth in the form of money.[66] Gesell suggested that this could be done by requiring that currency notes be stamped periodically as a condition of retaining their value. According to Keynes, the stamped-money idea is theoretically sound and may contain "the essence of what is needed," but it is not workable in the form proposed by Gesell. Nevertheless, Keynes felt that we should look to Gesell's work rather than to that of Marx for the ultimate solution of the economic problem. Beyond these hints, Keynes makes no attempt to point out what steps might be taken to reduce the rate of interest to zero in order to make it possible for investment to advance unimpeded to the point at which the marginal efficiency of capital would also be lowered to zero.

Although the concrete proposals for the long-run solution of the economic problem are not given by Keynes, his preference for Gesell rather than Marx, plus other aspects of his social philosophy, indicates the general nature of his solution. His goal is an alternative to socialism in the Marxian sense of government ownership of the means of production. His criticisms are directed toward the financial, rentier and speculative features of capitalism. In the long run the answer to the capitalist dilemma is to be discovered in the elimination of these faults rather than in the elimination of private ownership of the means of production.

The analyses of the capitalist process given by Keynes and Marx have a good deal in common. It is the operational meanings of their analyses as reflected in what to do about the situation that indicate the fundamental difference between

---

66. See Silvio Gesell, *The Natural Economic Order.* San Antonio: Free Economy Publishing Company, 1936.

the two systems of thought. In both theories, the successful functioning of the capitalist system depends on a high rate of capital accumulation because the unequal distribution of income and wealth leads to great potential savings which must be realized in the form of new capital assets if they are to be realized at all. The alternative is mass unemployment. These potential savings cannot be realized in the form of consumers goods and services because the unequal distribution of income is associated with a low propensity to consume. In its historical development, capitalism shows a tendency for the capacity to produce to outrun the capacity to consume. This means the gap between income and consumption at full employment is growing constantly larger. The capacity to consume refers, of course, to economic capacity and not physical capacity for consumption. As long as this inequality persists, there remains the necessity of capitalizing, in the form of capital assets, the surplus portion of large incomes, or suffering the only alternative of mass unemployment. Inequality arises primarily from the concentration of income from property as contrasted with income from labor. The social and economic problem cannot be solved as long as inequality exists.

Keynes' view that inequality of income is a barrier to the creation of new wealth reverses the traditional notion that the accumulation of wealth depends on the savings of the rich out of their superfluity. The old idea that equality and progress are incompatible is transformed by Keynes' theory into the revolutionary doctrine that greater equality is one of the essential conditions of progress. As he says, "One of the chief social justifications of great inequality is, therefore, removed." (p. 373) Keynes is not an equalitarian in the sense that he believes everyone should be rewarded equally. He saw social and psychological justification for "significant inequalities." However, the disparities are much greater than can be justified on social and psychological grounds, and also much greater than is compatible with a high level of aggregate demand.

Society cannot go on forever widening the gap between what it currently produces and what it currently consumes at full employment. Sooner or later the capacity to consume must be brought into harmony with the capacity to produce. This is not possible, however, in a society in which a relatively few owners receive nearly all the income from property and the great mass of non-owners receive only labor income. Getting rid of the deficiency of consumption means ultimately getting rid of gross inequality in the distribution of income. Up to this point, Keynes and Marx could agree. Beyond this point, however, there are two fundamental directions which economic evolution might follow. It is here that Keynes and Marx part company. Marx sees the only realistic solution of the contradiction between the capacity to produce and the capacity to consume in the socialization of the means of production. This will automatically socialize surplus incomes. Inequality will not disappear completely, but it will be greatly reduced and will cease to be a barrier to full employment. Investment will become a collective activity of society based on social need, rather than the consequence of private profit calculation.

The second road, the one which Keynes takes, regards the socialization of income-yielding property as unnecessary and undesirable. According to Keynes, capital assets yield income because they are scarce. When they cease to be scarce, they will cease to be a source of income to their owners. When property ceases to yield income, only labor, both mental and physical, will constitute a basis for receiving income. Therefore, if capital assets can be made sufficiently abundant, property income will disappear and with it the inequality of income distribution which is the great barrier to a high level of consumption and employment. However, the elimination of income from mere ownership would probably not eliminate the desire to save out of income at full employment. Presumably, the "socialisation of investment" would take care of the task of finding offsets to saving. Here is the perspective from which Keynes views the solution of the social and eco-

nomic problems of unemployment and inequality. This perspective leads quite logically to the view that labor is the sole
factor of production and to a sympathy with the labor theory
of value.[67] Even in accepting the labor theory of value, which
was a fundamental part of Marx's theory, Keynes differs from
Marx. Keynes is careful to include as functional labor the
full services of entrepreneurs, whereas Marx excluded from
functional labor a large part of the activities of entrepreneurs because he thought they were devoted to the exploita-
tion of wage earners under a system of private ownership of
the means of production and were unnecessary in a rationally
organized society.

If these inferences of the long view seem to raise more
questions than they answer, we can only express sympathy
with the reader and add that it is unfortunate Lord Keynes
did not live to grapple with the secular problem. If it seems
utopian to suppose that private enterprise can continue to
function after the rewards of ownership have ceased, we can
merely offer the observation that "socialists" of this variety
have been labeled "utopian" for the past hundred years. At
this point a warning is in order. We should not belittle the
value of Keynes' short-run analysis, which is all he intended
to give, just because the secular aspects of his theory are left
undeveloped. The *General Theory* may have great merit in
relation to problems of unemployment and inflation and not
be very useful as a tool of secular analysis.

The fulfillment of Keynes' long-term goal would indeed
constitute a minor revolution in class relations. The rentier
capitalist, the functionless investor, would disappear as a
class. Ownership would no longer constitute a basis for the
receipt of income. The process would take place gradually,
however, as the continuation of what has been going on in
Great Britain for several decades, and would require no
violent break with the past for its completion. To Keynes
this minor revolution is desirable not only because it would

---

67. See pages 194-195.

produce a more just society, but, more important, because it is the necessary price that must be paid in order to avert in the long run a major revolution of the Marxian variety. It represents the alternative to Marxism. Its basic purpose is to preserve private industrial capitalism, and in no sense does Keynes view it as the entering wedge for a gradual transition to collectivism. Financial capital, speculation, and rentierism, with all their abuses, are a cancerous growth on the body of private enterprise and are not an organic part of the system. Nevertheless, saving the patient requires a serious operation. In brief, Keynes believes the preservation of private capitalism requires the elimination of its worst faults. He also believes these faults can be abolished without at the same time destroying the foundations of private industrial capitalism.

References for Further Reading

Keynes, J. M., *The General Theory of Employment, Interest and Money*, Chapter 24. New York: Harcourt, Brace and Co., 1936.
——, *Essays in Persuasion*, especially Part IV. New York: Harcourt, Brace and Co., 1932.
——, *Laissez-faire and Communism*. New York: The New Republic, Inc., 1926.

Alexander, S. S., "Mr. Keynes and Mr. Marx," *The Review of Economic Studies*, February, 1940, Vol. VII, pages 123-135.
Ayres, C. E., "The Impact of the Great Depression on Economic Thinking," *The American Economic Review, Papers and Proceedings*, May, 1946, Vol. XXXVI, pages 112-125.
Clark, J. M., *Alternative to Serfdom*, Chapter IV, "Revolution in Economics," pages 91-117. New York: Alfred A. Knopf, 1948.
Dillard, Dudley, "Keynes and Proudhon," *The Journal of Economic History*, May, 1942, Vol. II, pages 63-76.
——, "Gesell's Monetary Theory of Social Reform," *The American Economic Review*, June, 1942, Vol. XXXII, pages 348-352.
Fan-Hung, "Keynes and Marx on the Theory of Capital Accumulation, Money and Interest," *The Review of Economic Studies*, October, 1939, Vol. VII, pages 28-41.
Gruchy, Allan G., "The Philosophical Basis of the New Keynesian Economics," *Ethics*, July, 1948, Vol. LVIII, pages 235-244.

Harrod, R. F., "John Maynard Keynes," *The Review of Economic Statistics*, November, 1946, Vol. XXVIII, pages 178-182. Reprinted in *The New Economics*, edited by S. E. Harris. New York: Alfred A. Knopf, 1947.

Klein, L. R., *The Keynesian Revolution*, Chapter VII on "Keynes and Social Reform." New York: The Macmillan Company, 1947.

Neisser, H. P., "Keynes as an Economist," *Social Research*, June, 1946, Vol. XIII, pages 225-235.

Robinson, E. A. G., "John Maynard Keynes, 1883-1946," *The Economic Journal*, March, 1947, Vol. LVII, pages 1-68.

Robinson, Joan, *An Essay on Marxian Economics*. London: Macmillan and Co., 1942.

Schumpeter, J. A., "John Maynard Keynes, 1883-1946," *The American Economic Review*, September, 1946, Vol. XXXVI, pages 495-518. Reprinted in *The New Economics*, edited by S. E. Harris. New York: Alfred A. Knopf, 1947.

Somerville, H., "Mr. Keynes and the Canonists," *Commonweal*, June 12, 1936, Vol. XXIV, pages 177-179.

Sweezy, Paul M., "John Maynard Keynes," *Science and Society*, Fall, 1946, Vol. X, pages 398-405. Reprinted in *The New Economics*, edited by S. E. Harris. New York: Alfred A. Knopf, 1947.

Trachtenberg, I., "Soviet Comment on Keynesian Theories of Full Employment," *Science and Society*, Fall, 1946, Vol. X, pages 405-409.

Wright, D. McC., "Future of Keynesian Economics," *The American Economic Review*, June, 1945, Vol. XXXV, pages 284-307.

Bibliography of John Maynard Keynes' Writings

Keynes was a prolific writer as the following bibliography attests. As editor of *The Economic Journal*, the quarterly journal of the Royal Economic Society, for more than thirty years, he undoubtedly wrote many unsigned notes and notices. As editor of the liberal British weekly, *The Nation and the Athenaeum*, he contributed numerous unsigned articles and editorials. As a member of several government commissions and committees (the Royal Commission on Indian Currency and Finance, 1914; the Macmillan Committee on Finance and Industry, 1931; and the Treasury group that drew up the *Plan for an International Clearing Union*, 1943), Keynes made further, important contributions. Since individual authorship cannot be clearly attributed in most of these cases, I have not listed them in the bibliography of Keynes' writings. Apart from these items and certain brief bits of correspondence and duplicate articles, I have included practically all of Keynes' publications. A bibliography that lists some anonymous articles believed to have been written by or discussed with Keynes before publication will be found in *The New Economics*, edited by Seymour E. Harris (New York: Alfred A. Knopf, 1947), pages 665-686.

Classified Bibliography
(arranged chronologically by each classification)

I. Books and Pamphlets
II. Articles

A. Money, Interest, Prices, and Inflation
B. International Economics, including Foreign Exchange and Gold
C. Unemployment, Employment, and Wages
D. Consumption, Saving, Investment, and Income
E. War and Peace, including War Debts and Reparations
F. Politics and Social Philosophy
G. Biographical
H. Miscellaneous

III. Book Reviews

I. Books and Pamphlets

Indian Currency and Finance. London: Macmillan and Co., Ltd., 1913. 263 pages.

The Economic Consequences of the Peace. New York: Harcourt, Brace and Howe, 1920. 298 pages.

A Treatise on Probability. London: Macmillan and Co., Ltd., 1921. 466 pages.

A Revision of the Treaty. New York: Harcourt, Brace and Co., 1922. 242 pages.

Monetary Reform. New York: Harcourt, Brace and Co., 1924. 227 pages. (The English edition is entitled *A Tract on Monetary Reform.*)

The Economic Consequences of Sterling Parity. New York: Harcourt, Brace and Co., 1925. 32 pages. (The English edition is entitled *The Economic Consequences of Mr. Churchill.*)

A Short View of Russia. London: Woolf, 1925. 27 pages. (Reprinted in *Laissez-Faire and Communism.*)

The End of Laissez-Faire. London: Woolf, 1926. 54 pages. (Reprinted in *Laissez-Faire and Communism.*)

Laissez-Faire and Communism. New York: New Republic, Inc., 1926. 144 pages. I. *The End of Laissez-Faire;* II. *A Short View of Russia.*

Réflexions sur le franc et sur quelques autres sujets. Paris: Simon Kra, 1928. 182 pages. (A collection of articles from *l'Information, l'Europe Nouvelle, The Economic Journal,* and *The Nation and the Athenaeum.*)

(with H. D. Henderson) *Can Lloyd George Do It? An Examination of the Liberal Pledge.* London: The Nation and the Athenaeum, 1929. 44 pages.

A Treatise on Money. London: Macmillan and Co., Ltd., 1930. Vol. I The Pure Theory of Money, 363 pages; Vol. II The Applied Theory of Money, 424 pages.

Essays in Persuasion. New York: Harcourt, Brace and Co., 1932. 376 pages.

Essays in Biography. London: Macmillan and Co., Ltd., 1933. 318 pages.

The Means to Prosperity. New York: Harcourt, Brace and Co., 1933. 37 pages.

The General Theory of Employment, Interest and Money. New York: Harcourt, Brace and Co., 1936. 403 pages.

How to Pay for the War. New York: Harcourt, Brace and Co., 1940. 88 pages.

II. Articles

A. Money, interest, prices, and inflation

"The Recent Economic Events in India," *The Economic Journal,* March, 1909, Vol. XIX, pages 51-67.

"Report of the National Monetary Commission of the United States," *The Economic Journal,* March, 1912, Vol. XXII, pages 150-151.

"Report of the Mint," *The Economic Journal,* December, 1912, Vol. XXII, pages 633-634.

"Currency in 1912," *The Economic Journal,* March, 1914, Vol. XXIV, pages 152-157. (Review of the *Forty-third Annual Report of the Deputy Master of the Mint.*)

"The City of London and the Bank of England, August, 1914," *The Quarterly Journal of Economics,* November, 1914, Vol. XXIX, pages 48-71.

"The Prospects of Money, November, 1914," *The Economic Journal,* December, 1914, Vol. XXIV, pages 610-634.

"Inflation as a Method of Taxation," *Manchester Guardian Commercial, Reconstruction in Europe,* July 27, 1922, Fifth Section, pages 268-269.

"The Consequences to Society of Changes in the Value of Money," *Manchester Guardian Commercial, Reconstruction in Europe,* July 27, 1922, Fifth Section, pages 321-328.

"Is Credit Abundant?—The Grand Trunk Railway," *The Nation and the Athenaeum,* July 7, 1923, Vol. XXXIII, page 470.

"Bank Rate at Four Per Cent," *The Nation and the Athenaeum,* July 14, 1923, Vol. XXXIII, page 502.

"Bank Rate and Stability of Prices—A Reply to Critics," *The Nation and the Athenaeum,* July 21, 1923, Vol. XXXIII, pages 511-512.

"A Comment on Professor Cannan's Article ('Limitation of Currency or Limitation of Credit?')," *The Economic Journal,* March, 1924, Vol. XXXIV, pages 65-68.

"Monetary Reform," *The Economic Journal,* June, 1924, Vol. XXXIV, pages 169-176.

"The Policy of the Bank of England," *The Nation and the Athenaeum,* July 19, 1924, Vol. XXXV, pages 500-501.

"The Bank Rate," *The Nation and the Athenaeum,* March 7, 1925, Vol. XXXVI, pages 790-792.

"The Amalgamation of the British Note Issues," *The Economic Journal,* June, 1928, Vol. XXXVIII, pages 321-328.

"The Bank Rate, Five-and-a-half Per Cent," *The Nation and the Athenaeum,* February 16, 1929, Vol. XLIV, pages 679-680.

"Mr. Keynes' Theory of Money: A Rejoinder" (to D. H. Robertson), *The Economic Journal,* September, 1931, Vol. XLI, pages 412-423.

"The Pure Theory of Money: A Reply to Dr. Hayek," *Economica,* November, 1931, Vol. XI, pages 387-397.

"Banks and the Collapse of Money Values," *Vanity Fair,* January, 1932, pages 21-23.

"Member Bank Reserves in the United States," *The Economic Journal,* March, 1932, Vol. XLII, pages 27-31.

"A Note on the Long-term Rate of Interest in Relation to the Conversion Scheme," *The Economic Journal,* September, 1932, Vol. XLII, pages 415-423.

"The Monetary Policy of the Labour Party," *The New Statesman and Nation,* September 17 and 24, 1932, Vol. IV, pages 306-307 and 338-339.

"Mr. Keynes's Control Scheme," *The American Economic Review,* December, 1933, Vol. XXIII, page 675.

"Report of the Monetary Committee, 1934, New Zealand," *The Economic Journal,* March, 1935, Vol. XLV, pages 192-196.

"Future of the Interest Rates," *The Times* (London), February 20, 1936, page 21.

"The Theory of the Rate of Interest," *Lessons of Monetary Experience, Essays in Honor of Irving Fisher,* edited by A. D. Gayer, pages 145-152. New York: Farrar and Rinehart, 1937.

"Alternative Theories of the Rate of Interest," *The Economic Journal,* June, 1937, Vol. XLVII, pages 241-252.

"The 'Ex-Ante' Theory of the Rate of Interest," *The Economic Journal,* December, 1937, Vol. XLVII, pages 663-669.

"Mr. Keynes and 'Finance,'" *The Economic Journal,* June, 1938, Vol. XLVIII, pages 318-322.

"The United States and the Keynes Plan," *The New Republic,* July 29, 1940, Vol. CIII, pages 156-159.

B. International economics, including foreign exchange and gold

"Return of Estimated Value of Foreign Trade of the United Kingdom at Prices of 1900," *The Economic Journal,* December, 1912, Vol. XXII, pages 630-631.

"The Stabilization of the European Exchanges," I and II, *The Manchester Guardian Commercial, Reconstruction in Europe,* April 20, 1922, Number One, pages 3-5; and December 7, 1922, Eleventh Number, pages 658-661.

"The Theory of the Exchanges and 'Purchasing Power Parity,'" *The Manchester Guardian Commercial, Reconstruction in Europe,* April 20, 1922, Number One, pages 6-8.

"The Forward Market in Foreign Exchange," *Manchester Guardian Commercial, Reconstruction in Europe,* April 20, 1922, Number One, pages 11-15.

"Professor Jevons on the Indian Exchange," *The Economic Journal,* March, 1923, Vol. XXXIII, pages 60-65.

"Trustee Investments—Home, Colonial, and Indian," *The Nation and the Athenaeum,* June 2, 1923, Vol. XXXIII, page 318.

"Free Trade for England," *The New Republic,* December 19, 1923, Vol. XXXVII, pages 86-87.

"Gold in 1923," *The New Republic,* February 27, 1924, Vol. XXXVIII, pages 10-11.

"The Prospects of Gold," *The New Republic,* March 12, 1924, Vol. XXXVIII, pages 66-67.

"The Franc," *The New Republic,* March 26, 1924, Vol. XXXVIII, pages 120-121.

"The Return Towards Gold," *The New Republic,* March 18, 1925, Vol. XLII, pages 92-94.

"The Problem of the Gold Standard," *The Nation and the Athenaeum,* March 21, 1925, Vol XXXVI, pages 866-870.

"The Gold Standard," *The Nation and the Athenaeum,* May 2, 1925, Vol. XXXVII, pages 129-130.

"Is the Pound Overvalued?" *The New Republic,* May 6, 1925, Vol. XLII, pages 286-287.

"The Gold Standard—A Correction," *The Nation and the Athenaeum,* May 9, 1925, Vol. XXXVII, pages 169-170.

"England's Gold Standard," *The New Republic,* May 20, 1925, Vol. XLII, pages 339-340.

"The Gold Standard Act," *The Economic Journal,* June, 1925, Vol. XXXV, pages 312-313.

"The Arithmetic of the Sterling Exchange," *The Nation and the Athenaeum,* June 13, 1925, Vol. XXXVII, page 338.

"Great Britain's Cross of Gold," *The New Republic,* September 16, 1925, Vol. XLIV, pages 88-90.

"The French Franc," *The New Republic,* January 27, 1926, Vol. XLV, pages 266-268.

"The First Fruits of the British Gold Standard," *The New Republic,* June 2, 1926, Vol. XLVII, pages 54-55.

"The Future of the Franc," *The New Republic,* August 11, 1926, Vol. XLVII, pages 328-329.

"Will England Restrict Foreign Investments?" *The New Republic,* December 1, 1926, Vol. XLIX, pages 34-36.

"A Model Form for Statements of International Balances," *The Economic Journal,* September, 1927, Vol. XXXVII, pages 472-476.

"The British Balance of Trade, 1925-27," *The Economic Journal,* December, 1927, Vol. XXXVII, pages 551-565.

"Note on the British Balance of Trade," *The Economic Journal,* March, 1928, Vol. XXXVIII, pages 146-147.

"The United States' Balance of Trade in 1927," *The Economic Journal,* September, 1928, Vol. XXXVIII, pages 487-489.

"Is There Enough Gold?" *The Nation and the Athenaeum,* January 19, 1929, Vol. XLIV, pages 545-546.

"Proposal for a Revenue Tariff," *The New Statesman and Nation,* March 7, 1931, Vol. I, pages 53-54.

"Revenue Tariff for Great Britain," *The New Republic,* April 8, 1931, Vol. LXVI, pages 196-197.

"Paradox of British Economic Policy: Will England Introduce a Revenue Tariff?" *Journal of the Institute of Bankers in South Africa,* May, 1931, Vol. XXVIII, pages 72-76.

"The Prospects of the Sterling Exchange," *Yale Review,* March, 1932, Vol. XXI, pages 433-447.

"Reflections on the Sterling Exchange," *Lloyds Bank Limited Monthly Review,* April, 1932, Vol. III, pages 143-160.

"The World's Economic Outlook," *Atlantic Monthly*, May, 1932, Vol. CXLIX, pages 521-526.

"The World Economic Conference, 1933," *The New Statesman and Nation*, December 24, 1932, Vol. IV, pages 825-826.

"National Self-Sufficiency," *Yale Review*, Summer, 1933, Vol. XXII, pages 755-769.

"The Solid Business of the Conference: A Plan to End the Chaos of the Exchanges," *Journal of the Institute of Bankers in South Africa*, July, 1933, Vol. XXX, pages 226-230.

"President Roosevelt's Gold Policy," *The New Statesman and Nation*, January 20, 1934, Vol. VII, pages 76-77.

"The Bank for International Settlements, Fourth Annual Report (1933-4)," *The Economic Journal*, September, 1934, Vol. XLIV, pages 514-518.

"The Bank for International Settlements, Fifth Annual Report (1934-5)," *The Economic Journal*, September, 1935, Vol. XLV, pages 594-597.

"The Future of the Foreign Exchanges," *Lloyds Bank Limited Monthly Review*, October, 1935, Vol. VI, pages 527-535.

"The Supply of Gold," *The Economic Journal*, September, 1936, Vol. XLVI, pages 412-418.

"International Clearing Union," (Speech before the House of Lords), May 18, 1943, *Hansard Lords*, Vol. CXXVII, pages 527-537. (Reprinted in *The New Economics*, edited by S. E. Harris. New York: Alfred A. Knopf, 1947.)

"The Objective of International Price Stability," *The Economic Journal*, June-September, 1943, Vol. LIII, pages 185-187.

"International Monetary Fund," (Speech before the House of Lords), May 23, 1944, *Hansard Lords*, Vol. CXXXI, pages 838-849. (Reprinted in *The New Economics*, edited by S. E. Harris. New York: Alfred A. Knopf, 1947.)

"The Bank for Reconstruction and Development," (Speech delivered as Chairman of the Second Commission of the Bank, July 3, 1944). (Published in *The New Economics*, edited by S. E. Harris, Chapter XXIX, pages 396-400. New York: Alfred A. Knopf, 1947.)

"A Rejoinder to Professor Graham," (On the Objective of International Price Stability), *The Economic Journal*, December, 1944, Vol. LIV, pages 429-430.

"Anglo-American Financial Arrangements," (Speech before the House of Lords), December 18, 1945, *Hansard Lords*, Vol. CXXXVIII, pages 777-794. (Reprinted in *The New Economics*,

edited by S. E. Harris. New York: Alfred A. Knopf, 1947.)
"The Balance of Payments of the United States," *The Economic Journal,* June, 1946, Vol. LVI, pages 172-187.

C. Unemployment, employment, and wages

"Currency Policy and Unemployment," *The Nation and the Athenaeum,* August 11, 1923, Vol. XXXIII, pages 611-612.

"Does Unemployment Need a Drastic Remedy?" *The Nation and the Athenaeum,* May 24, 1924, Vol. XXXV, pages 235-236.

"A Drastic Remedy for Unemployment: Reply to Critics," *The Nation and the Athenaeum,* June 7, 1924, Vol. XXXV, pages 311-312.

"Back to the Coal Problem," *The Nation and the Athenaeum,* May 15, 1926, Vol. XXXIX, page 159.

"The Question of High Wages," *Political Quarterly,* January, 1930, Vol. I, pages 110-124.

"British Industry, Unemployment, and High Wages," *Barrons,* March 24, 1930, Vol. X, pages 22-23.

"The Industrial Crisis," *The Nation and the Athenaeum,* May 10, 1930, Vol. XLVII, pages 163-164.

"The Great Slump of 1930," *The Nation and the Athenaeum,* December 20 and 27, 1930, Vol. XLVIII, pages 402, 427-428.

"An Economic Analysis of Unemployment," in *Unemployment as a World-Problem,* edited by Quincy Wright, Chapter I, pages 3-42. Chicago: University of Chicago Press, 1931.

"Causes of World Depression," *The Forum and Century,* January, 1931, Vol. LXXXV, pages 21-25.

"Some Consequences of the Economy Report," *The New Statesman and Nation,* August 15, 1931, Vol. II, pages 189-190.

"The World's Economic Crisis and the Way of Escape," Halley Stewart Lecture, 1931, Chapter III, pages 57-75, in *The World's Economic Crisis and the Way of Escape.* New York: The Century Co., 1932.

"A Plan to Save the World," *Journal of the Institute of Bankers in South Africa,* February, 1933, Vol. XXIX, pages 735-741.

"A Programme for Unemployment," *The New Statesman and Nation,* February 4, 1933, Vol. V, pages 121-122.

"The Multiplier," *The New Statesman and Nation,* April 1, 1933, Vol. V, pages 405-407.

"Economic Revival," *The New York Times,* April 2, 1933, Section VIII, page 3.

"Public Works: Earnings, Direct and Indirect," *The Times* (London), July 28, 1933, page 10.

"From Keynes to Roosevelt: Our Recovery Plan Assayed," (An open letter to President Roosevelt), *The New York Times*, December 31, 1933, Section VIII, page 2.

"Mr. Roosevelt's Experiments," *The Times* (London), January 2, 1934, pages 11-12.

"U. S. Recovery Needs," *The New York Times*, June 10, 1934, Section IV, page 1E.

"A Self-adjusting Economic System?" *The New Republic*, February 20, 1935, Vol. LXXXII, pages 35-37.

"How to Avoid a Slump," *The Times* (London), January 12, 13, 14, 1937, pages 13f, 13f, 13f.

"The General Theory of Employment," *The Quarterly Journal of Economics*, February, 1937, Vol. LI, pages 209-223.

"Professor Pigou on Money Wages in Relation to Unemployment," *The Economic Journal*, December, 1937, Vol. XLVII, pages 743-745.

"Public Works, Improvisation or Planning?" *The Times* (London), January 3, 1938, page 13.

"Relative Movements of Real Wages and Output," *The Economic Journal*, March, 1939, Vol. XLIX, pages 34-51.

D. Consumption, saving, investment, and income

"Saving and Usury," *The Economic Journal*, March, 1932, Vol. XLII, pages 135-137.

"Mr. Robertson on 'Saving' and 'Hoarding'," *The Economic Journal*, December, 1933, Vol. XLIII, pages 699-701.

"Fluctuations in Net Investment in the United States," *The Economic Journal*, September, 1936, Vol. XLVI, pages 540-547.

"Mr. Keynes' Consumption Function: Reply," *The Quarterly Journal of Economics*, August, 1938, Vol. LII, pages 708-709. (A reply to an article by G. R. Holden, in the same volume, pages 281-296. See a further brief comment by Keynes in the same journal, November, 1938, Vol. LIII, page 160.)

"Mr. Keynes on the Distribution of Incomes and 'Propensity to Consume': A Reply," *The Review of Economic Statistics*, August, 1939, Vol. XXI, page 129. (See Hans Staehle, in the same journal, August, 1938, Vol. XX, pages 128-141; and August, 1939, Vol. XXI, pages 129-130.)

"The Process of Capital Formation," *The Economic Journal*, September, 1939, Vol. XLIX, pages 569-574.

"Professor Tinbergen's Method: The Statistical Testing of Business-Cycle Theories," *The Economic Journal*, September, 1939, Vol.

XLIX, pages 558-568. (See "Comment" by Keynes in response to a reply by Tinbergen, *The Economic Journal*, March, 1940, Vol. L, pages 154-156.)

"The Concept of National Income: A Supplementary Note," *The Economic Journal*, March, 1940, Vol. L, pages 60-65.

E. War and peace, including war debts and reparations

"War and the Financial System, August, 1914," *The Economic Journal*, September, 1914, Vol. XXIV, pages 460-486.

"The Economics of War in Germany," *The Economic Journal*, September, 1915, Vol. XXV, pages 443-452.

"Editorial Foreword," to European Reconstruction, *Manchester Guardian Commercial, Reconstruction in Europe*, April 20, 1922, Number One, page 2. (Keynes was general editor of this special publication of the *Manchester Guardian Commercial*.)

"The Reconstruction of Europe: A General Introduction," *The Manchester Guardian Commercial, Reconstruction in Europe*, May 18, 1922, Second Number, pages 66-67.

"The Genoa Conference," *The Manchester Guardian Commercial, Reconstruction in Europe*, June 15, 1922, Third Number, pages 132-133.

"Is a Settlement of the Reparation Question Possible Now?" *The Manchester Guardian Commercial, Reconstruction in Europe*, September 28, 1922, Eighth Number, pages 462-464.

"Speculation in the Mark and Germany's Balances Abroad," *The Manchester Guardian Commercial, Reconstruction in Europe*, September 28, 1922, Eighth Number, pages 480-482.

"The Underlying Principles," *The Manchester Guardian Commercial, Reconstruction in Europe*, January 4, 1923, Twelfth Number, pages 717-718.

"British Policy in Europe," *The Nation and the Athenaeum*, May 5, 1923, Vol. XXXIII, pages 148-150.

"The German Offer and the French Reply," *The Nation and the Athenaeum*, May 12, 1923, Vol. XXXIII, pages 188-189.

"The German Loan Delusion," *The New Republic*, June 13, 1923, Vol. XXXV, pages 62-64.

"A Reparations Plan," *The New Republic*, August 8, 1923, Vol. XXXV, pages 280-281.

"The Experts' Reports. I. The Dawes Report," and "II. The McKenna Report," *The Nation and the Athenaeum*, April 12, 1924, and April 19, 1924. Vol. XXXV, pages 40-41 and 76-77.

"How Can the Dawes Plan Work?" *The New Republic*, April 23, 1924, Vol. XXXVIII, pages 224-226.

"The American Debt," *The Nation and the Athenaeum*, August 4, 1924, Vol. XXXV, pages 584-587.

"What the Dawes Plan Will Do," *The New Republic*, October 22, 1924, Vol. XL, pages 195-196.

"The Interallied Debts," *The New Republic*, January 21, 1925, Vol. XLI, pages 221-222.

"Germany's Coming Problem," *The New Republic*, February 17, 1926, Vol. XLV, pages 348-349.

"Mr. Churchill on the Peace," *The Nation and the Athenaeum*, March 9, 1929, Vol. XLIV, pages 782-783.

"The German Transfer Problem," *The Economic Journal*, March, 1929, Vol. XXXIX, pages 1-7.

"The Reparations Problem: A Discussion: II. A Rejoinder," *The Economic Journal*, June. 1929, Vol. XXXIX, pages 179-182.

"Views on the Transfer Problem: III. A Reply," *The Economic Journal*, September, 1929, Vol. XXXIX, pages 404-408.

"The Reparations Crisis," *The New Republic*, May 1, 1929, Vol. LVIII, pages 296-297.

"The Report of the Young Committee," *The Nation and the Athenaeum*, June 15, 1929, Vol. XLIV, pages 359-361.

"Reaping the Whirlwind of the Peace Treaty," *The Golden Book Magazine*, January, 1932, Vol. XV, pages 31-32.

"An End of Reparations?" *The New Statesman and Nation*, January 16, 1932, Vol. III, pages 57-58.

"Britain for Cancellation," *The New Republic*, January 27, 1932, Vol. LXIX, pages 284-285.

"A Policy for Lausanne," *The Times* (London), June 15, 1932, page 15.

"A Positive Peace Programme," *The New Statesman and Nation*, March 26 and April 9, 1938, Vol. XV, pages 509-510, and 605.

"A British Peace Program," *The New Republic*, April 13, 1938, Vol. XCIV, pages 295-296.

"The Policy of Government Storage of Foodstuffs and Raw Materials," *The Economic Journal*, September, 1938, Vol. XLVIII, pages 449-460.

"Crisis Finance," *The Times* (London), April 17 and 18, 1939, pages 13-14 and 15-16.

"The Income and Fiscal Potential of Great Britain," *The Economic Journal*, December, 1939. Vol. XLIX, pages 626-635.

F. Politics and social philosophy

"Russia," *Manchester Guardian Commercial, Reconstruction in Europe,* July 6, 1922, Fourth Number, pages 200-201.

"Mr. Baldwin's Task," *The New Republic,* August 1, 1923, Vol. XXXV, pages 252-253.

"Public and Private Enterprise," *The Nation and the Athenaeum,* June 21, 1924, Vol. XXXV, pages 374-375.

"The Balance of Political Power in Great Britain," *The New Republic,* November 26, 1924, Vol. XLI, pages 18-19.

"Mr. Churchill on Rates and the Liberal Industrial Inquiry," *The Nation and the Athenaeum,* April 28, 1928, Vol. XLIII, pages 99-100.

"Soviet Russia," *The New Republic,* October 28, November 4, and November 11, 1925, Vol. XLIV, pages 246-248, 275-277, and 301-303.

"Liberalism and Labor in England," *The New Republic,* March 3, 1926, Vol. XLVI, pages 38-39.

"The Treasury Contribution to the White Paper," *The Nation and the Athenaeum,* May 18, 1929, Vol. XLV, pages 227-228.

"Sir Oswald Moseley's Manifesto," *The Nation and the Athenaeum,* December 13, 1930, Vol. XLVIII, page 367.

"A Criticism of Mr. Snowden's Budget," *Journal of the Institute of Bankers in South Africa,* June, 1931, Vol. XXXVIII, pages 106-107.

"The Budget," *The New Statesman and Nation,* September 19, 1931, Vol. II, page 329.

"Enjoying Russia" (review of Low's drawings), *The New Statesman and Nation,* December 10, 1932, Vol. IV, page 770.

"Shaw on Wells on Stalin," *The New Statesman and Nation,* November 10, 1934, Vol. VIII, pages 653-654.

"British Foreign Policy," *The New Statesman and Nation,* July 10, 1937, Vol. XIV, pages 61-62. (In the same journal see also Keynes' correspondence on British foreign policy, July 18, August 8, August 15, August 29, and September 12, 1936, Vol. XII, pages 82-83, 188, 219, 284, and 348.)

"Mr. Chamberlain's Foreign Policy," *The New Statesman and Nation,* October 8, 1938, Vol. XVI, pages 518-519.

"Democracy and Efficiency" (discussion with Kingsley Martin), *The New Statesman and Nation,* January 28, 1939, Vol. XVII, pages 121-122.

G. Biographical

"Frederic Hillersdon Keeling," *The Economic Journal*, September, 1916, Vol. XXVI, pages 403-404.

"Alfred Marshall, 1842-1924," *The Economic Journal*, September, 1924, Vol. XXXIV, pages 311-372.

"Bibliographical List of the Writings of Alfred Marshall," *The Economic Journal*, December, 1924, Vol. XXXIV, pages 627-637. (Reprinted in *Memorials of Alfred Marshall*.)

"Francis Ysidro Edgeworth, 1845-1926," *The Economic Journal*, March, 1926, Vol. XXXVI, pages 140-150. (Reprinted in *Essays in Biography*.)

"F. P. Ramsey," *The Economic Journal*, March, 1930, Vol. XL, pages 153-154.

"C. P. Sanger," *The Economic Journal*, March, 1930, Vol. XL, pages 154-155.

"The Earl of Balfour," *The Economic Journal*, June, 1930, Vol. XL, pages 336-338.

"Commemoration of T. R. Malthus," *The Economic Journal*, June, 1935, Vol. XLV, pages 230-234.

"Sir Henry Cunynghame," *The Economic Journal*, June, 1935, Vol. XLV, pages 398-406.

"Andrew Andreades (1876-1935)," *The Economic Journal*, September, 1935, Vol. XLV, pages 597-599.

"William Stanley Jevons, 1835-1882," *Journal of the Royal Statistical Society*, 1936, Vol. XCIX, Part III, pages 516-548, 554-555.

"Herbert Somerton Foxwell," *The Economic Journal*, December, 1936, Vol. XLVI, pages 589-614.

"Adam Smith as Student and Professor," *Economic History (Economic Journal Supplement)*, February, 1938, Vols. III-IV, pages 33-46.

"George Broomhall, 1857-1938," *The Economic Journal*, September, 1938, Vol. XLVIII, pages 576-578.

"Alfred Hoare, 1850-1938," *The Economic Journal*, December, 1938, Vol. XLVIII, pages 753-756.

(with Clara Collet) "Henry Higgs," *The Economic Journal*, December, 1940, Vol. L, pages 546-558.

"Mary Paley Marshall," *The Economic Journal*, June-September, 1944, Vol. LIV, pages 268-284.

H. Miscellaneous

"The Principal Averages, and the Laws of Error Which Lead to Them," *Journal of the Royal Statistical Society*, February, 1911, Vol. LXXIV, pages 322-331.

"The Influence of Parental Alcoholism," *Journal of the Royal Statistical Society*, February, 1911, Vol. LXXIV, pages 339-345.

"Report of the Commissioners of Inland Revenue for the Year Ended 31st March, 1912," *The Economic Journal*, December, 1912, Vol. XXII, pages 632-633.

"Report of the Committee on Irish Finance," "Government of Ireland Bill: Outline of Financial Provisions," and "Return Showing the Debt Incurred for Purely Irish Purposes," (reviews of official documents), *The Economic Journal*, September, 1912, Vol. XXII, pages 498-502.

"An Economist's View of Population," *Manchester Guardian Commercial, Reconstruction in Europe*, August 17, 1922, Sixth Number, pages 340-341.

(assisted by R. B. Lewis) "Stocks of Staple Commodities," *London and Cambridge Economic Service*, Special Memorandum No. 1, April, 1923, pages 2-20.

"Is Britain Overpopulated?" *The New Republic*, October 31, 1923, Vol. XXXVI, pages 247-248.

"A Reply to Sir William Beveridge's 'Population and Unemployment'," *The Economic Journal*, December, 1923, Vol. XXXIII, pages 476-486. (See Sir William Beveridge, *ibid.*, pages 447-475.)

"Investment Policy for Insurance Companies," *The Nation and the Athenaeum*, May 17, 1924, Vol. XXXV, page 226.

"Stocks of Staple Commodities," *London and Cambridge Economic Service*, Special Memorandum No. 6, June, 1924, pages 2-18.

(with J. W. F. Rowe) "Stocks of Staple Commodities," *London and Cambridge Economic Service*, Special Memorandum No. 12, July, 1925, pages 2-18; Special Memorandum No. 16, February, 1926, pages 2-18; Special Memorandum No. 22, March, 1927, pages 2-23; and Special Memorandum No. 29, August, 1929, pages 2-25.

"Coal: A Suggestion," *The Nation and the Athenaeum*, April 24, 1926, Vol. XXXIX, pages 91-92.

"The Colwyn Report on National Debt and Taxation," *The Economic Journal*, June, 1927, Vol. XXXVII, pages 198-212.

(with J. W. F. Rowe and G. L. Schwartz) "Stocks of Staple Commodities," *London and Cambridge Economic Service*, Special Memorandum No. 32, September, 1930, pages 2-30.

"Professor Laski and the Issue of Freedom," *The New Statesman and Nation*, July 21, 1934, Vol. VIII, pages 86-87.

"Some Economic Consequences of a Declining Population," *Eugenics Review,* April, 1937, Vol. XXIX, pages 13-17.
(with Piero Sraffa) "Introduction" to an *Abstract of a Treatise of Human Nature,* by David Hume, pages v-xxxii. Cambridge: University Press, 1938.

III. Book Reviews

The Rupee Problem, by Montagu de Pomeroy Webb. *The Economic Journal,* September, 1910, Vol. XX, pages 438-440.
The Purchasing Power of Money, by Irving Fisher. *The Economic Journal,* September, 1911, Vol. XXI, pages 393-398.
The Economic Transition in India, by T. Morrison. *The Economic Journal,* September, 1911, Vol. XXI, pages 426-431.
Theory of Political Economy, Fourth Edition, by W. Stanley Jevons. *The Economic Journal,* March, 1912, Vol. XXII, pages 78-80.
The Economic Principles of Confucius and His School, by Chen Huan-Chang. *The Economic Journal,* December, 1912, Vol. XXII, pages 584-588.
The Course of Prices in New Zealand, by James W. McIlbraith, and *Report of Commission on the Cost of Living in New Zealand. The Economic Journal,* December, 1912, Vol. XXII, pages 595-598.
The Standard of Value, by Sir David M. Barbour. *The Economic Journal,* June, 1913, Vol. XXIII, pages 390-393.
Gold, Prices, and Wages, by John A. Hobson. *The Economic Journal,* June, 1913, Vol. XXIII, pages 393-398.
Le Thaler de Marie Thérèse, by Marcel-Maurice Fischel. *The Economic Journal,* June, 1914, Vol. XXIV, pages 257-260.
Theorie des Geldes und der Umlaufsmittel, by Ludwig von Mises, and *Geld und Kapital,* by Friedrich Bendixen. *The Economic Journal,* September, 1914, Vol. XXIV, pages 417-419.
What is Money? by Mitchell Innes. *The Economic Journal,* September, 1914, Vol. XXIV, pages 419-421.
The Works and Life of Walter Bagehot, by Mrs. Russell Barrington. *The Economic Journal,* September, 1915, Vol. XXV, pages 369-375.
Currency and Credit, by R. G. Hawtrey. *The Economic Journal,* September, 1920, Vol. XXX, pages 362-365.
Indian Finance and Banking, by G. Findlay Shirras. *The Economic Journal,* September, 1920, Vol. XXX, pages 396-397.

The Future of Exchange and the Indian Currency, by H. Stanley Jevons. *The Economic Journal,* March, 1923, Vol. XXXIII, pages 60-65.

The Behavior of Prices: A Report of an Investigation, by F. C. Mills. *The Economic Journal,* December, 1928, Vol. XXXVIII, pages 606-608.

Inter-relationships of Supply and Price, by G. F. Warren and F. A. Pearson. *The Economic Journal,* March, 1929, Vol. XXXIX, pages 92-95.

Unemployment and Inflation, by Alfred Hoare. *The Economic Journal,* September, 1933, Vol. XLIII, pages 474-475.

Consumers' Credits and Unemployment, by J. E. Meade. *The Economic Journal,* March, 1938, Vol. XLVIII, pages 67-71.

English Economic History, Mainly Since 1700, by C. R. Fay. *The Economic Journal,* June-September, 1940, Vol. L, pages 259-261.

INDEX

CPSIA information can be obtained
at www.ICGtesting.com
Printed in the USA
BVHW061937240722
642887BV00009B/704

9 781162 766065